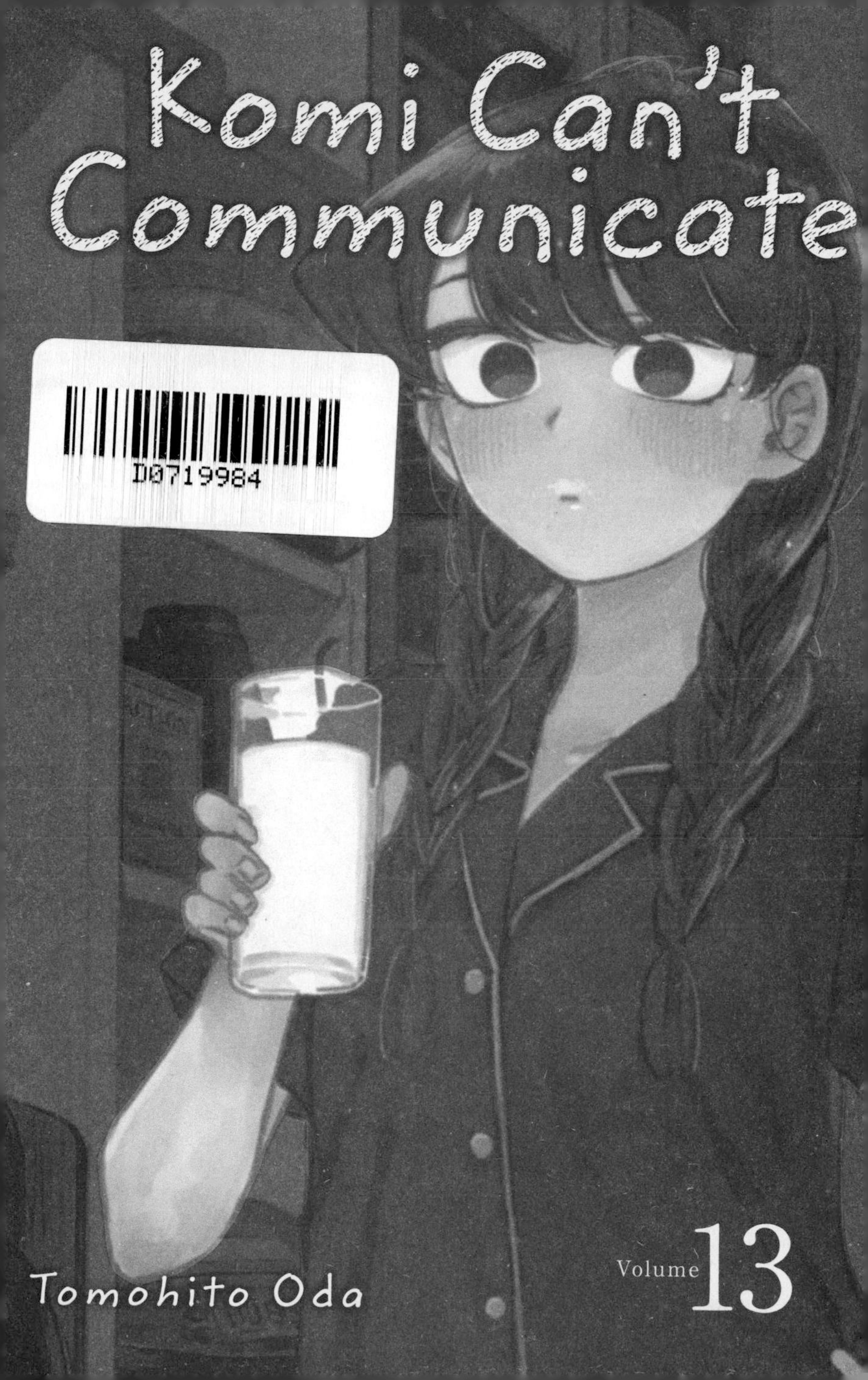
Komi Can't Communicate
Volume 13
Tomohito Oda

Contents

Komi Can't Communicate

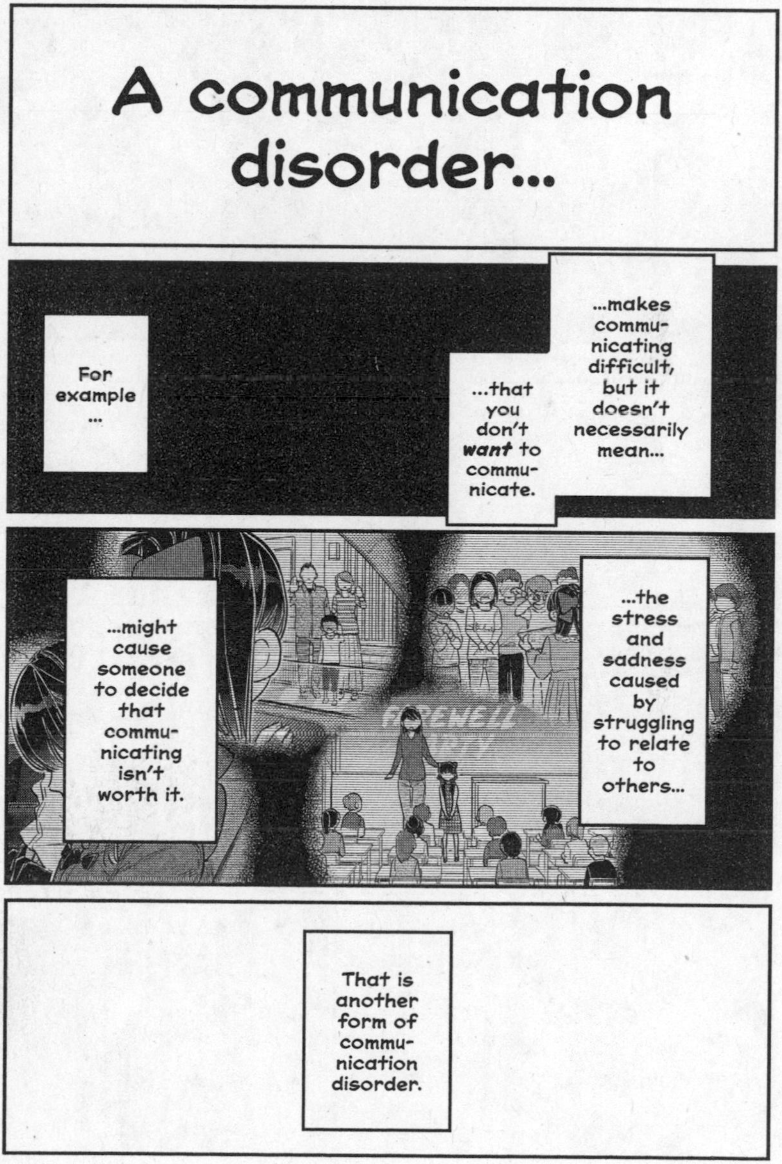

A communication disorder...
...makes communicating difficult, but it doesn't necessarily mean...
...that you don't *want* to communicate.
For example...
...the stress and sadness caused by struggling to relate to others...
...might cause someone to decide that communicating isn't worth it.
That is another form of communication disorder.

Communication 171: While Mother Is Out

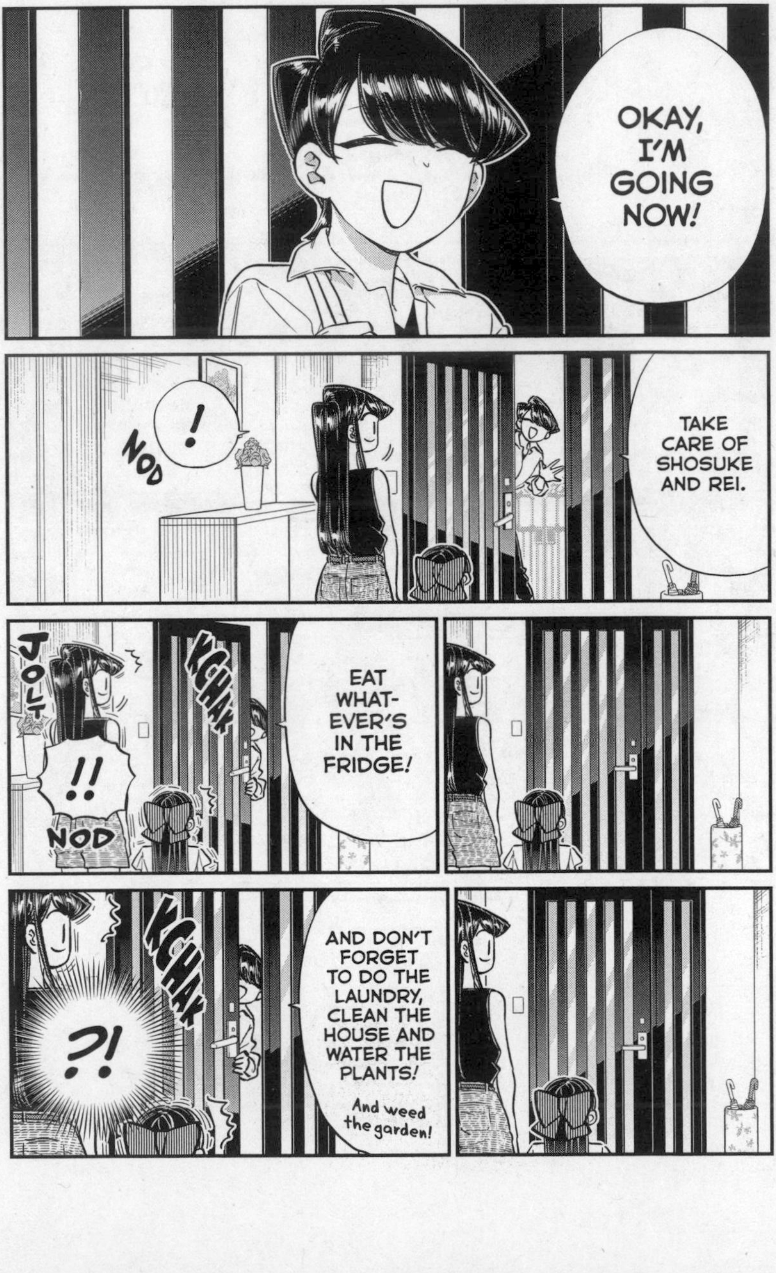
OKAY, I'M GOING NOW!
TAKE CARE OF SHOSUKE AND REI.
!
NOD
EAT WHATEVER'S IN THE FRIDGE!
KCHAK
JOLT
!!
NOD
AND DON'T FORGET TO DO THE LAUNDRY, CLEAN THE HOUSE AND WATER THE PLANTS!
And weed the garden!
KCHAK
?!

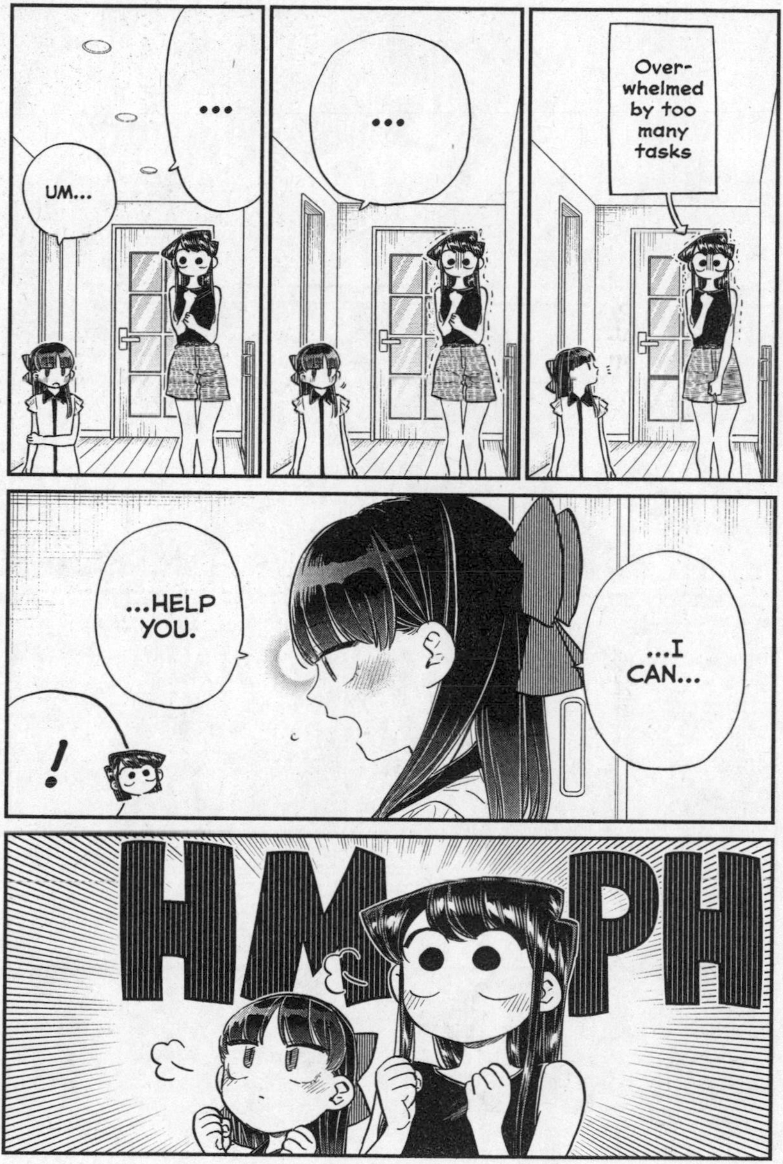
Over-whelmed by too many tasks
...
...
UM...
...I CAN...
...HELP YOU.
!
HMPH

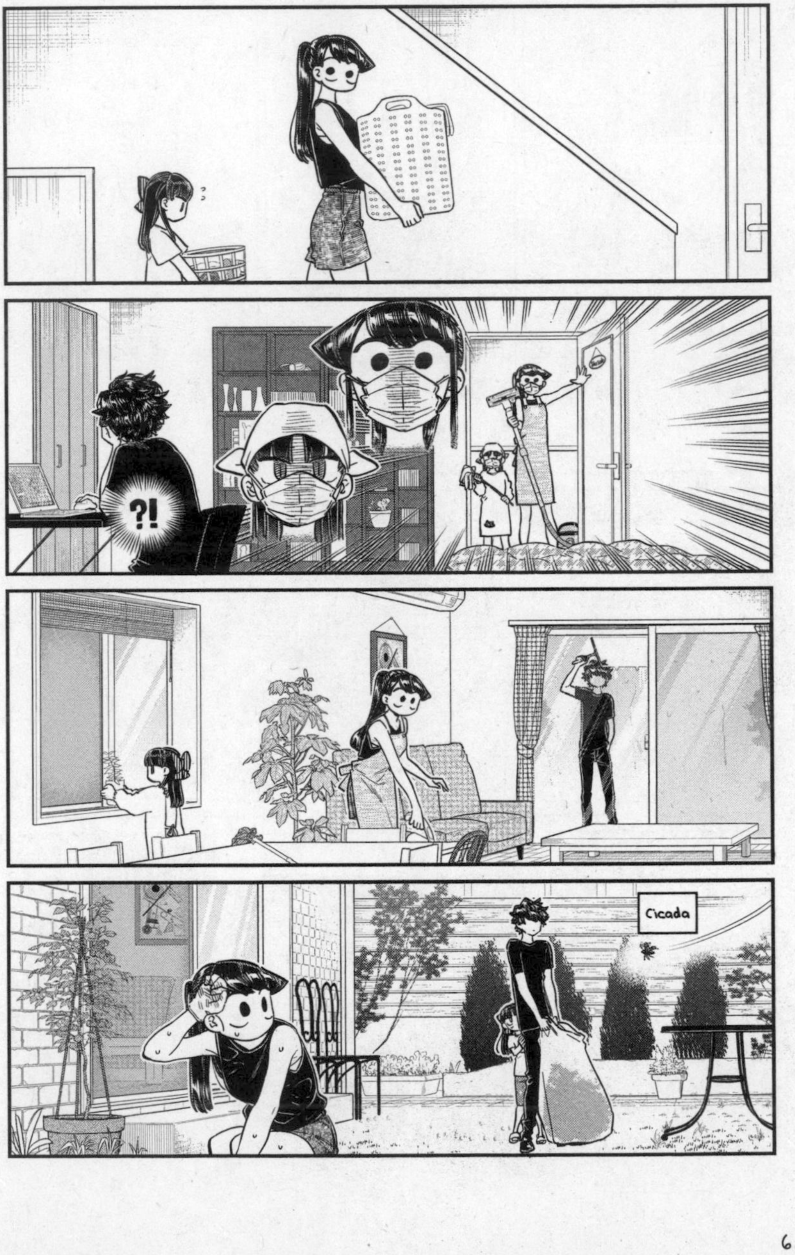
?!
Cicada

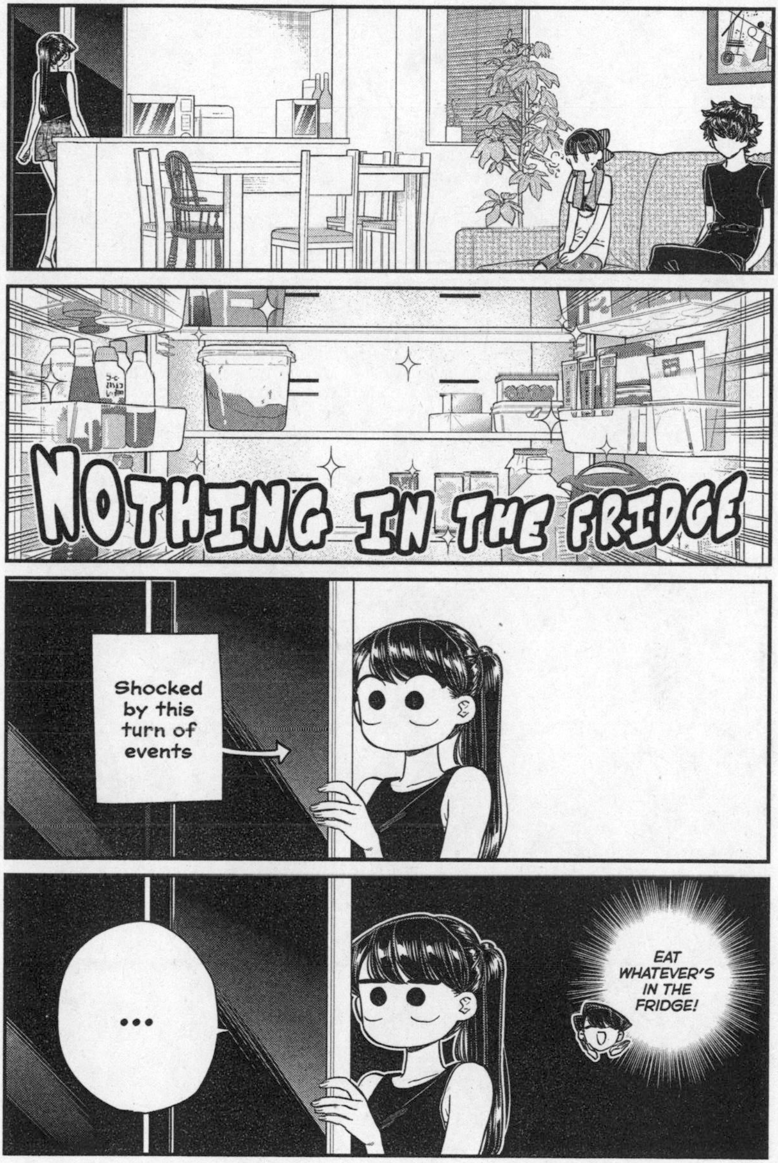
NOTHING IN THE FRIDGE
Shocked by this turn of events
EAT WHATEVER'S IN THE FRIDGE!
...

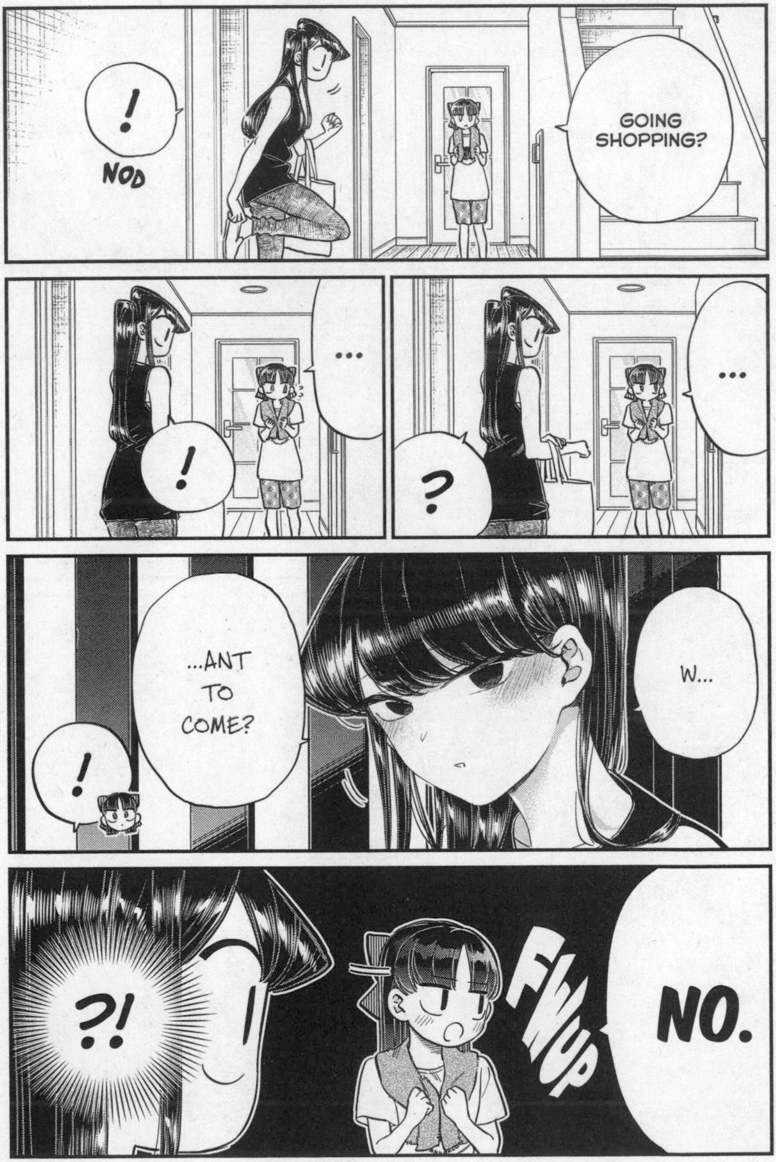
GOING SHOPPING?
!
NOD
...
?
...
!
W...
...ANT TO COME?
!
NO.
FWUP
?!

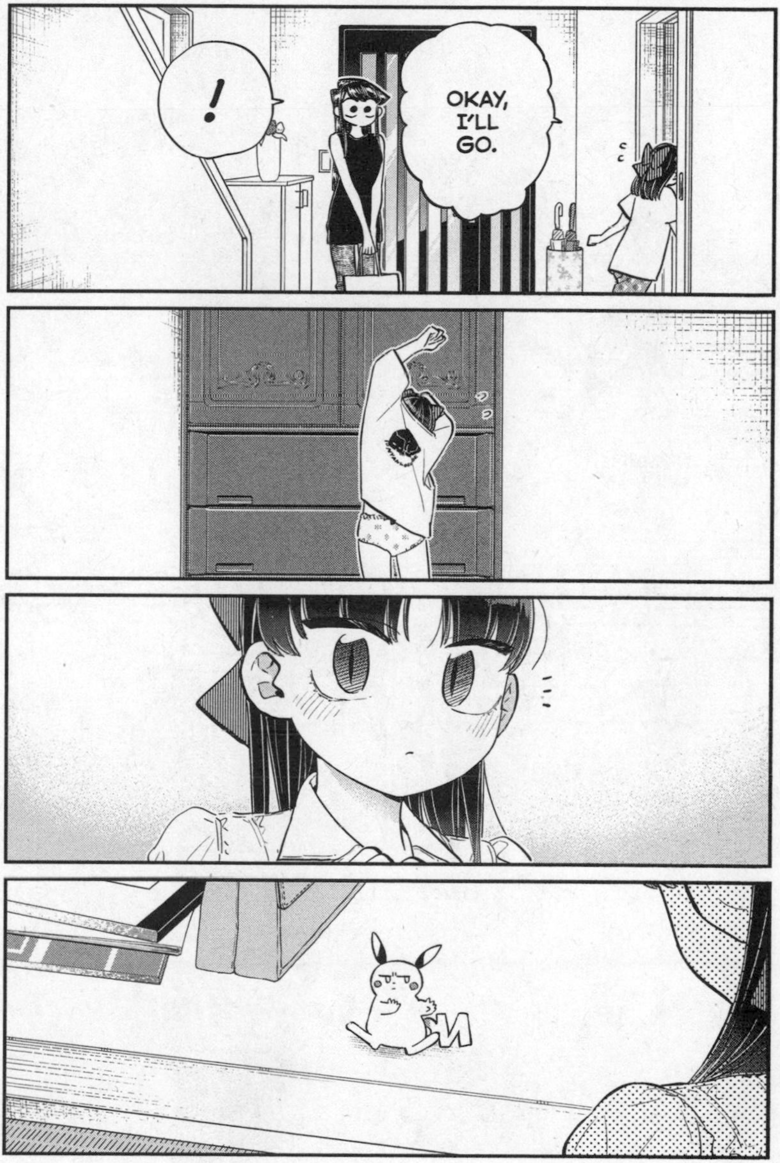
OKAY, I'LL GO.
!

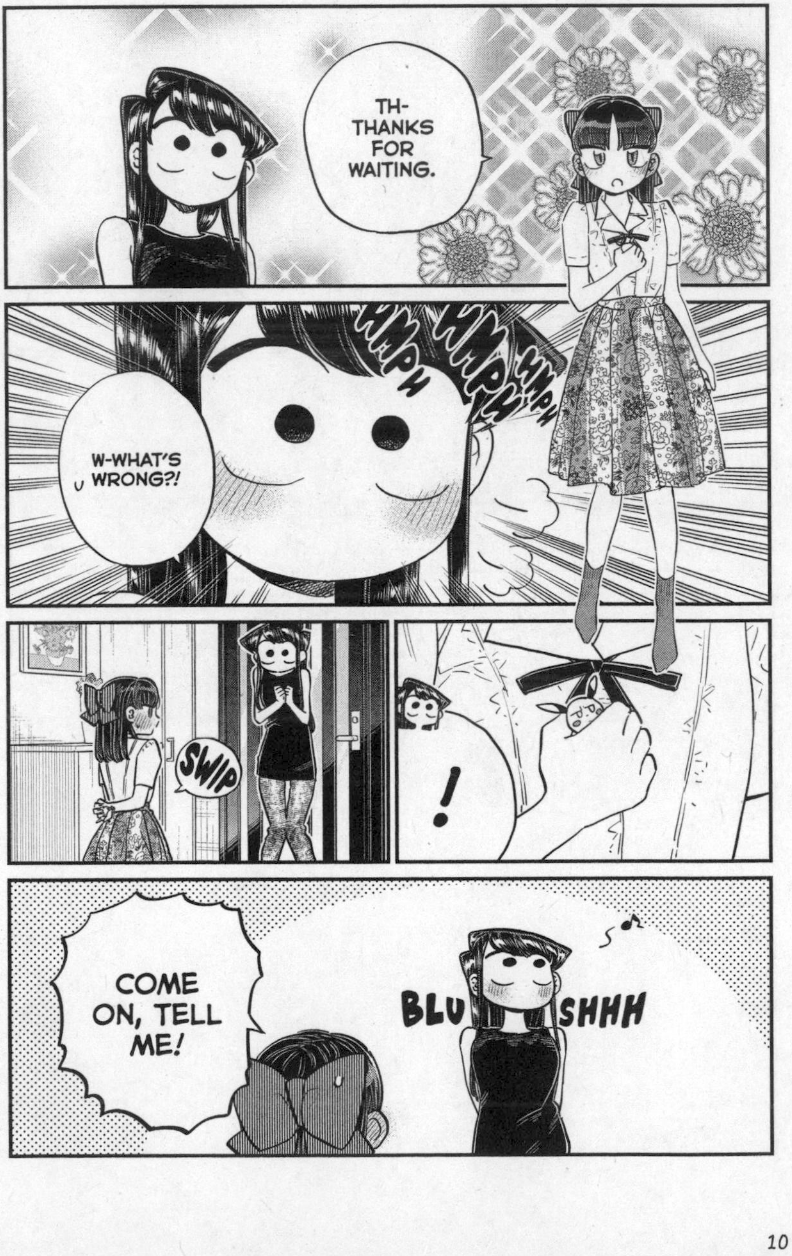
TH-THANKS FOR WAITING.
HMPH HMPH HMPH HMPH
W-WHAT'S WRONG?!
!
SWIP
BLUSHHH
COME ON, TELL ME!

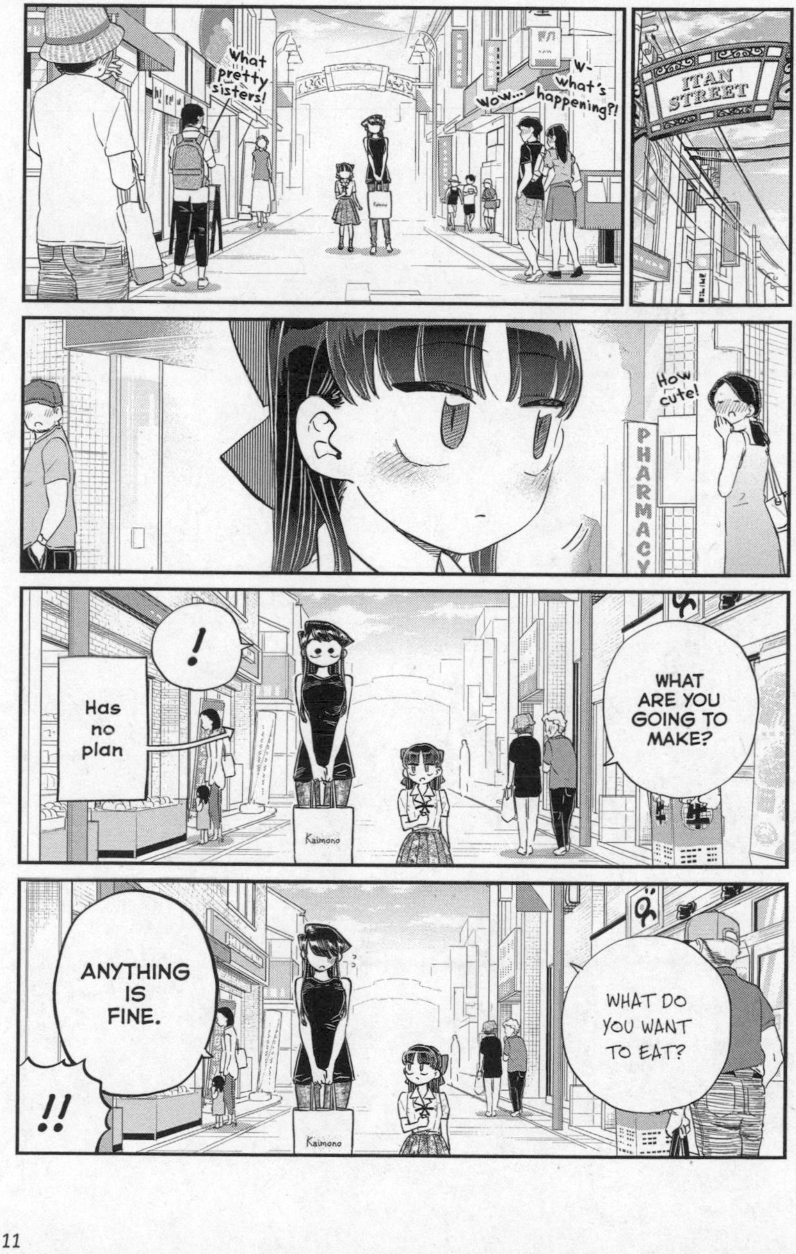
ITAN STREET
W-what's happening?!
Wow...
What pretty sisters!
How cute!
PHARMACY
WHAT ARE YOU GOING TO MAKE?
!
Has no plan
Kaimono
WHAT DO YOU WANT TO EAT?
ANYTHING IS FINE.
!!
Kaimono

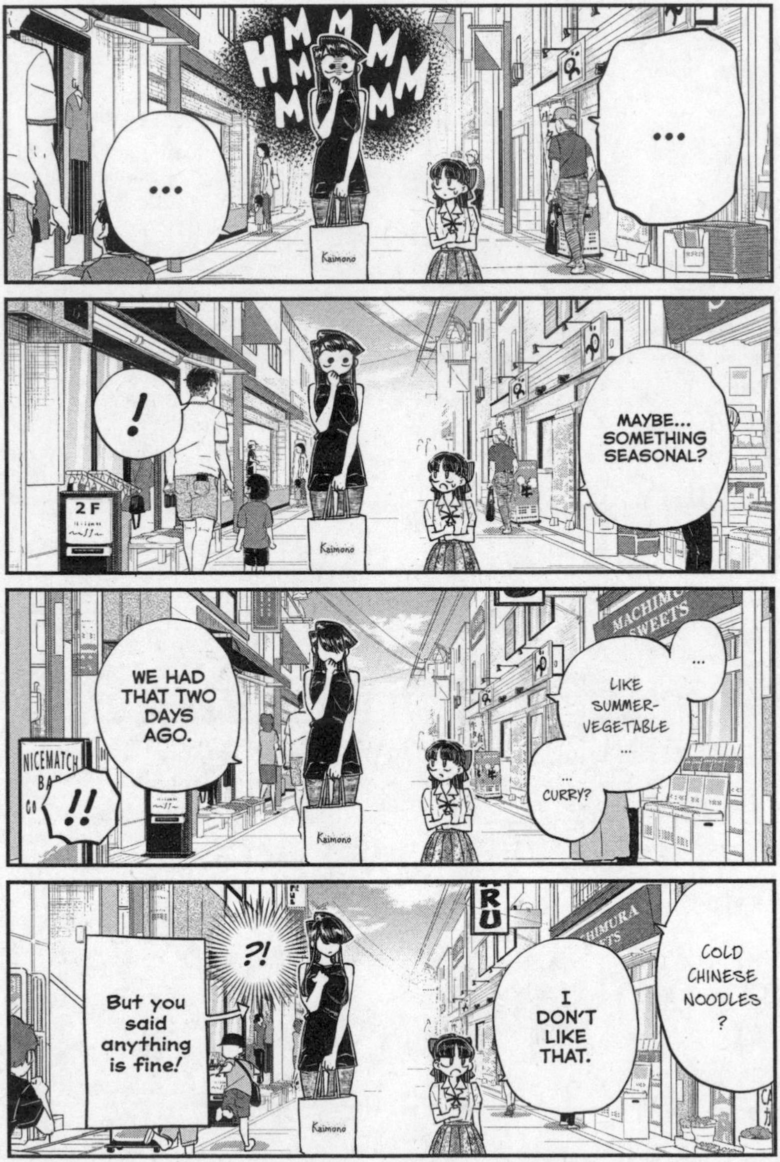
...
HMMMMMMM
...
Kaimono
MAYBE... SOMETHING SEASONAL?
!
2F
... LIKE SUMMER-VEGETABLE ... ... CURRY?
WE HAD THAT TWO DAYS AGO.
!!
COLD CHINESE NOODLES ?
I DON'T LIKE THAT.
?!
But you said anything is fine!

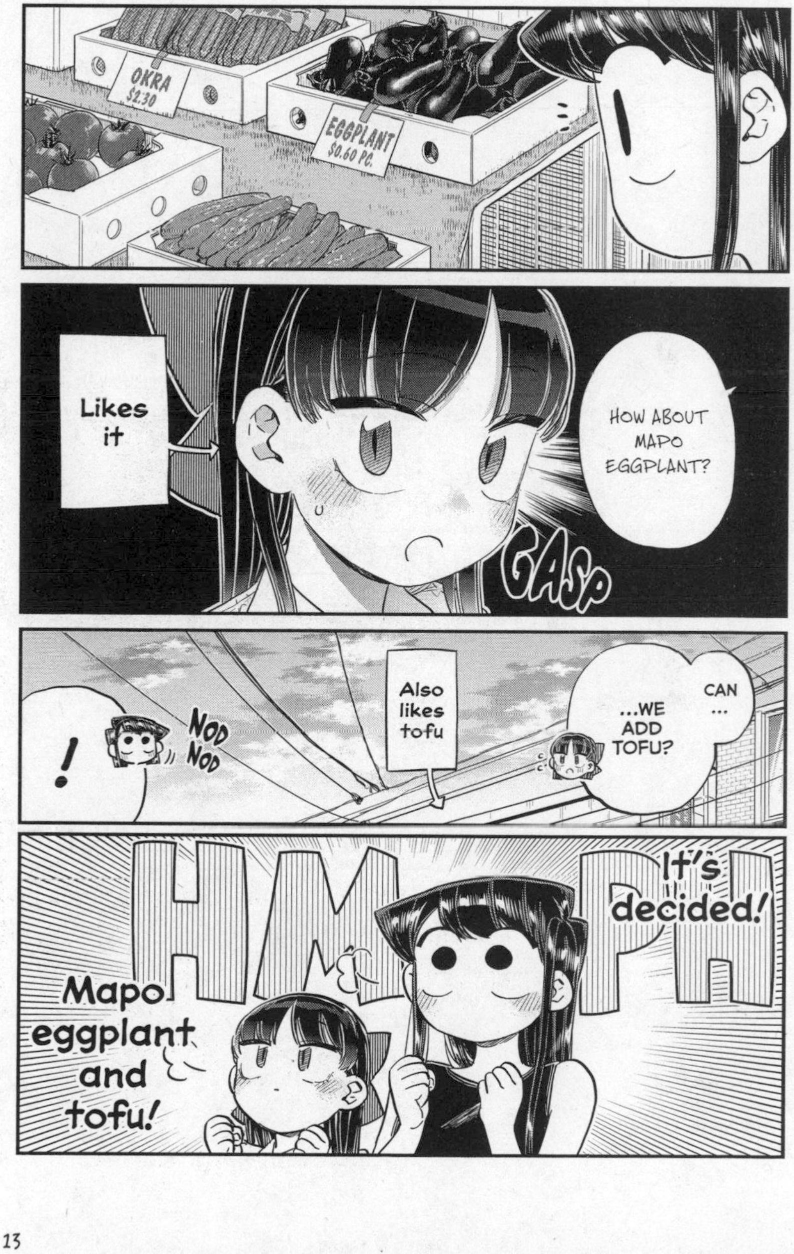
OKRA $2.30
EGGPLANT $0.60 PC.
HOW ABOUT MAPO EGGPLANT?
GASP
Likes it
CAN ...
...WE ADD TOFU?
Also likes tofu
NOD NOD
!
HMPH
It's decided!
Mapo eggplant and tofu!

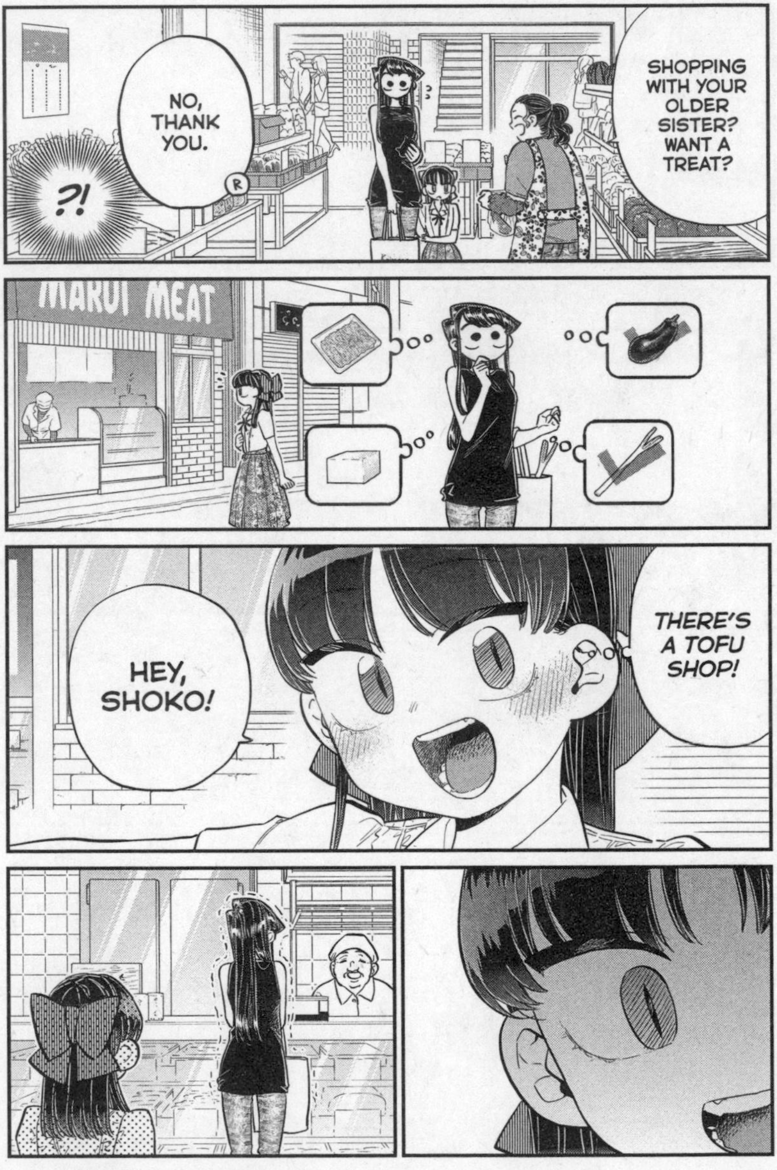
SHOPPING WITH YOUR OLDER SISTER? WANT A TREAT?
NO, THANK YOU.
?!
MARUI MEAT
THERE'S A TOFU SHOP!
HEY, SHOKO!

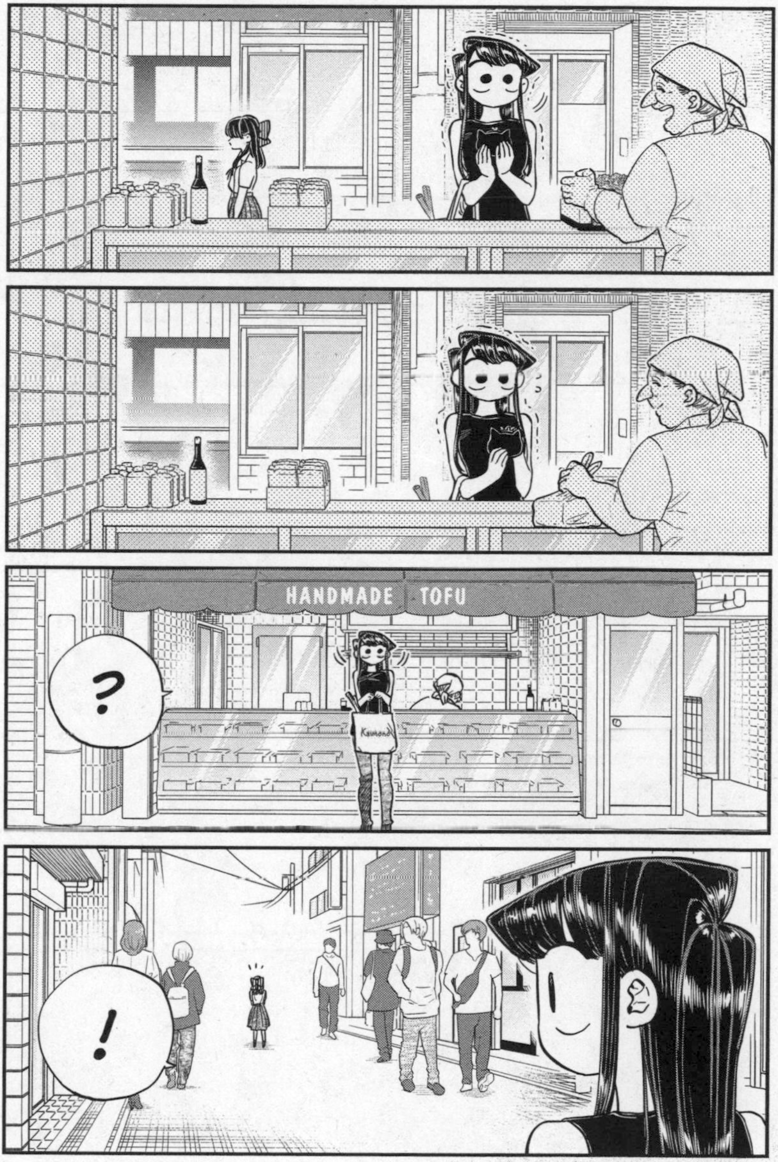
HANDMADE TOFU
Kaimono
?
!

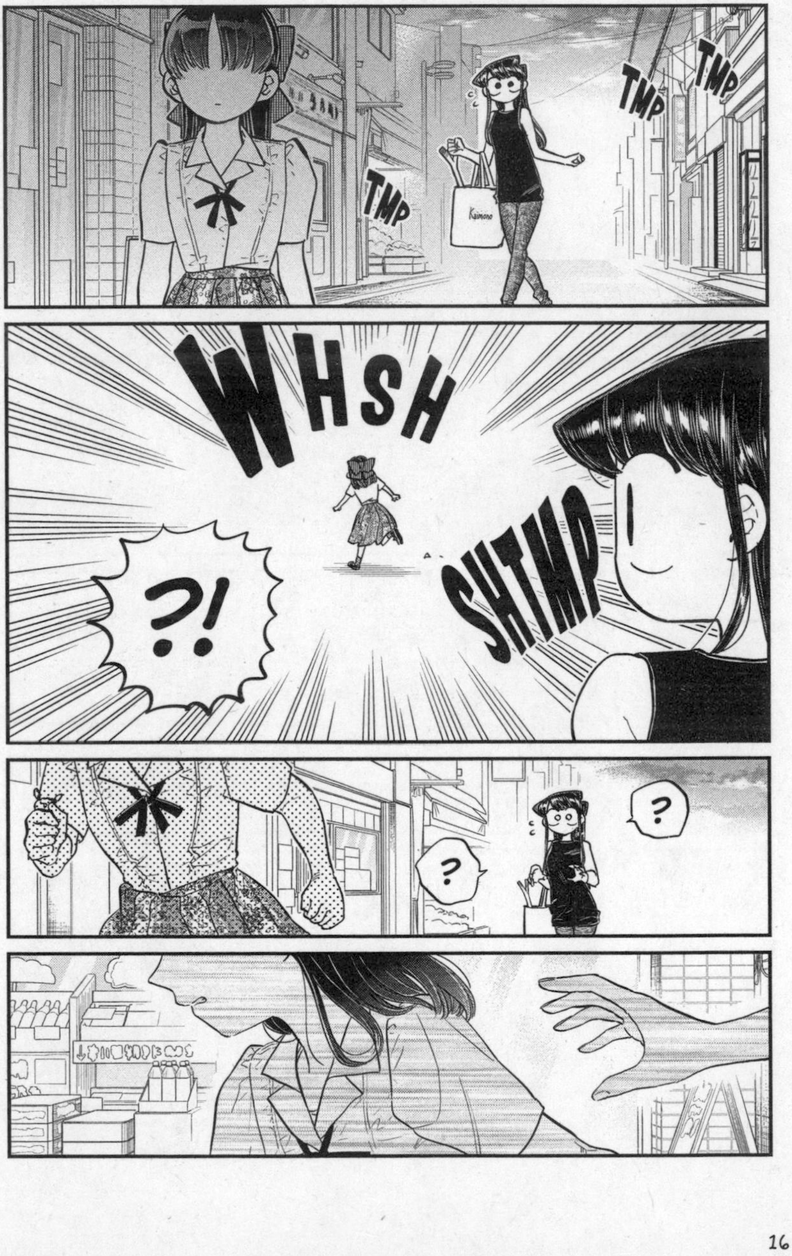
TMP
TMP
Kaimono
TMP
SHTMP
WHSH
?!
?
?

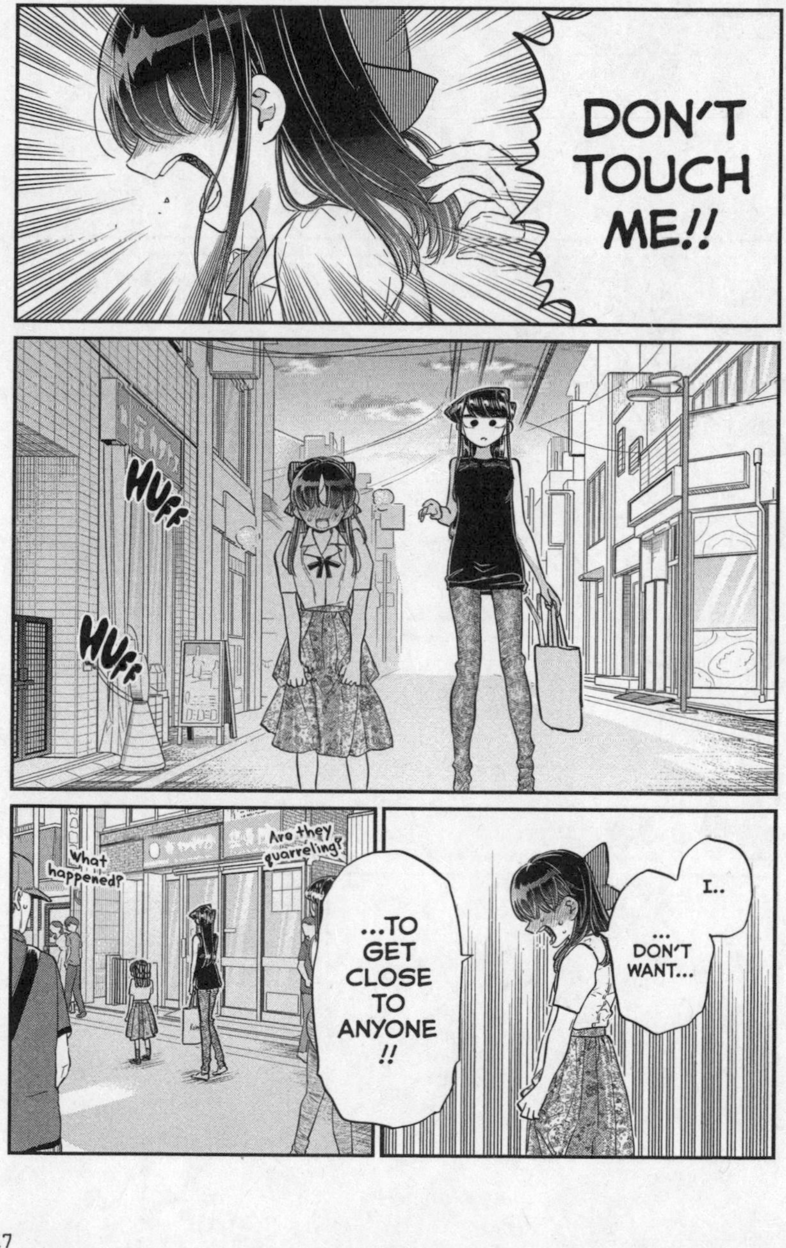
DON'T TOUCH ME!!
HUFF
HUFF
I..
...DON'T WANT...
...TO GET CLOSE TO ANYONE!!
Are they quarreling?
What happened?

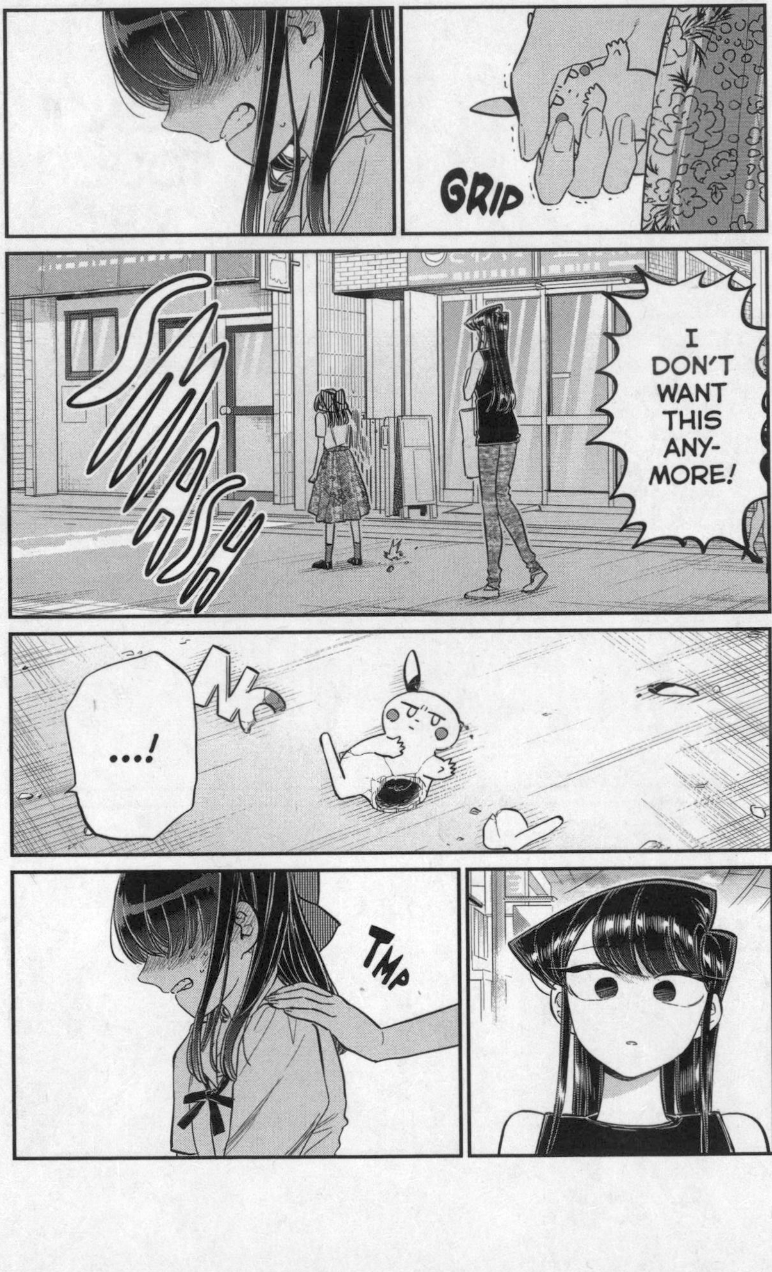
GRIP
I DON'T WANT THIS ANY-MORE!
SMASH
...!
TMP

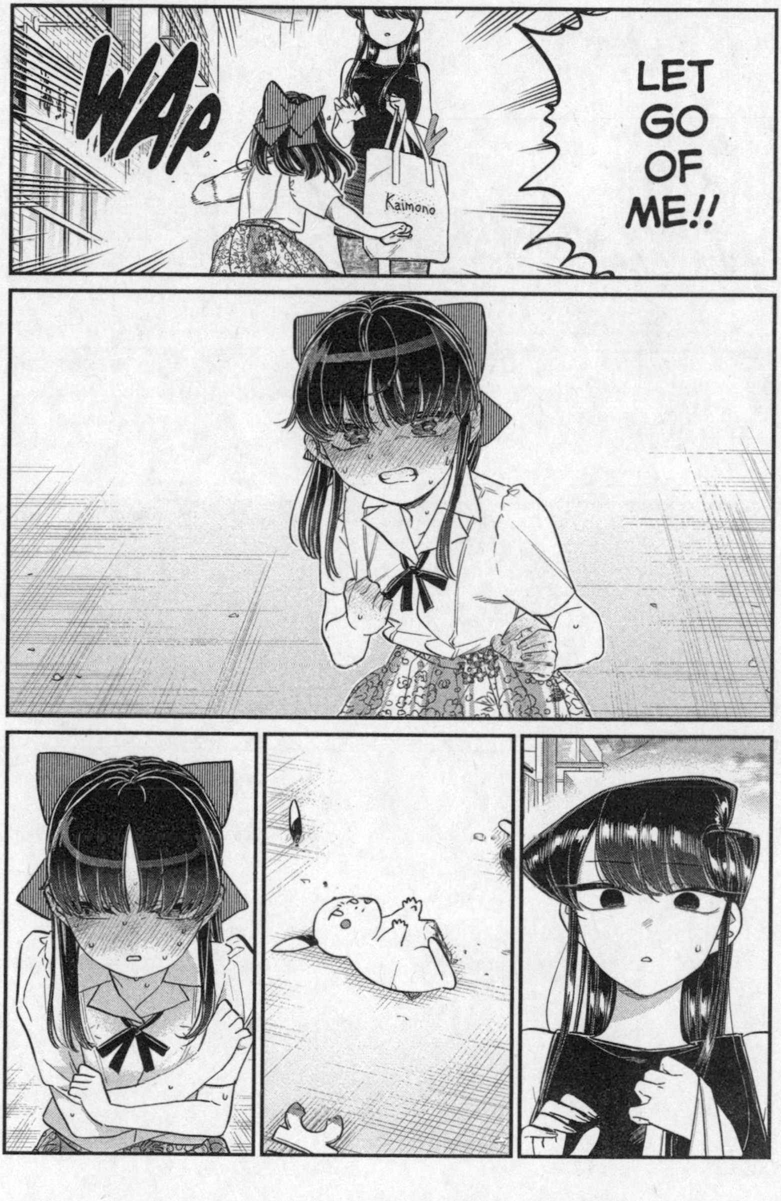
LET GO OF ME!!
Kaimono
WAP

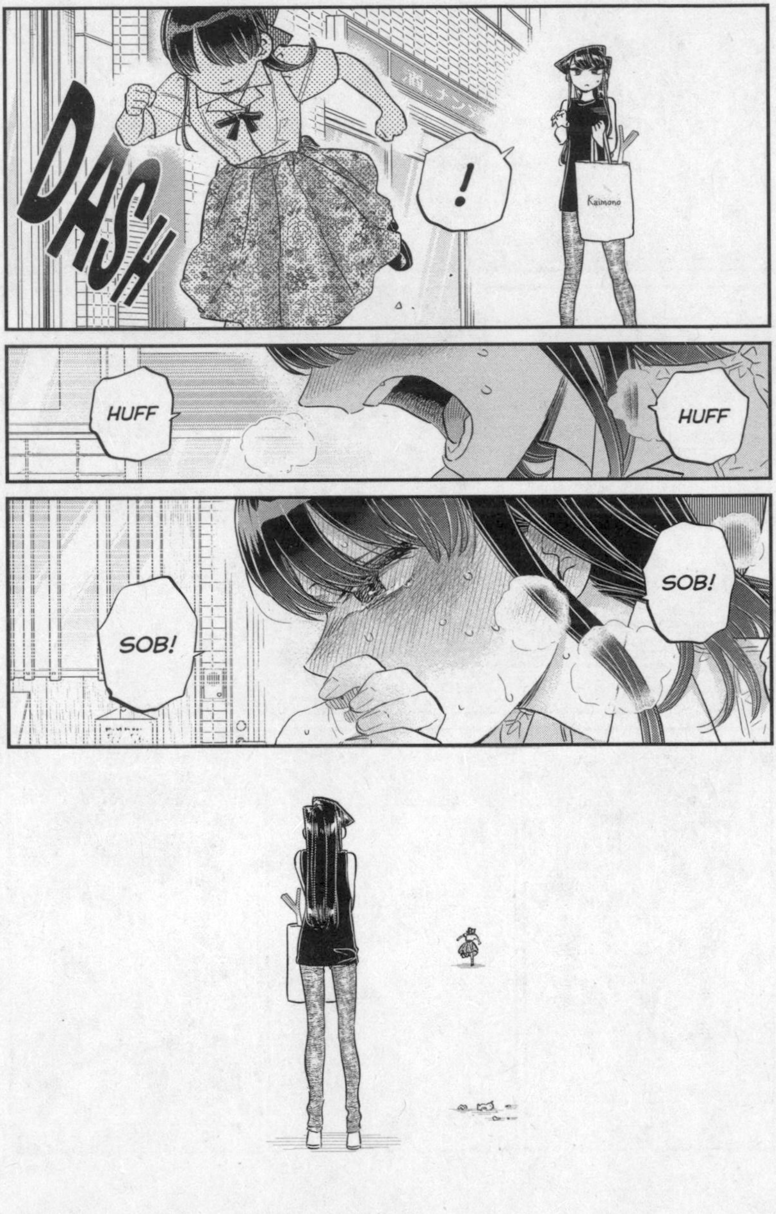
Kaimono
!
DASH
HUFF
HUFF
SOB!
SOB!

Communication 171 — The End

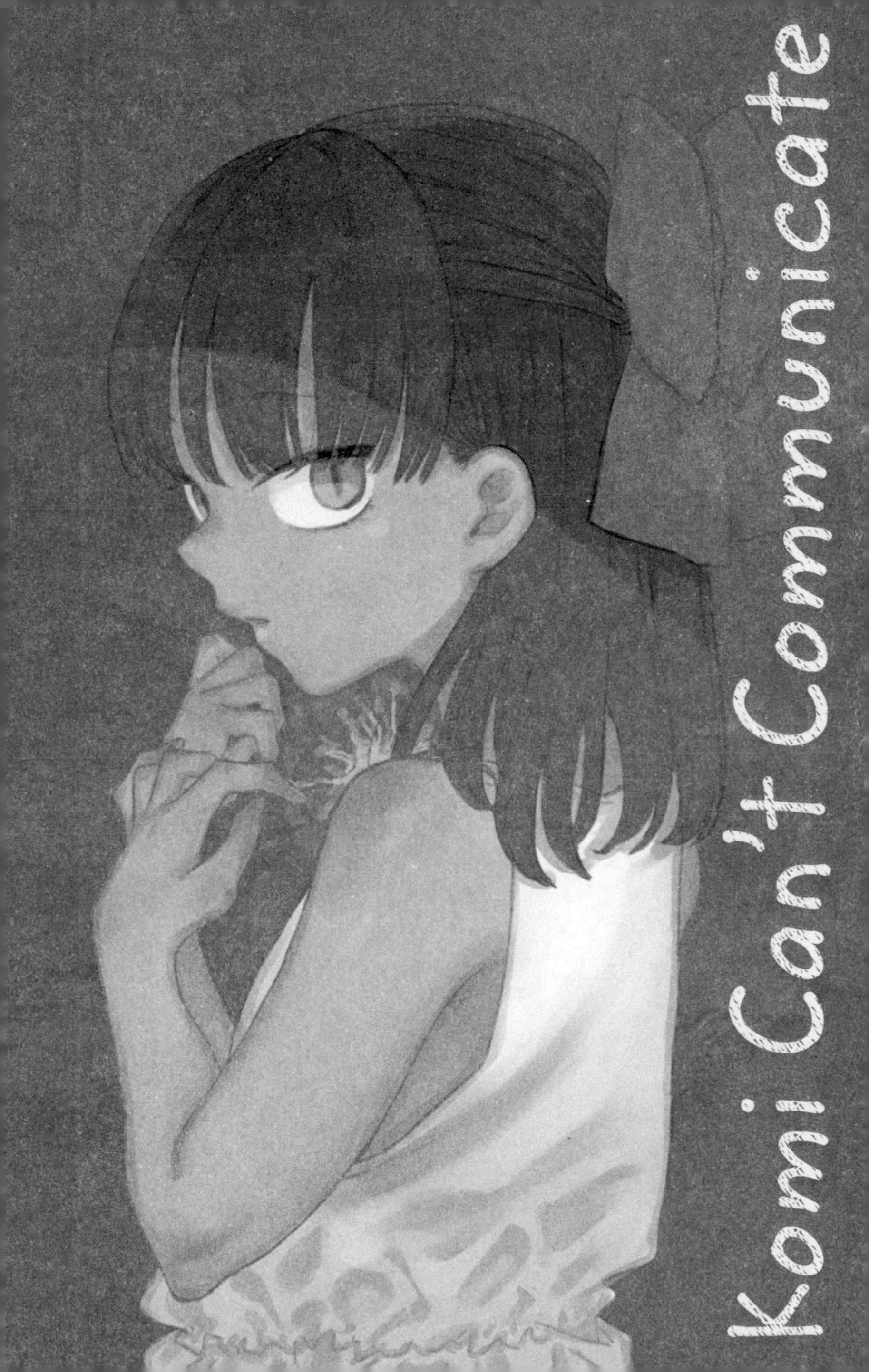
Komi Can't Communicate

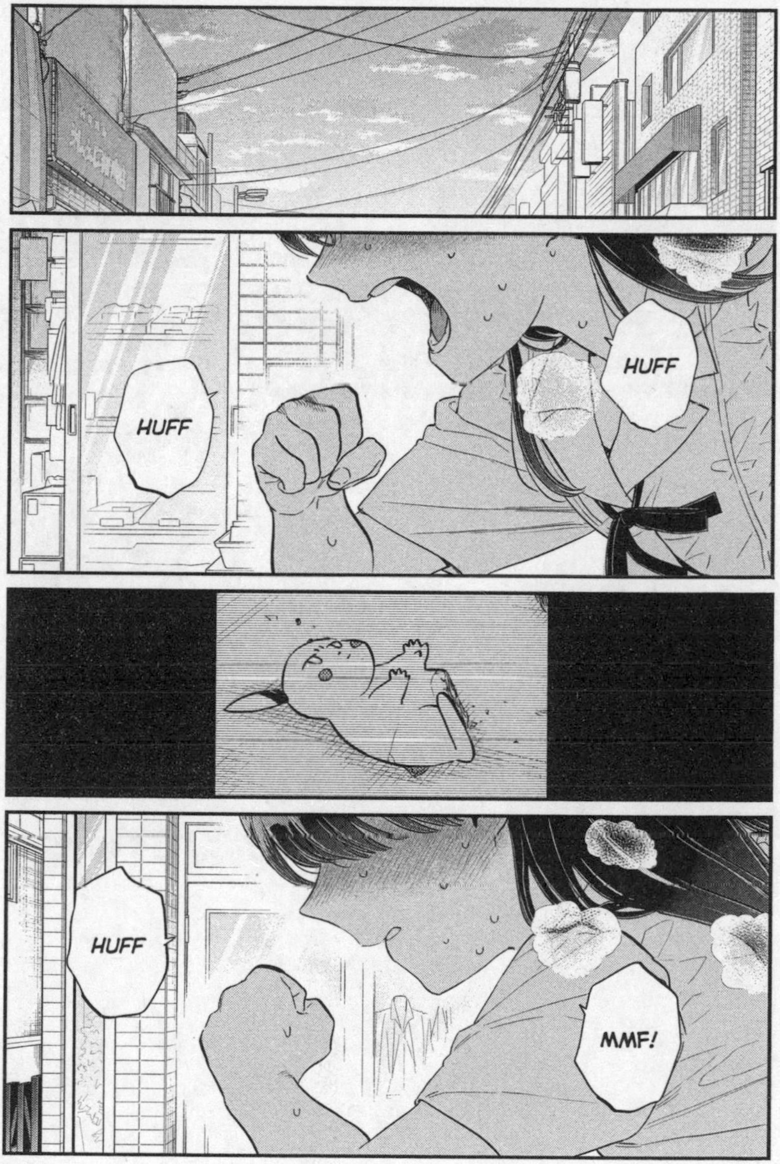
HUFF
HUFF
HUFF
MMF!

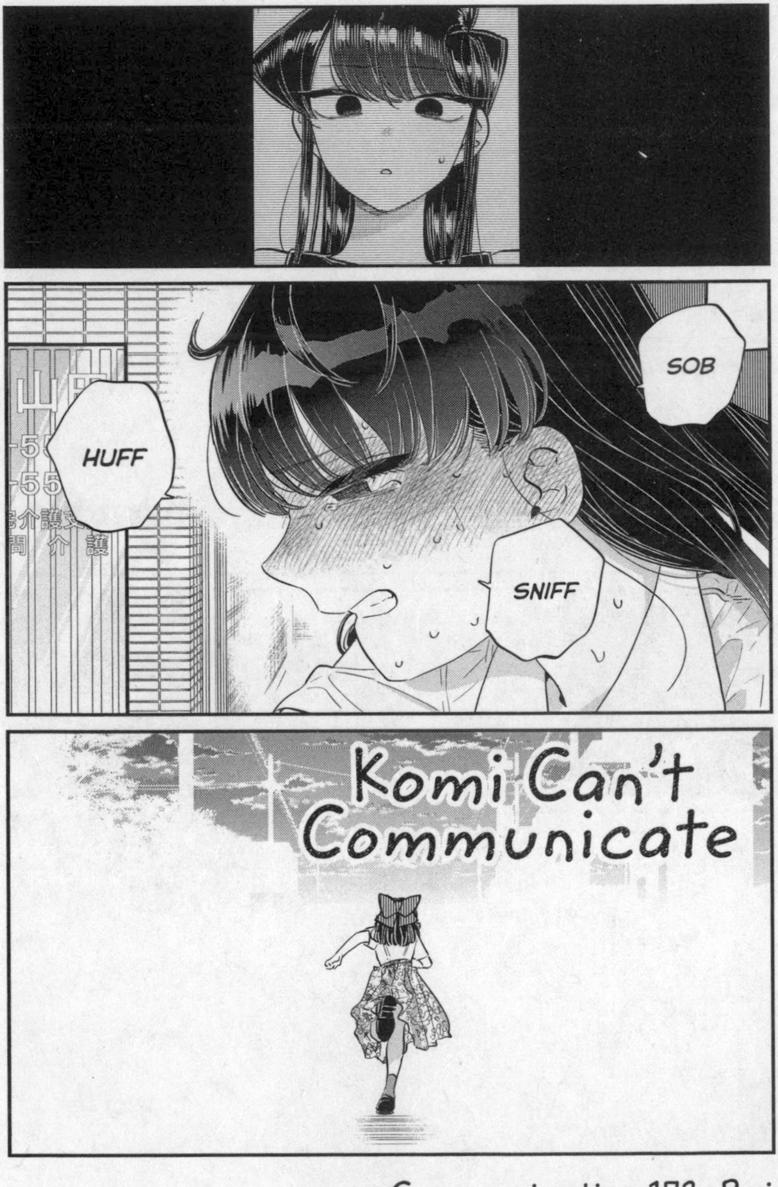
SOB
SNIFF
HUFF
Komi Can't Communicate

Communication 172: Rei

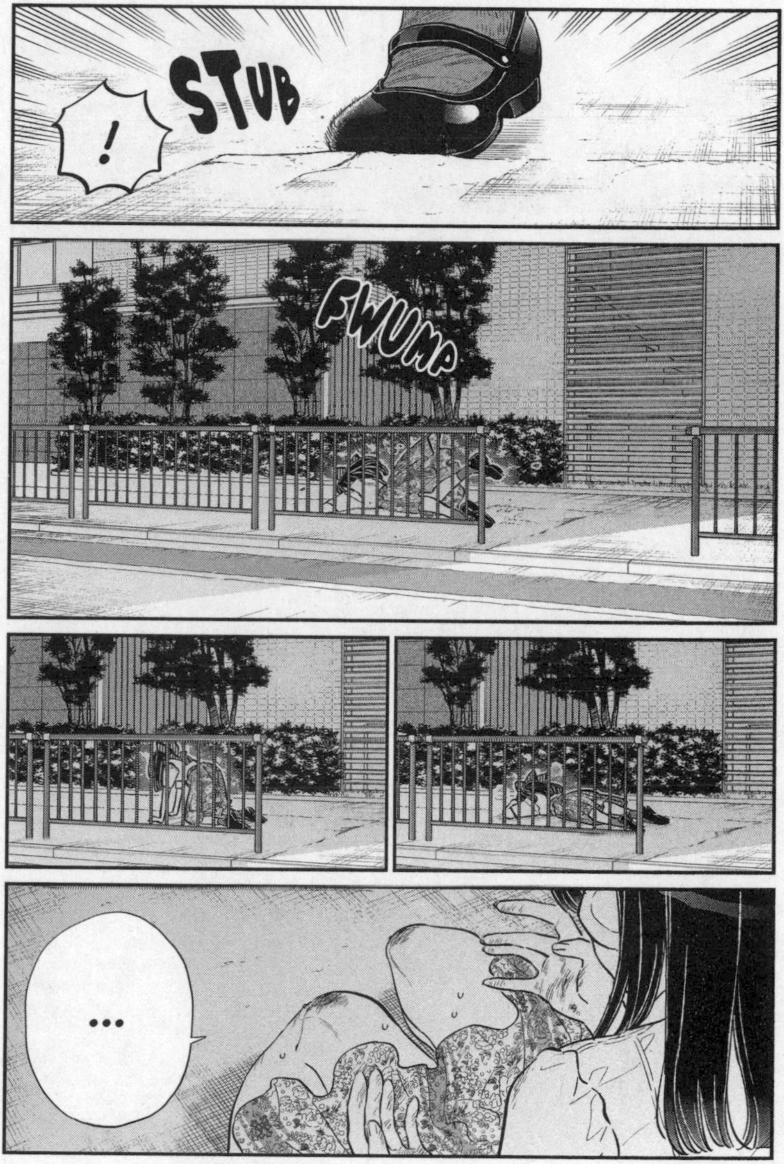
STUB
!
FWUMP
...

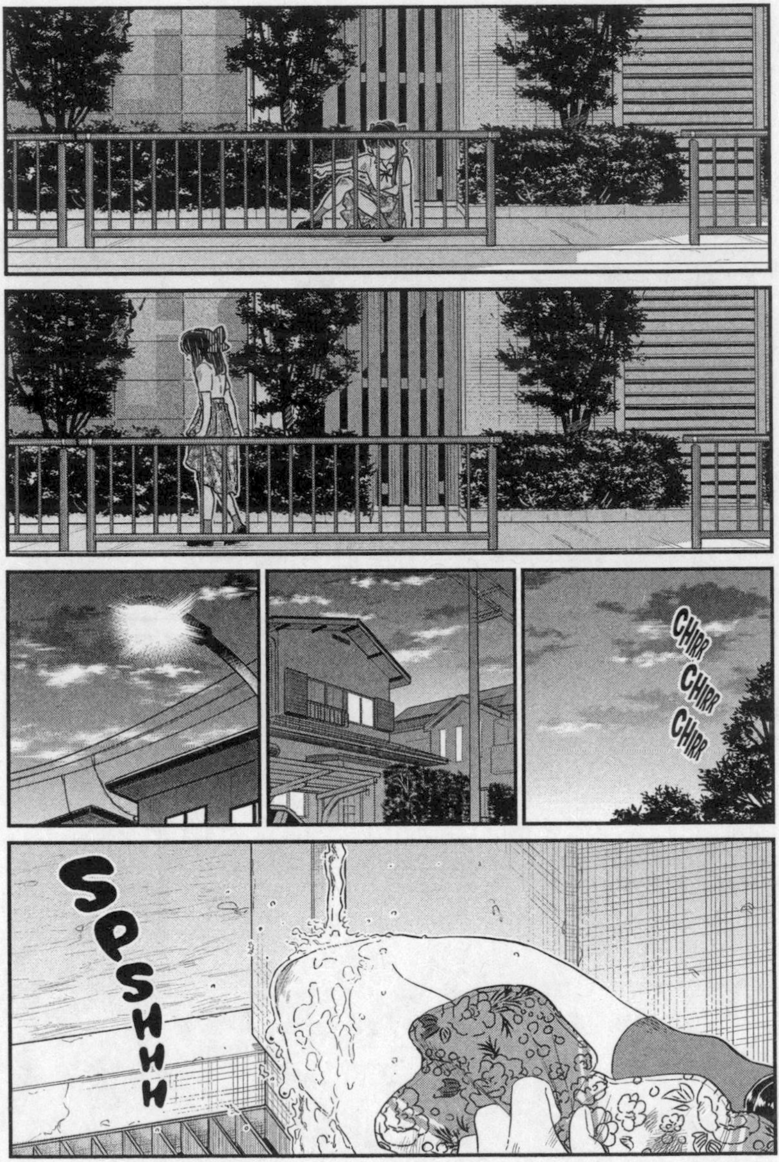
CHIRR CHIRR CHIRR
SPSHHH

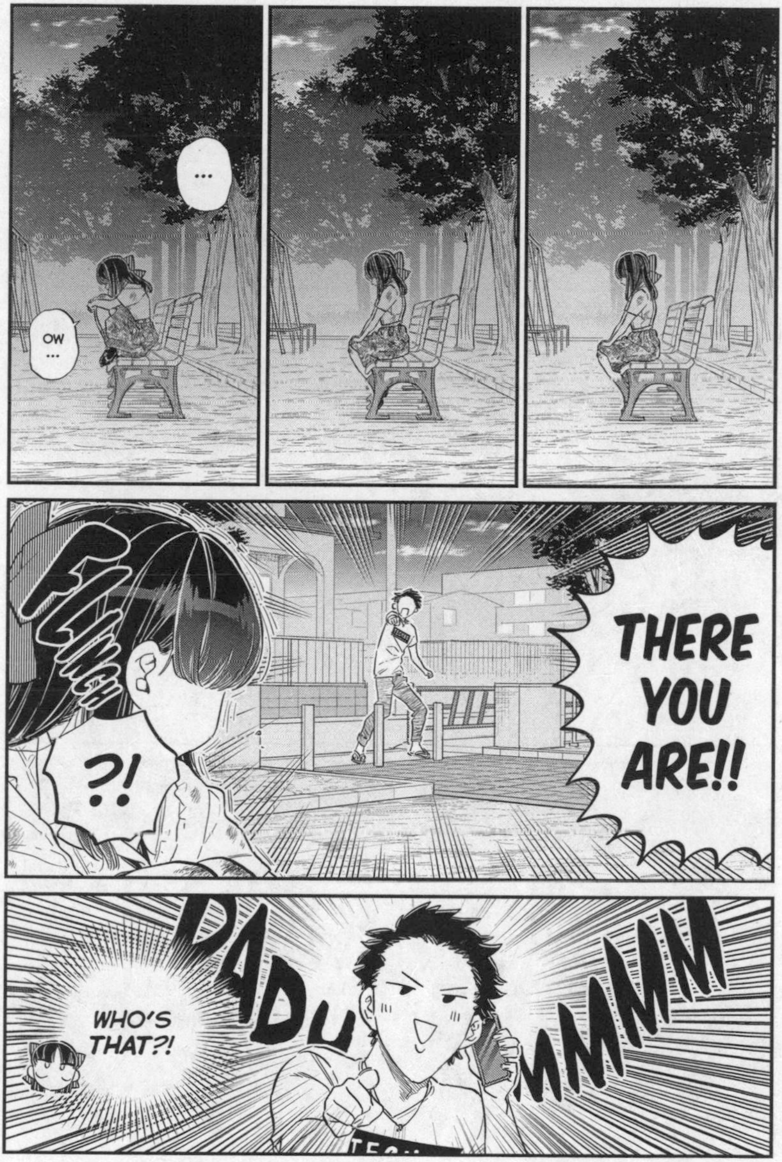
...
OW ...
THERE YOU ARE!!
FLINCH
?!
DADUMMMM
WHO'S THAT?!

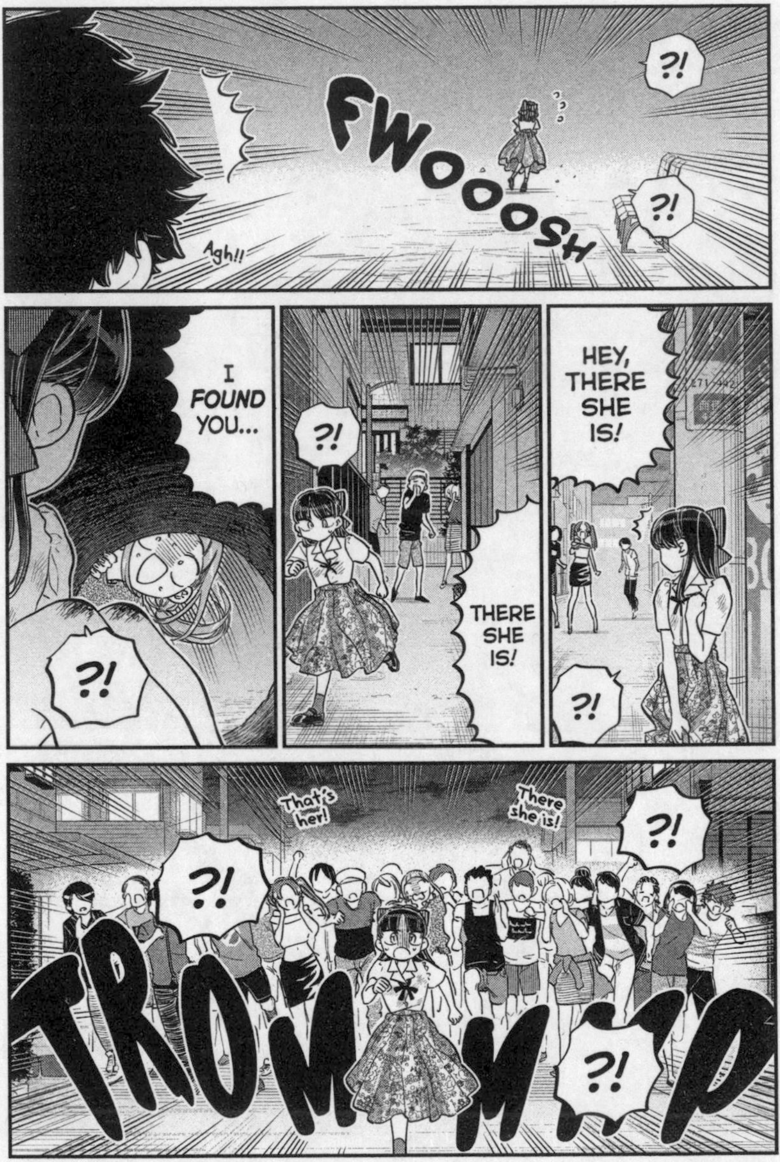
?!
?!
FWOOOSH
Agh!!
HEY, THERE SHE IS!
?!
?!
THERE SHE IS!
I FOUND YOU...
?!
?!
There she is!
That's her!
?!
TROMMP
?!

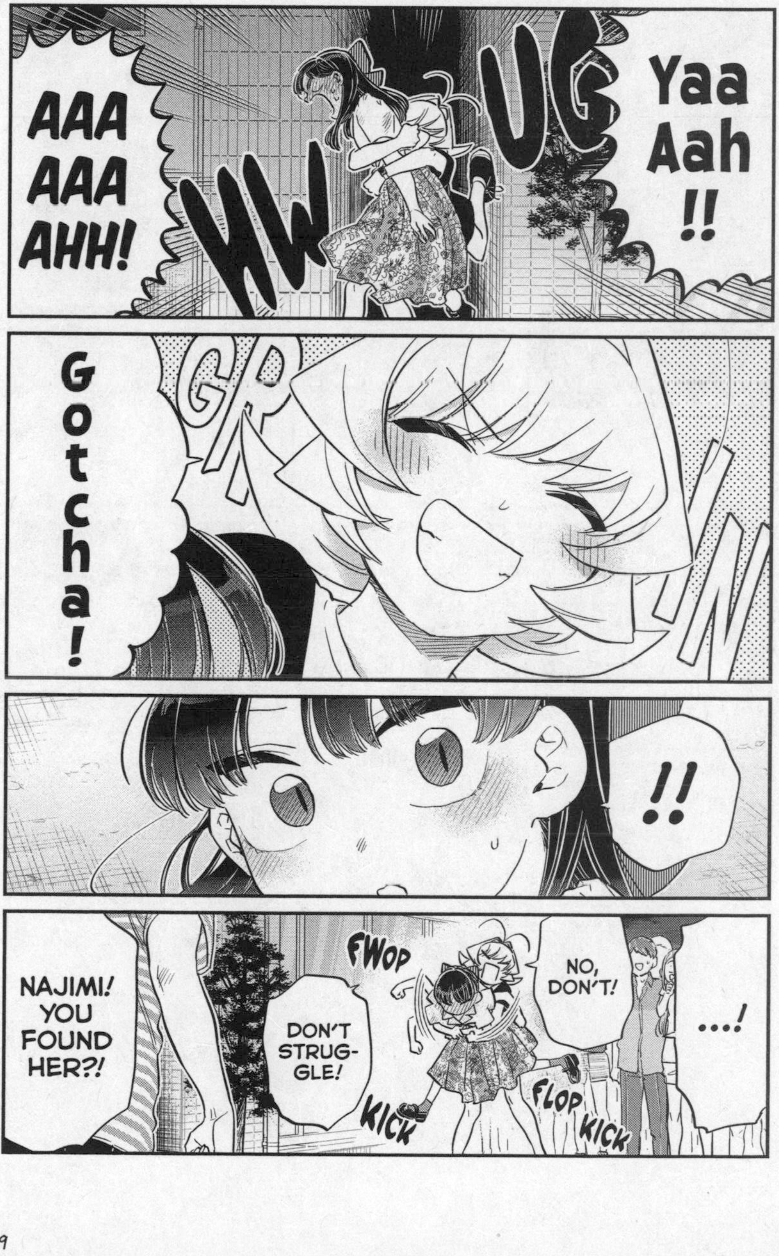
Yaa Aah !!
HWUG
AAA AAA AHH!
GRIN
Gotcha!
!!
...!
NO, DON'T!
FWOP
DON'T STRUG-GLE!
FLOP
KICK
KICK
NAJIMI! YOU FOUND HER?!

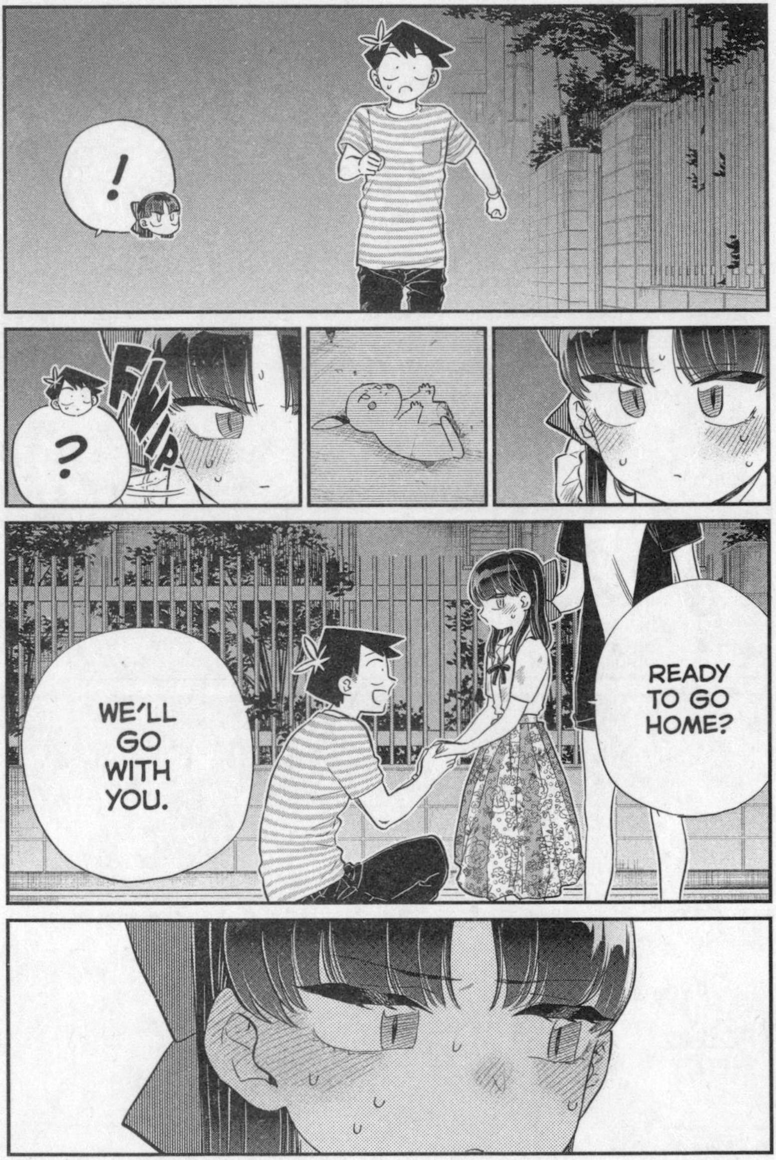
!
FWIP
?
READY TO GO HOME?
WE'LL GO WITH YOU.

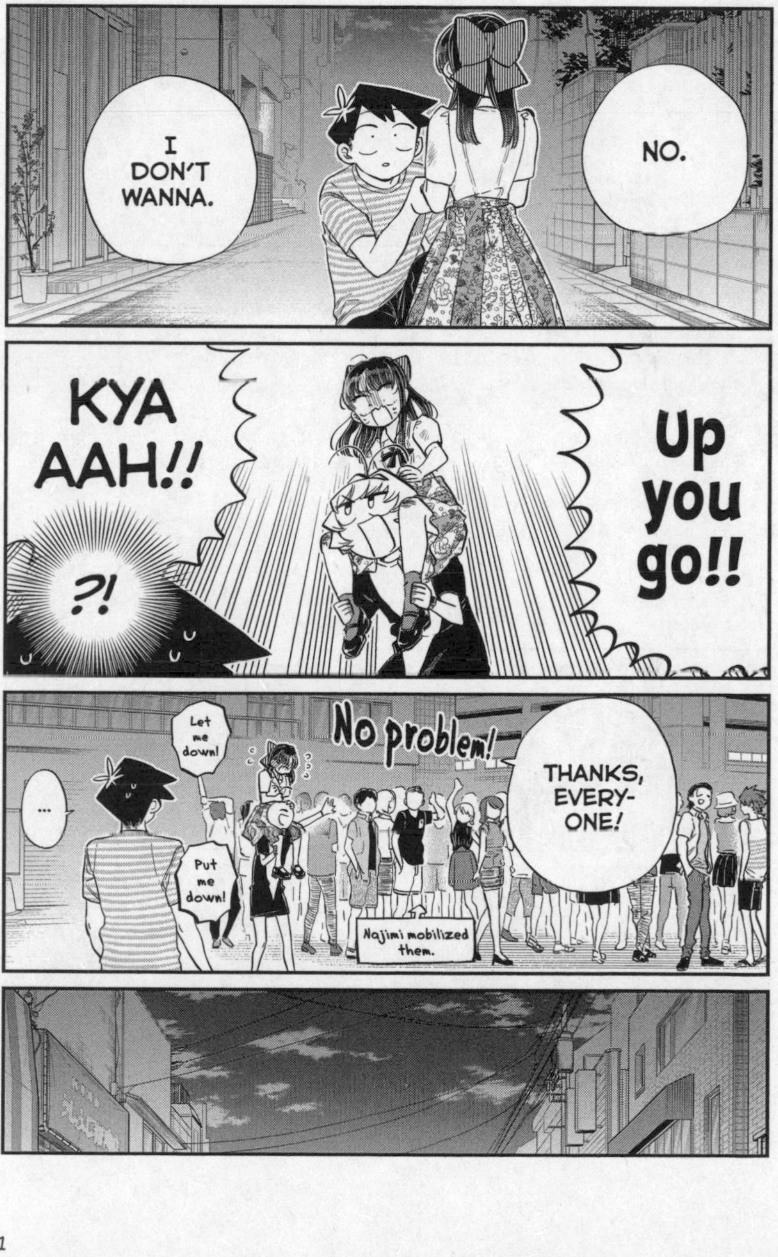
NO.
I DON'T WANNA.
Up you go!!
KYA AAH!!
?!
THANKS, EVERY-ONE!
No problem!
Najimi mobilized them.
Let me down!
Put me down!
...

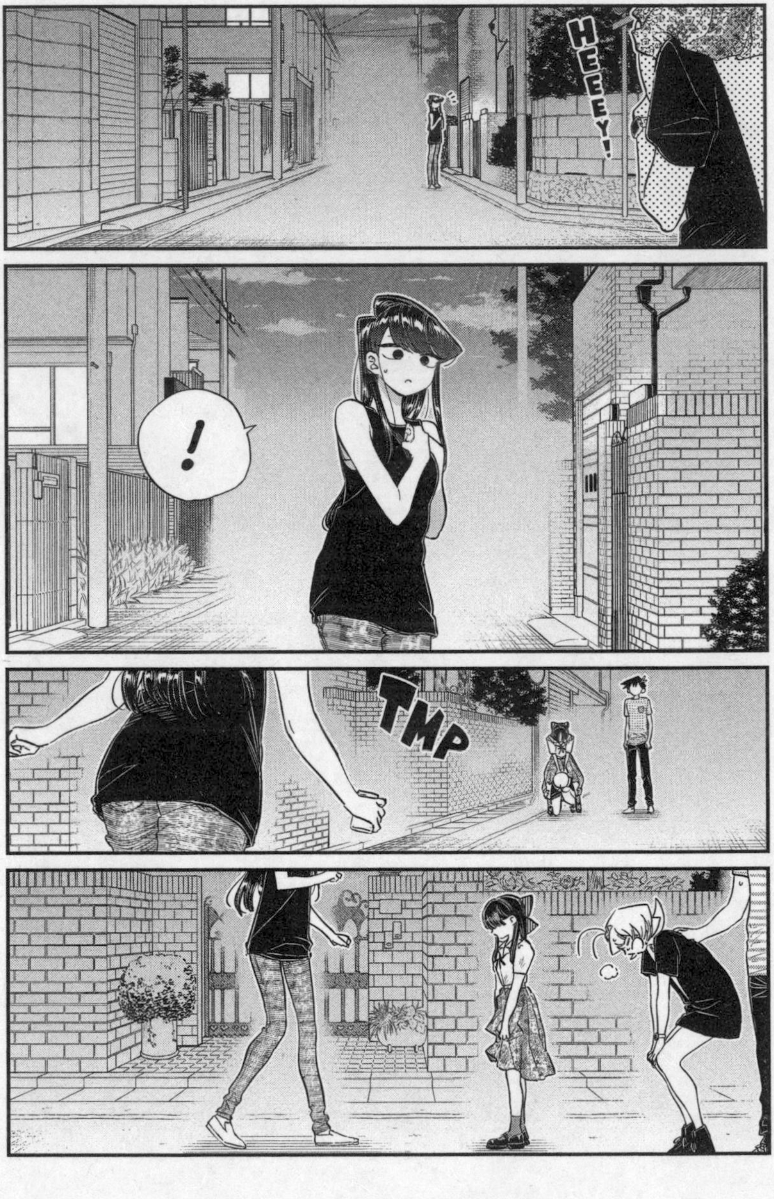
HEEEY!
!
TMP

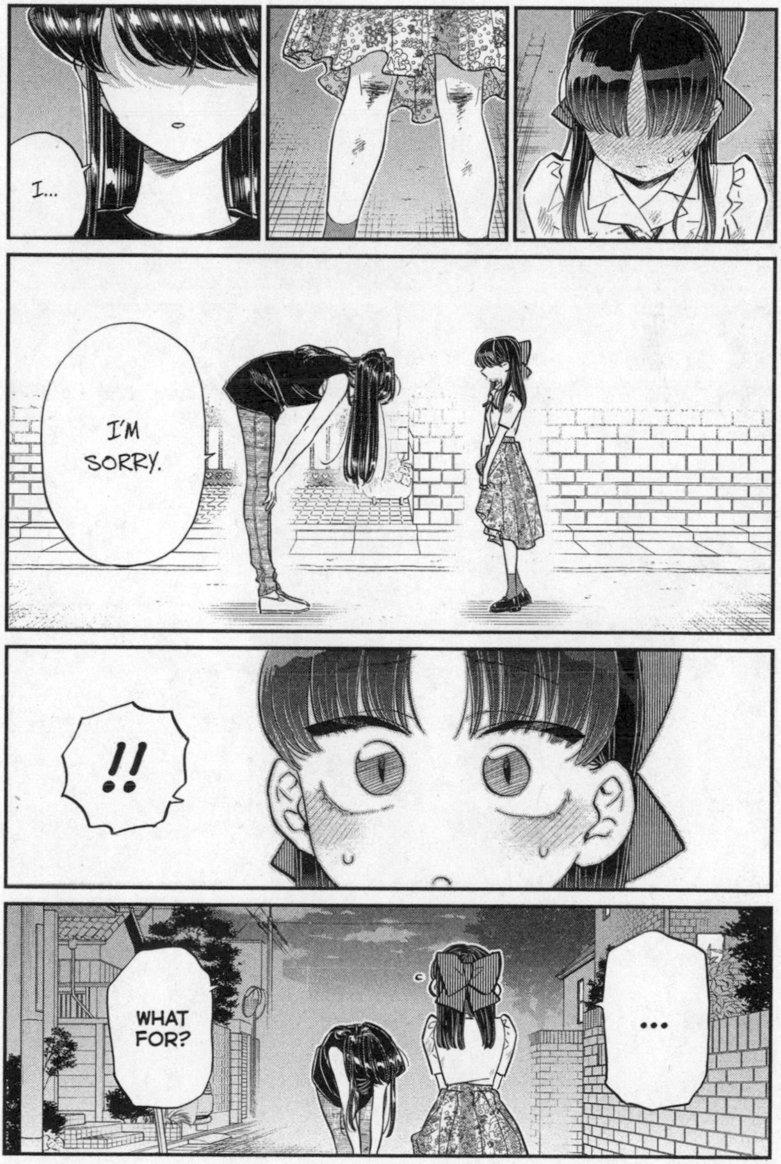
I...
I'M SORRY.
!!
...
WHAT FOR?

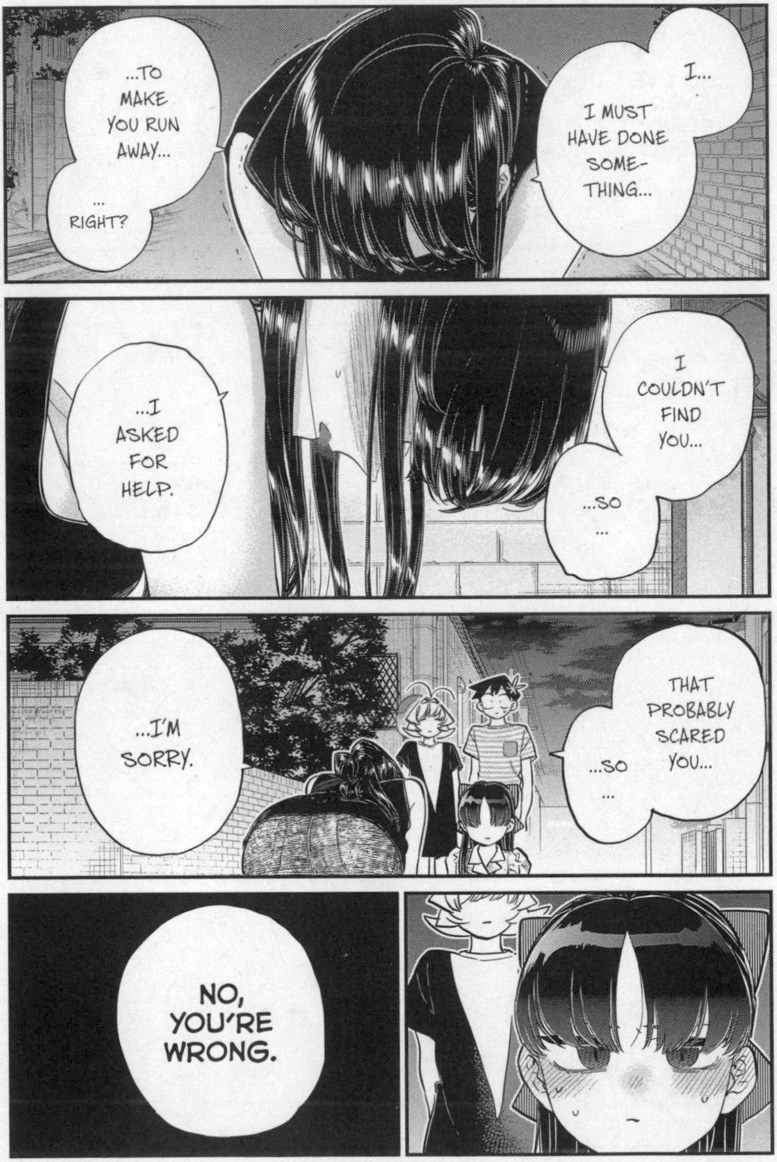
I...
I MUST HAVE DONE SOME-THING...
...TO MAKE YOU RUN AWAY...
...RIGHT?
I COULDN'T FIND YOU...
...SO ...
...I ASKED FOR HELP.
THAT PROBABLY SCARED YOU...
...SO ...
...I'M SORRY.
NO, YOU'RE WRONG.

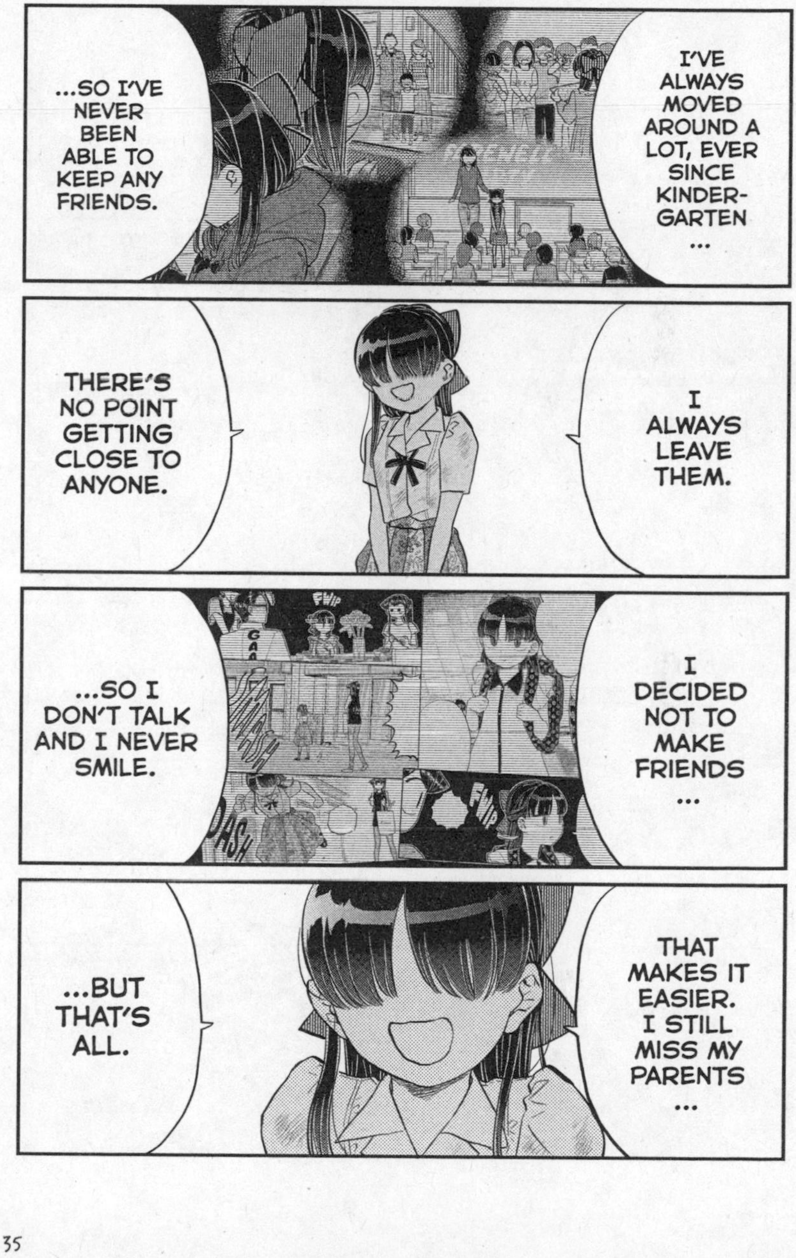
I'VE ALWAYS MOVED AROUND A LOT, EVER SINCE KINDER-GARTEN...
...SO I'VE NEVER BEEN ABLE TO KEEP ANY FRIENDS.
I ALWAYS LEAVE THEM.
THERE'S NO POINT GETTING CLOSE TO ANYONE.
I DECIDED NOT TO MAKE FRIENDS...
FWIP
DASH
...SO I DON'T TALK AND I NEVER SMILE.
THAT MAKES IT EASIER. I STILL MISS MY PARENTS...
...BUT THAT'S ALL.

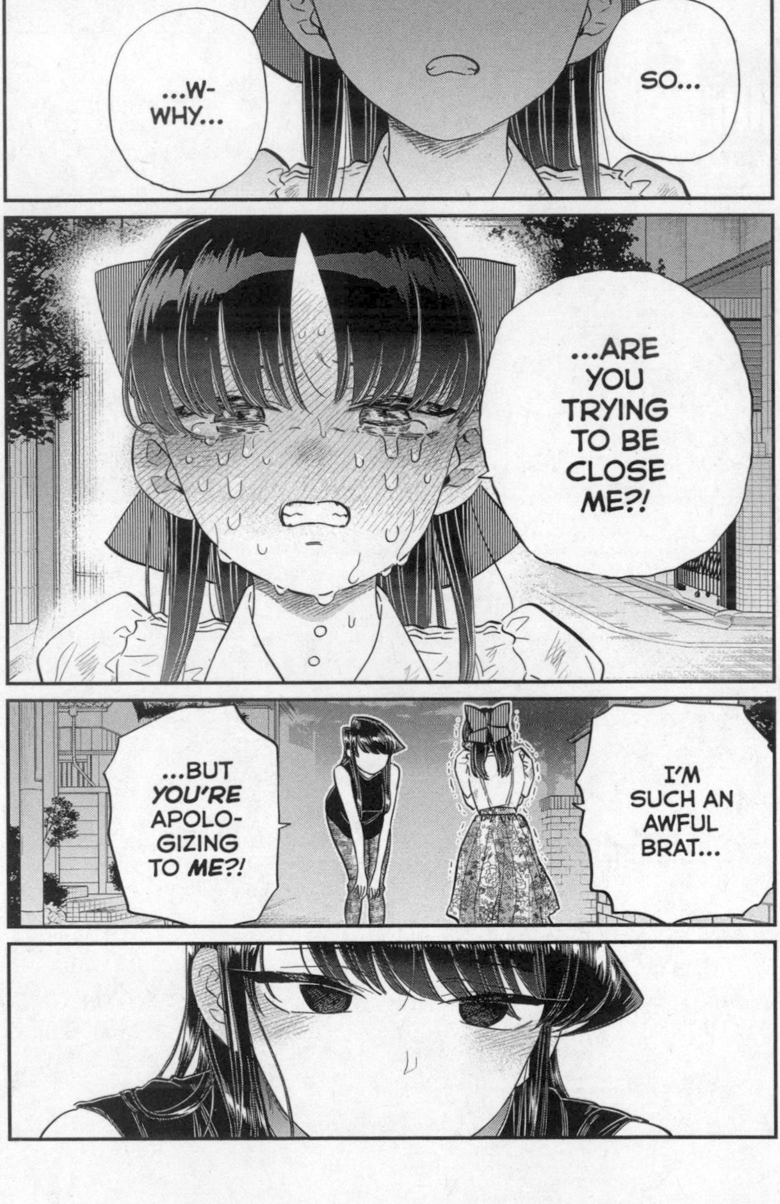
SO...
...W-WHY...
...ARE YOU TRYING TO BE CLOSE ME?!
I'M SUCH AN AWFUL BRAT...
...BUT YOU'RE APOLOGIZING TO ME?!

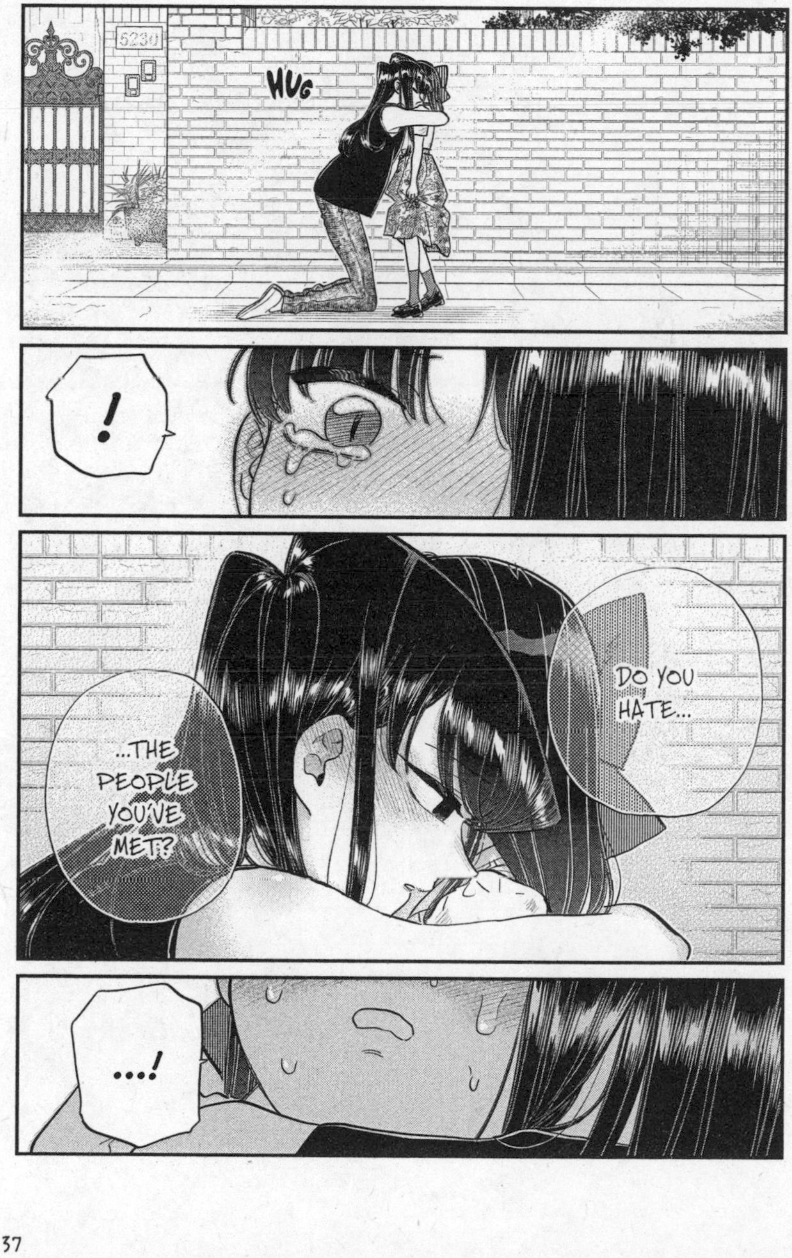
HUG
5230
!
DO YOU HATE...
...THE PEOPLE YOU'VE MET?
...!

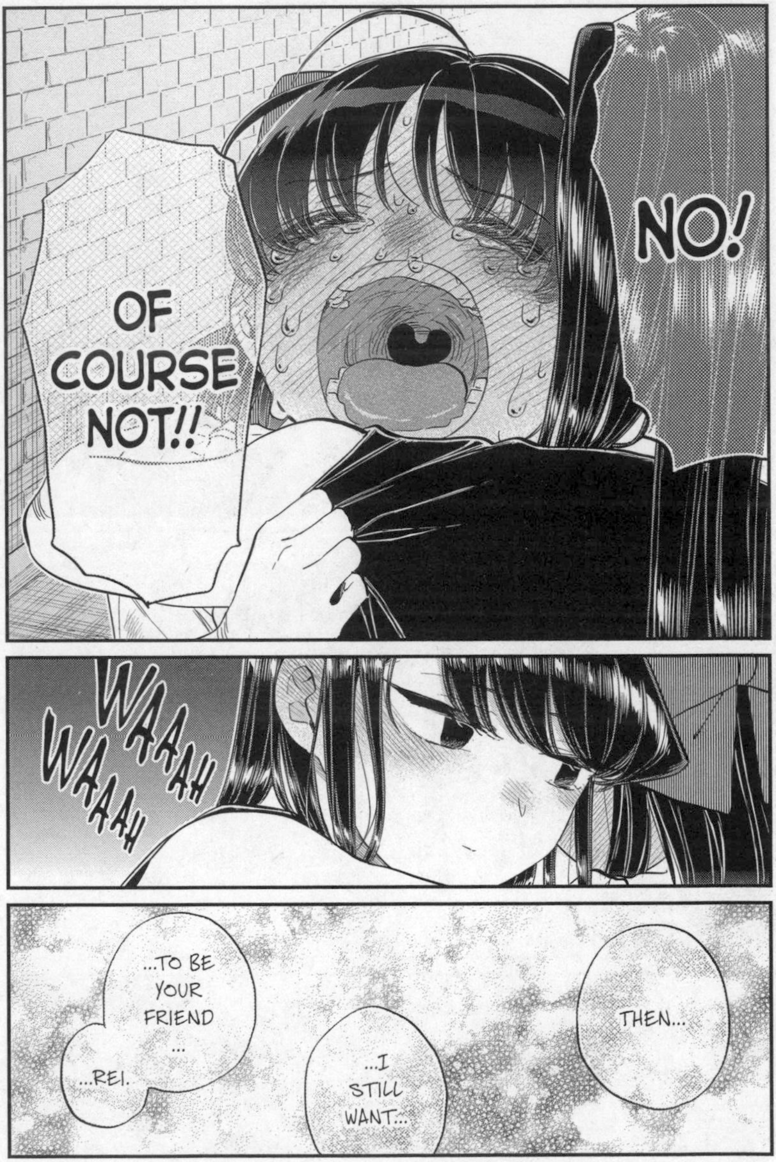
NO!
OF COURSE NOT!!
WAAAH WAAAH
THEN...
...I STILL WANT...
...TO BE YOUR FRIEND ...
...REI.

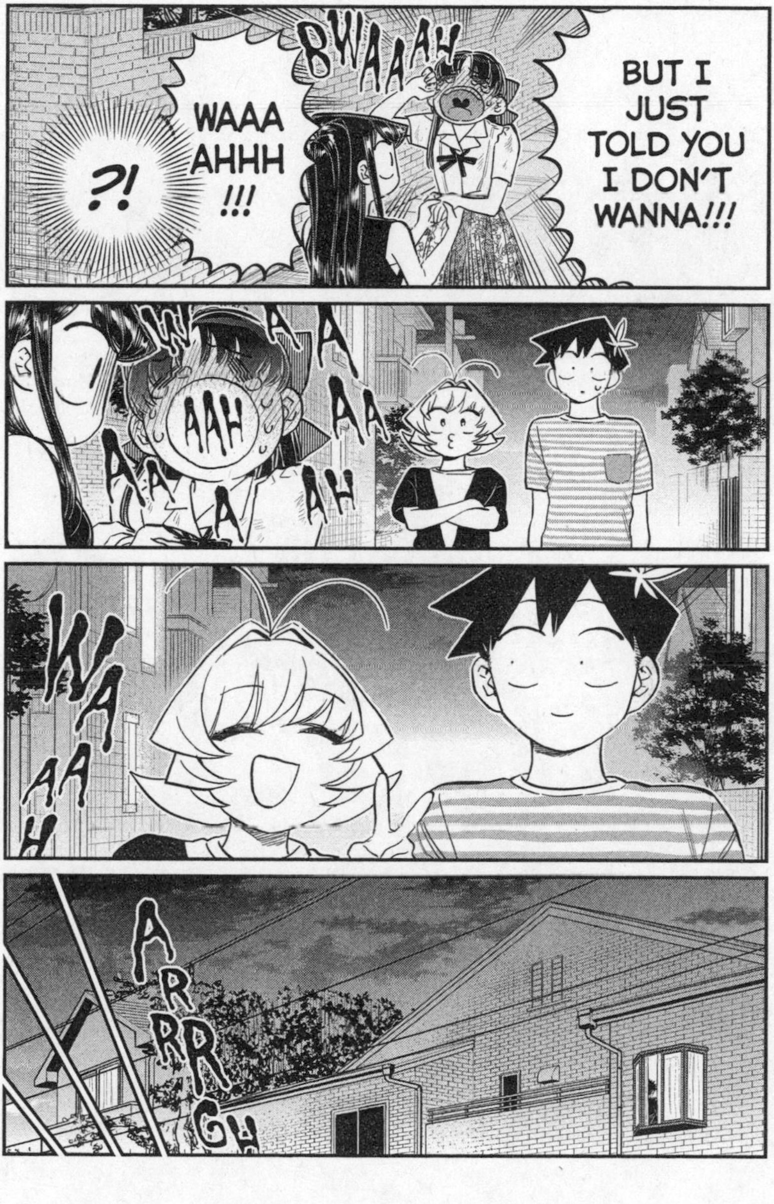
BUT I JUST TOLD YOU I DON'T WANNA!!!
BWAAAAH
WAAA AHHH !!!
?!
WAAAAAAAH
AAH
AAAAH
WAAAAH
ARRRGH

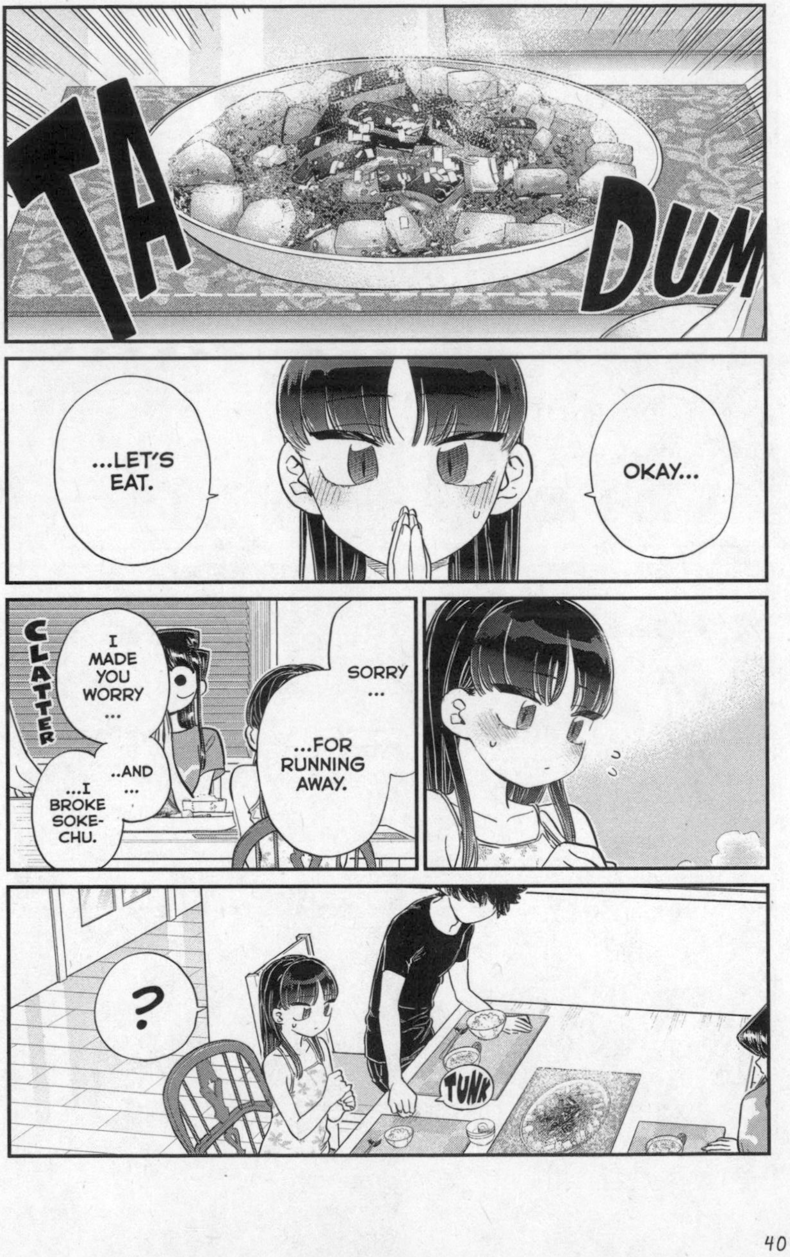
TA DUM
OKAY...
...LET'S EAT.
SORRY ...
...FOR RUNNING AWAY.
I MADE YOU WORRY ...
CLATTER
..AND ...
...I BROKE SOKE-CHU.
TUNK
?

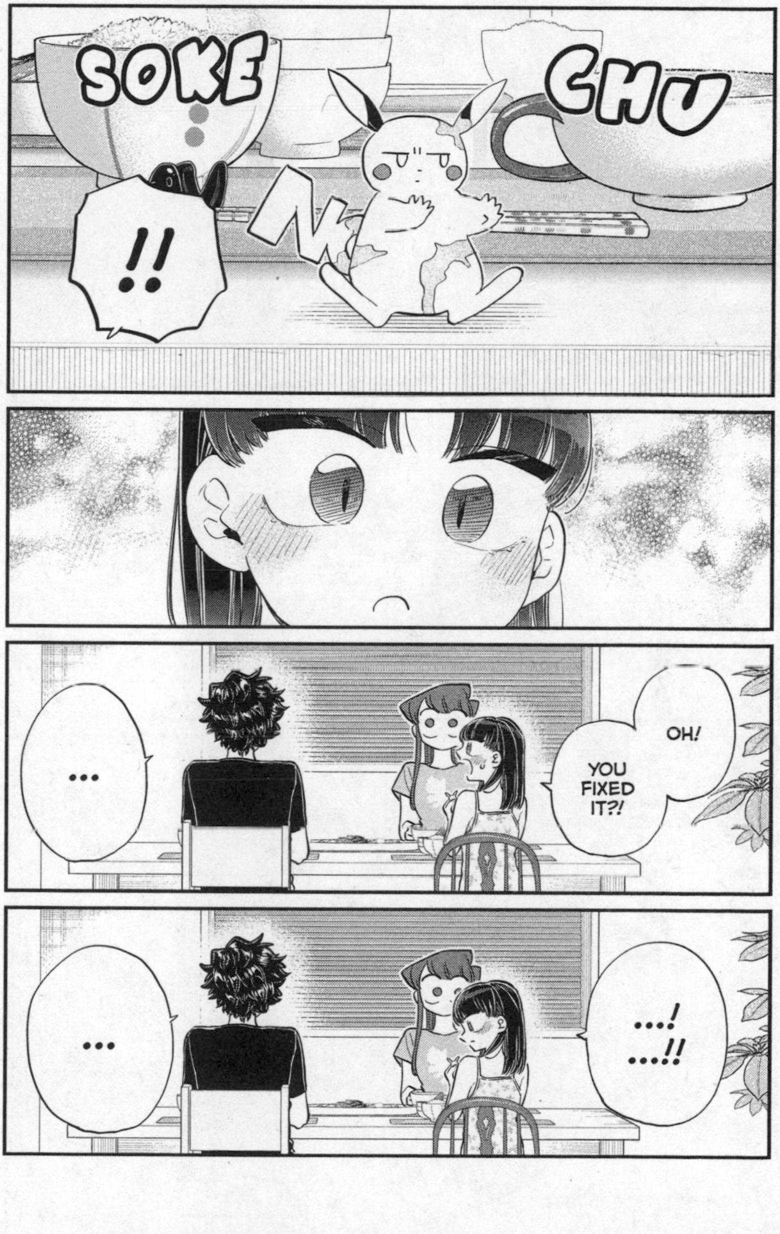
CHU
SOKE
N
!!
OH! YOU FIXED IT?!
...
...! ...!!
...

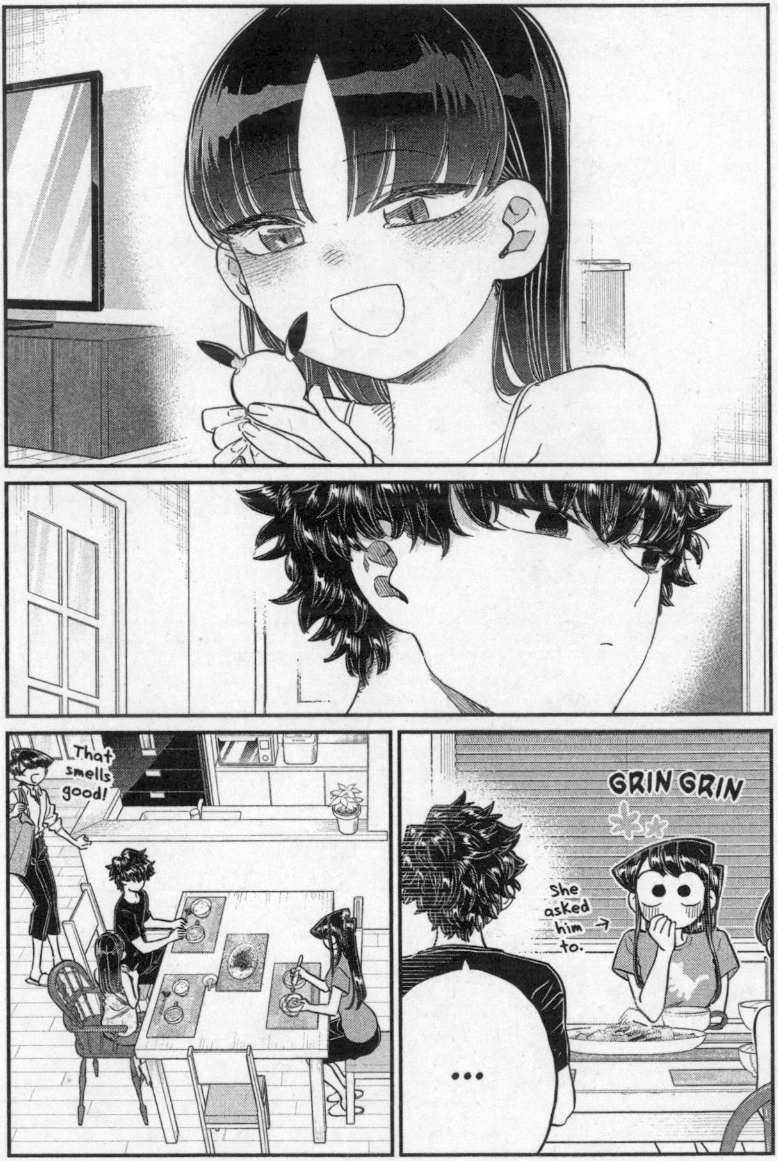
GRIN GRIN
She asked him to.
...
That smells good!

Communication 172 — The End

Komi Can't Communicate

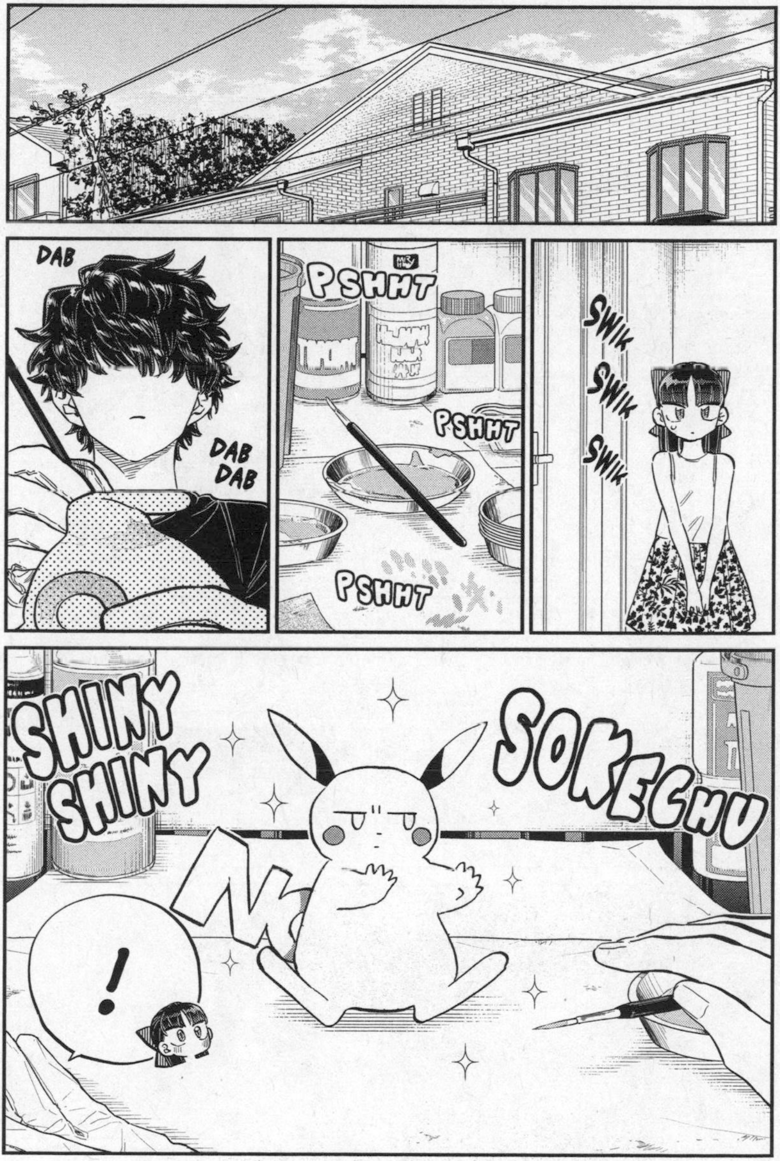
SWIK
SWIK
SWIK
PSHHT
PSHHT
PSHHT
DAB
DAB DAB
SOKECHU
SHINY SHINY
!

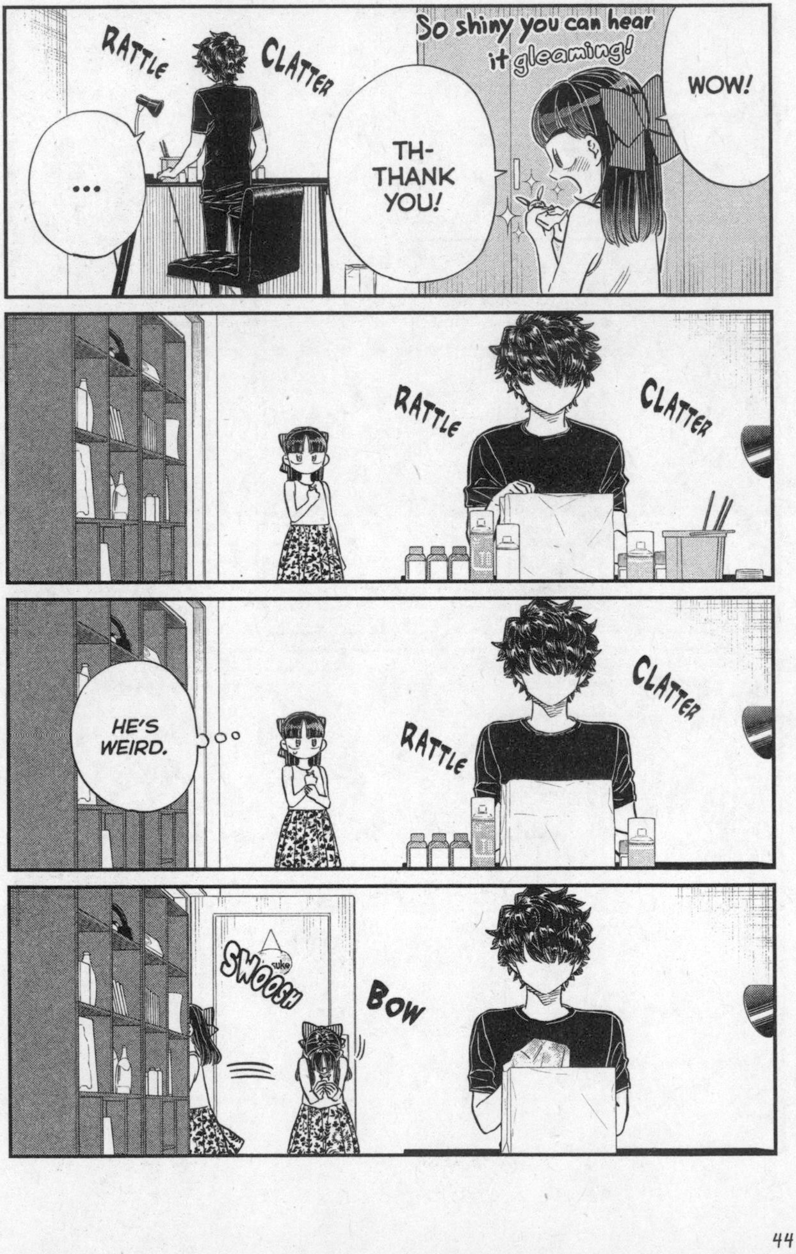
WOW!
So shiny you can hear it gleaming!
TH- THANK YOU!
CLATTER
RATTLE
...
CLATTER
RATTLE
CLATTER
RATTLE
HE'S WEIRD.
BOW
SWOOSH

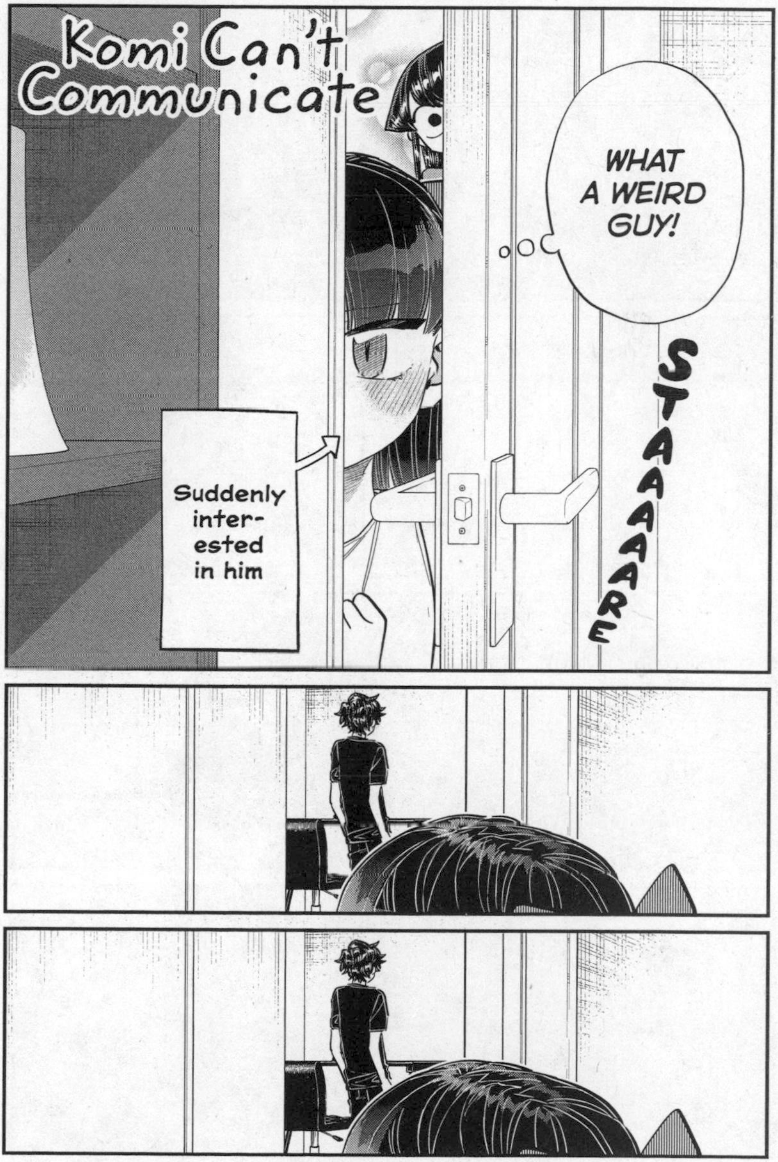
WHAT A WEIRD GUY!
Komi Can't Communicate
STAAAAARE
Suddenly inter-ested in him

Communication 173: Following Rei

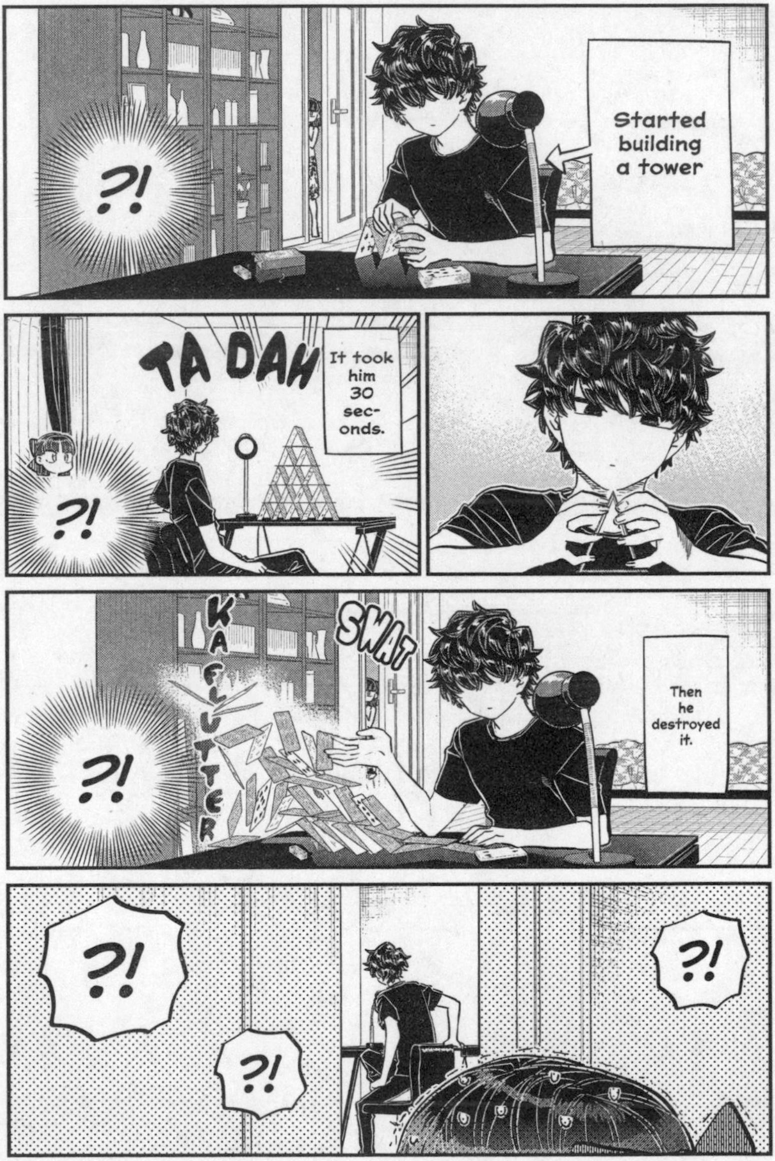
Started building a tower
?!
It took him 30 sec- onds.
TA DAH
?!
Then he destroyed it.
SWAT
KAFLUTTER
?!
?!
?!
?!

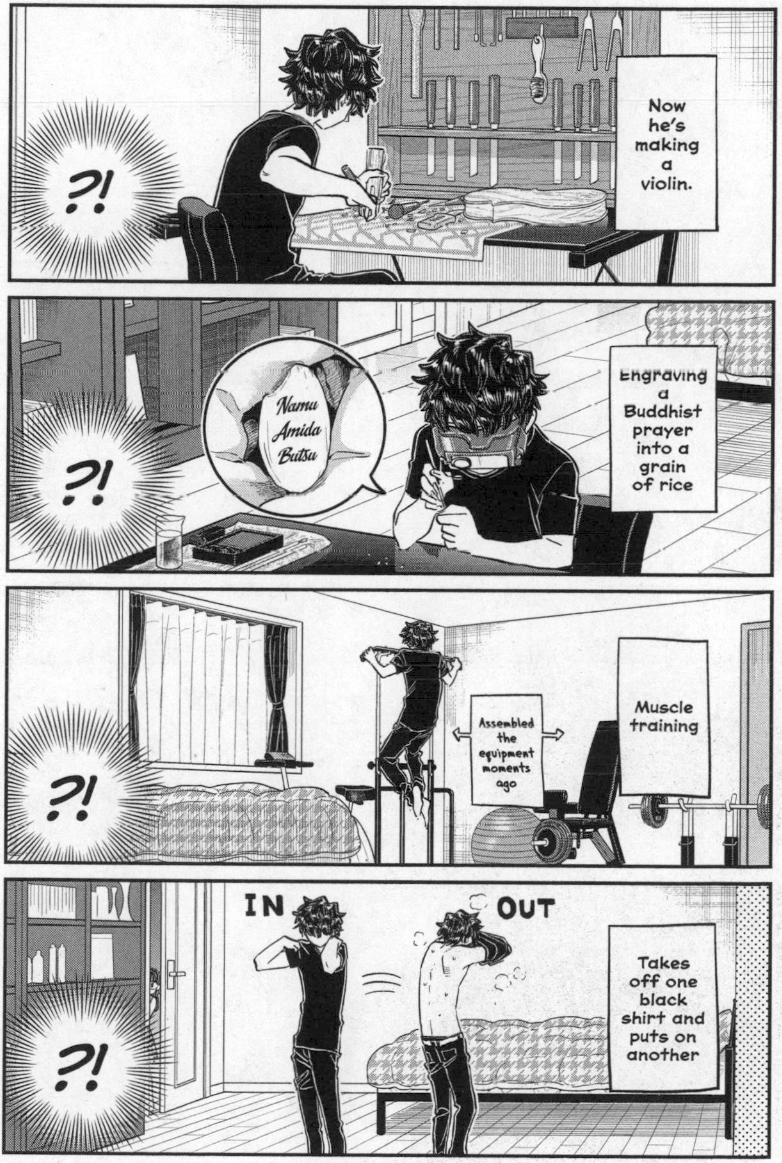
Now he's making a violin.
?!
Engraving a Buddhist prayer into a grain of rice
Namu Amida Butsu
?!
Muscle training
Assembled the equipment moments ago
?!
Takes off one black shirt and puts on another
OUT
IN
?!

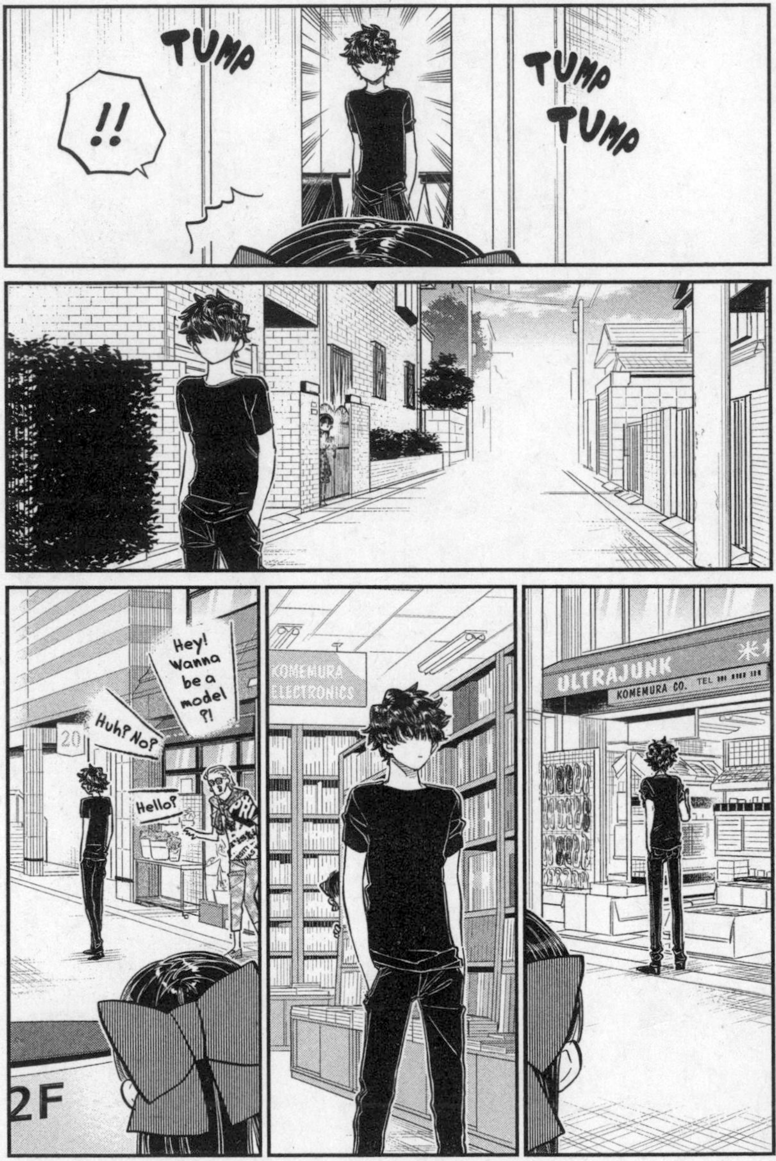
TUMP
TUMP
TUMP
!!
ULTRAJUNK
KOMEMURA CO. TEL
KOMEMURA ELECTRONICS
Hey! Wanna be a model?!
Huh? No?
20
Hello?
2F

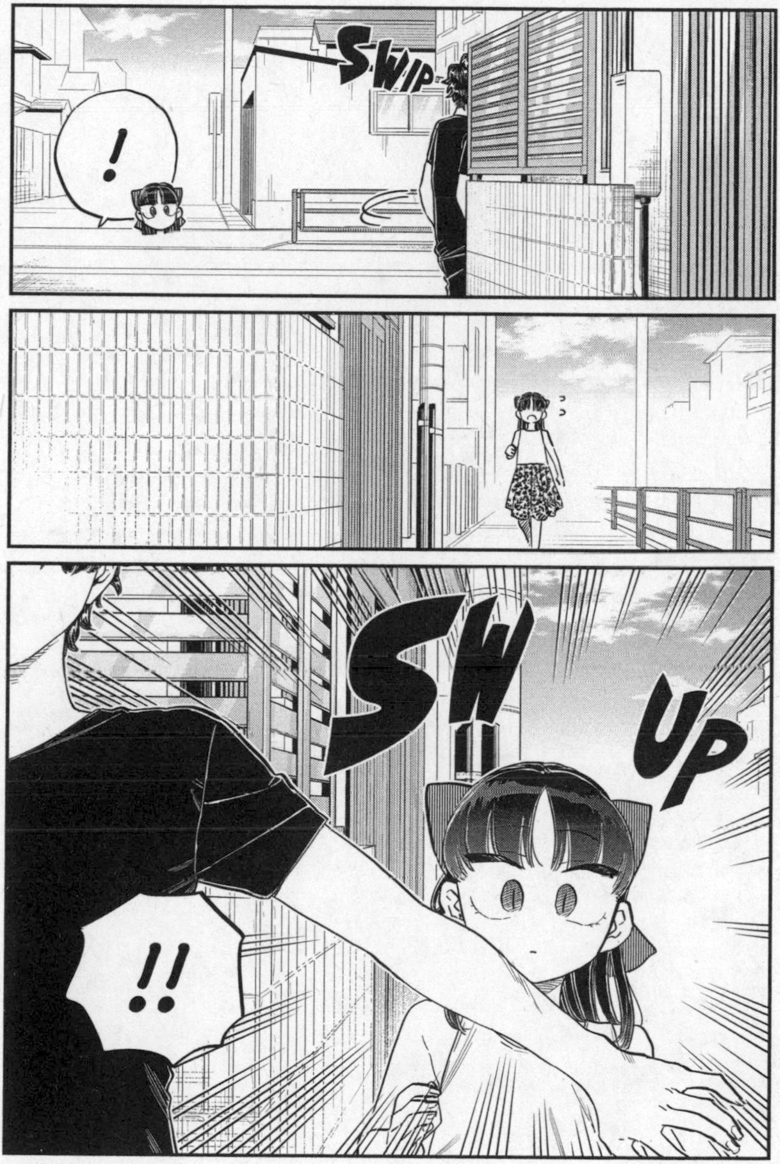
SWIP
!
SWUP
!!

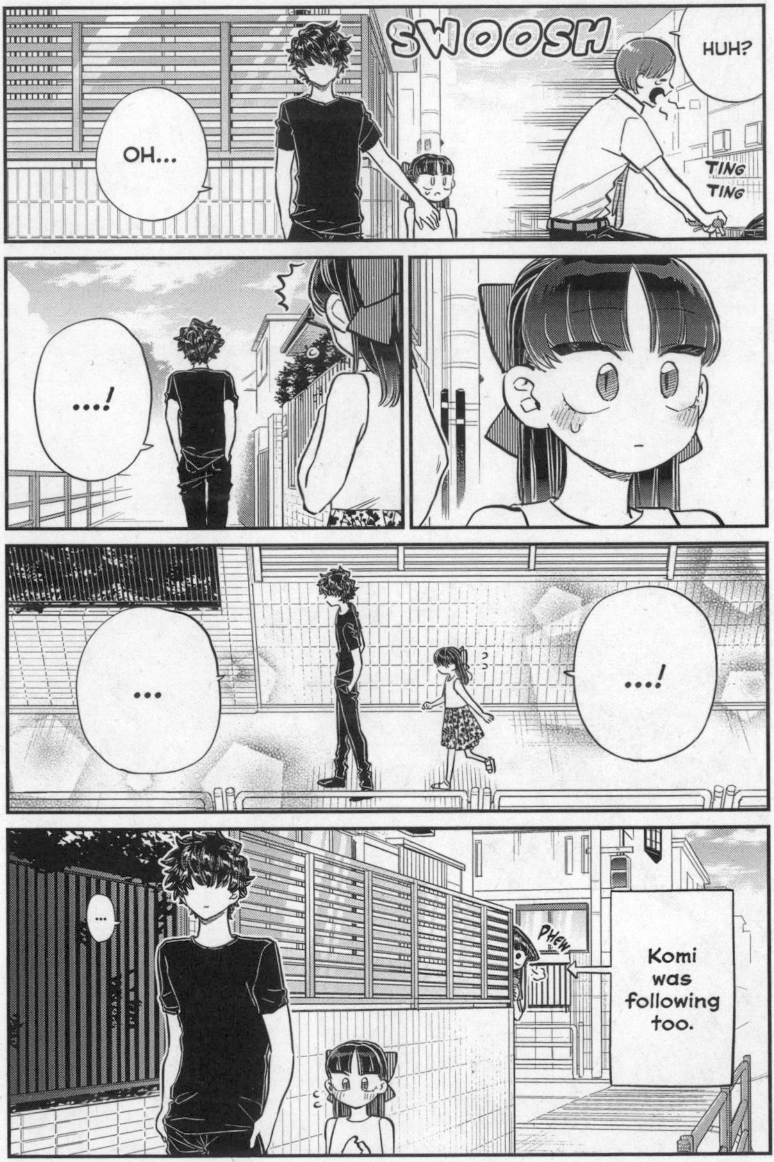
HUH?
SWOOSH
TING TING
OH...
...!
...!
...
Komi was following too.
PHEW
...

Communication 173 — The End

Komi Can't Communicate

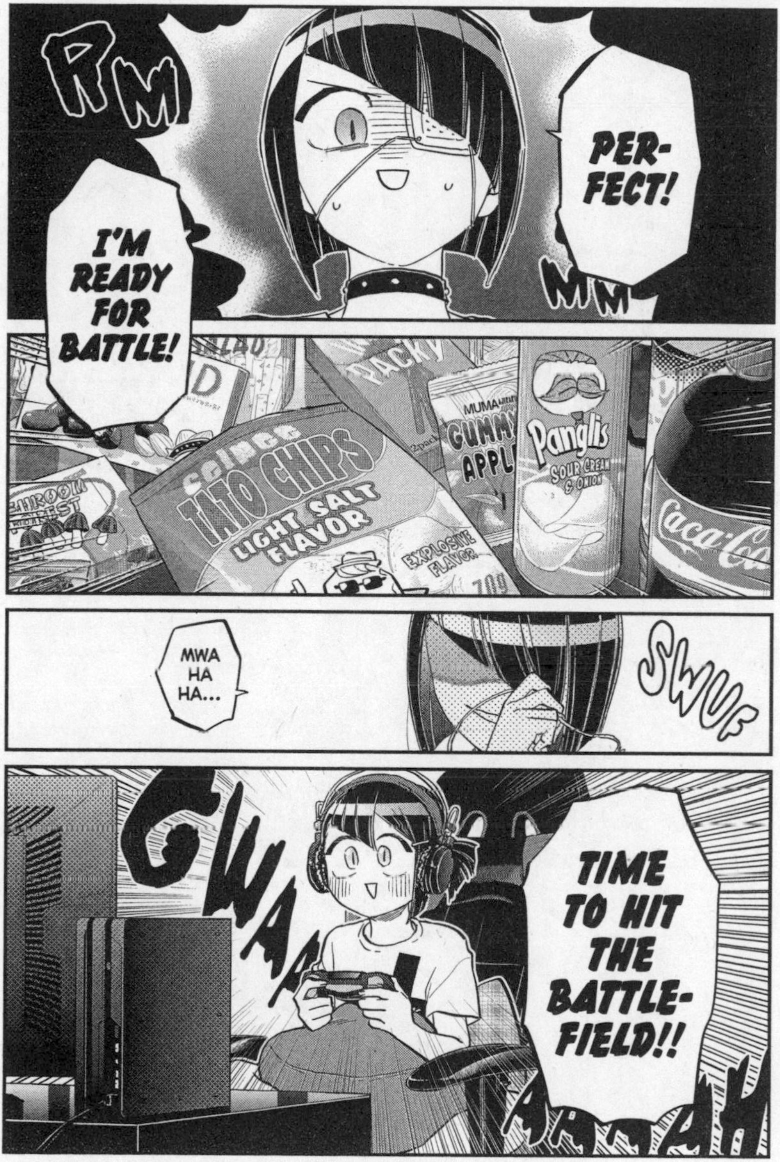
PER-FECT!
RM
MM
I'M READY FOR BATTLE!
Panglis
SOUR CREAM & ONION
GUMMY APPLE
PACKY
Caca-Cola
TATO CHIPS
LIGHT SALT FLAVOR
EXPLOSIVE FLAVOR
SWUF
MWA HA HA...
TIME TO HIT THE BATTLE-FIELD!!
GWAA
AAAAH

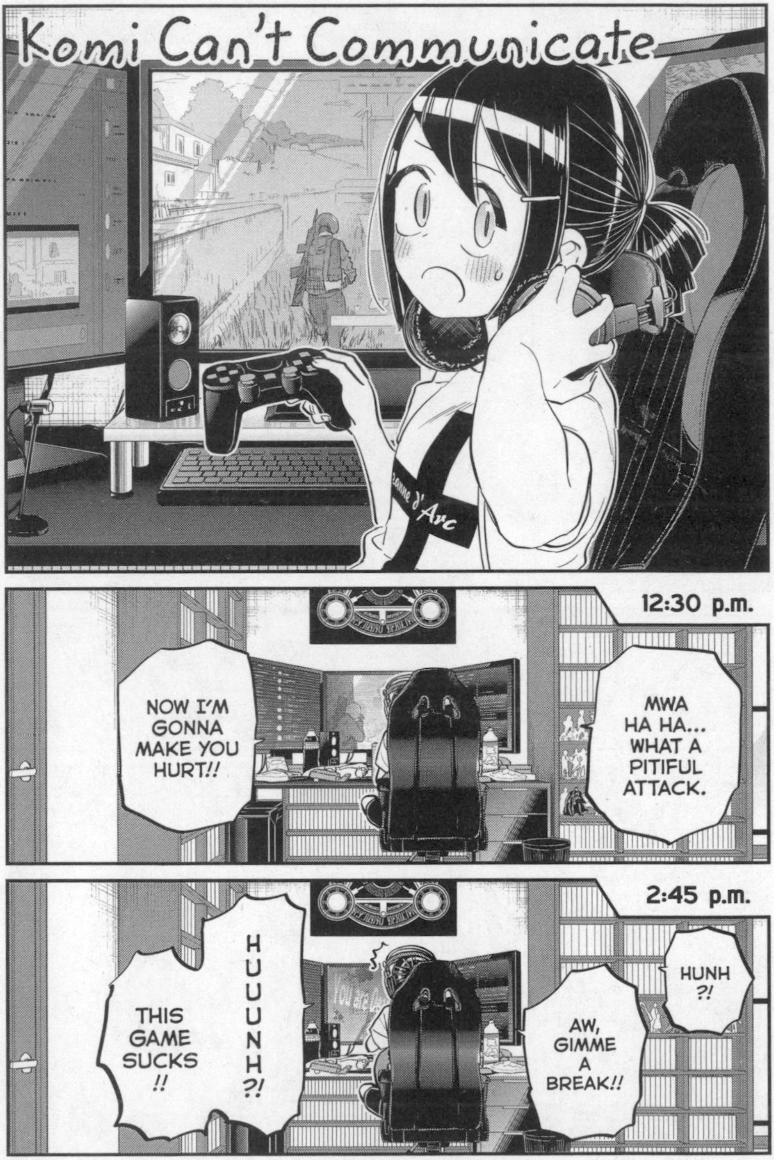
Komi Can't Communicate
12:30 p.m.
MWA HA HA... WHAT A PITIFUL ATTACK.
NOW I'M GONNA MAKE YOU HURT!!
2:45 p.m.
HUNH ?!
AW, GIMME A BREAK!!
HUUUUNH?!
THIS GAME SUCKS !!

Communication 174: Nakanaka's Grand Summer Day

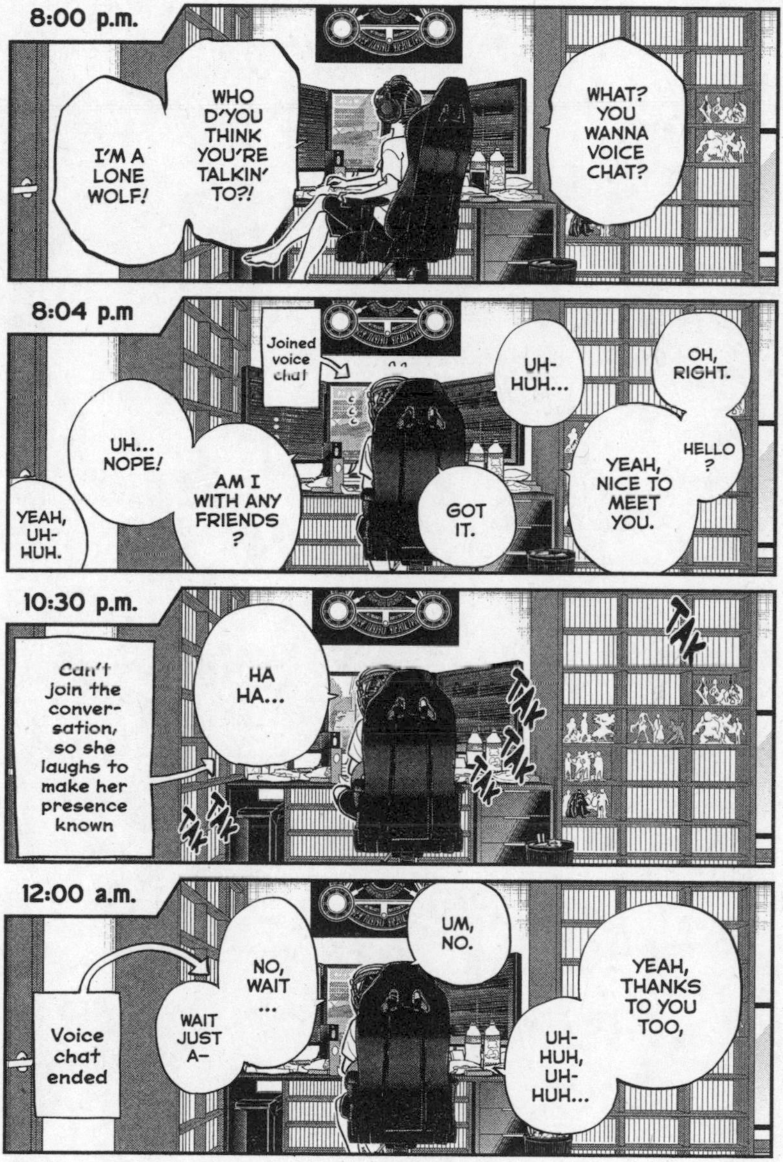
8:00 p.m.
WHAT? YOU WANNA VOICE CHAT?
WHO D'YOU THINK YOU'RE TALKIN' TO?!
I'M A LONE WOLF!
8:04 p.m
OH, RIGHT.
HELLO?
UH-HUH...
YEAH, NICE TO MEET YOU.
GOT IT.
Joined voice chat
AM I WITH ANY FRIENDS?
UH... NOPE!
YEAH, UH-HUH.
10:30 p.m.
TAK
TAK TAK TAK
HA HA...
TAK TAK
Can't join the conversation, so she laughs to make her presence known
12:00 a.m.
YEAH, THANKS TO YOU TOO,
UH-HUH, UH-HUH...
UM, NO.
NO, WAIT...
WAIT JUST A-
Voice chat ended

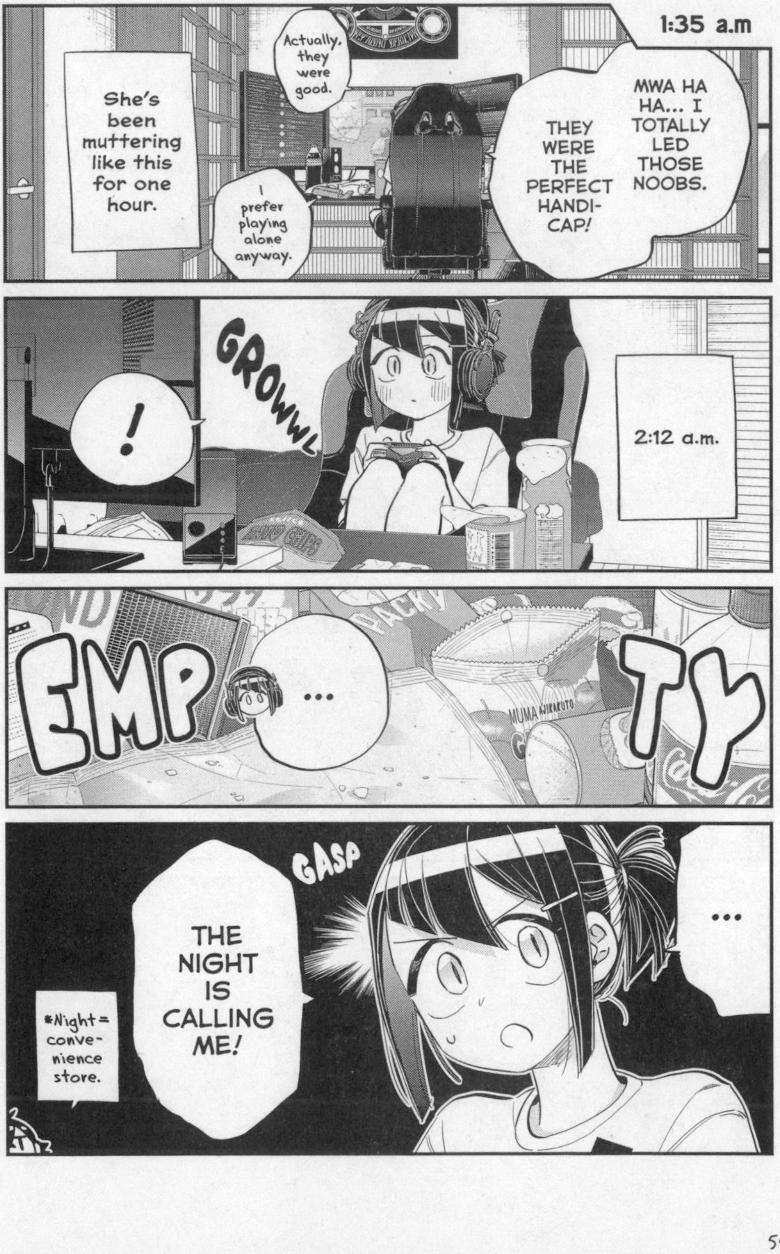
1:35 a.m
MWA HA HA... I TOTALLY LED THOSE NOOBS.
THEY WERE THE PERFECT HANDI-CAP!
Actually, they were good.
I prefer playing alone anyway.
She's been muttering like this for one hour.
2:12 a.m.
GROWWL
!
EMPTY
PACKY
MUMA AJIRAKUTO
...
...
GASP
THE NIGHT IS CALLING ME!
*Night = conve-nience store.

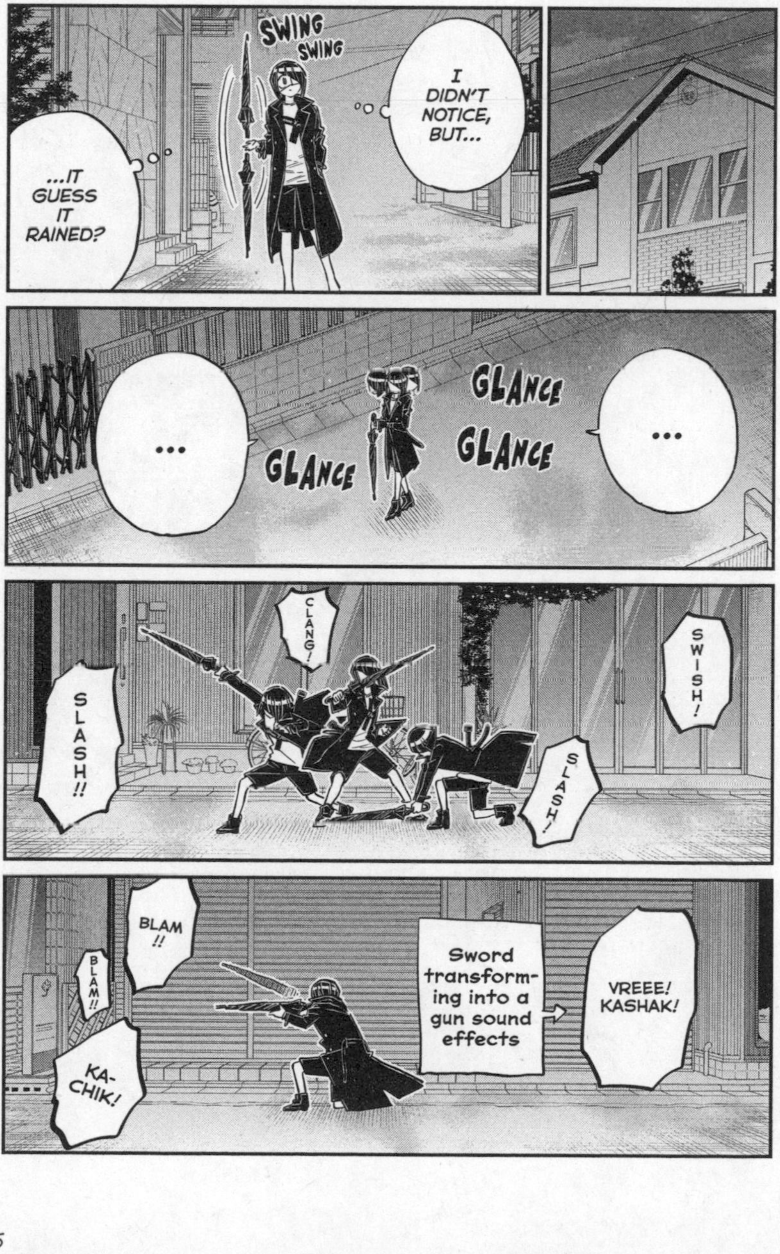
I DIDN'T NOTICE, BUT...
SWING
SWING
...IT GUESS IT RAINED?
...
GLANCE
GLANCE
GLANCE
...
SWISH!
SLASH!
CLANG!
SLASH!!
VREEE! KASHAK!
Sword transforming into a gun sound effects
BLAM!!
BLAM!!
KA-CHIK!

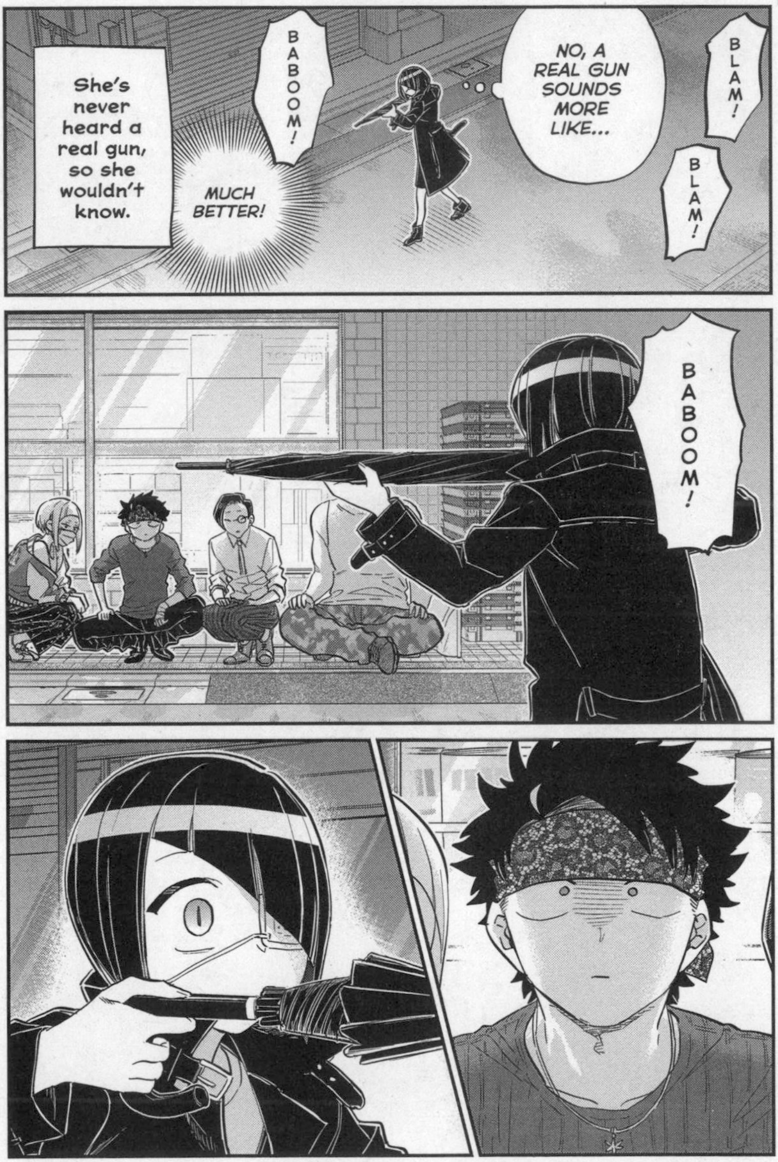
BLAM!
BLAM!
NO, A REAL GUN SOUNDS MORE LIKE...
BABOOM!
MUCH BETTER!
She's never heard a real gun, so she wouldn't know.
BABOOM!

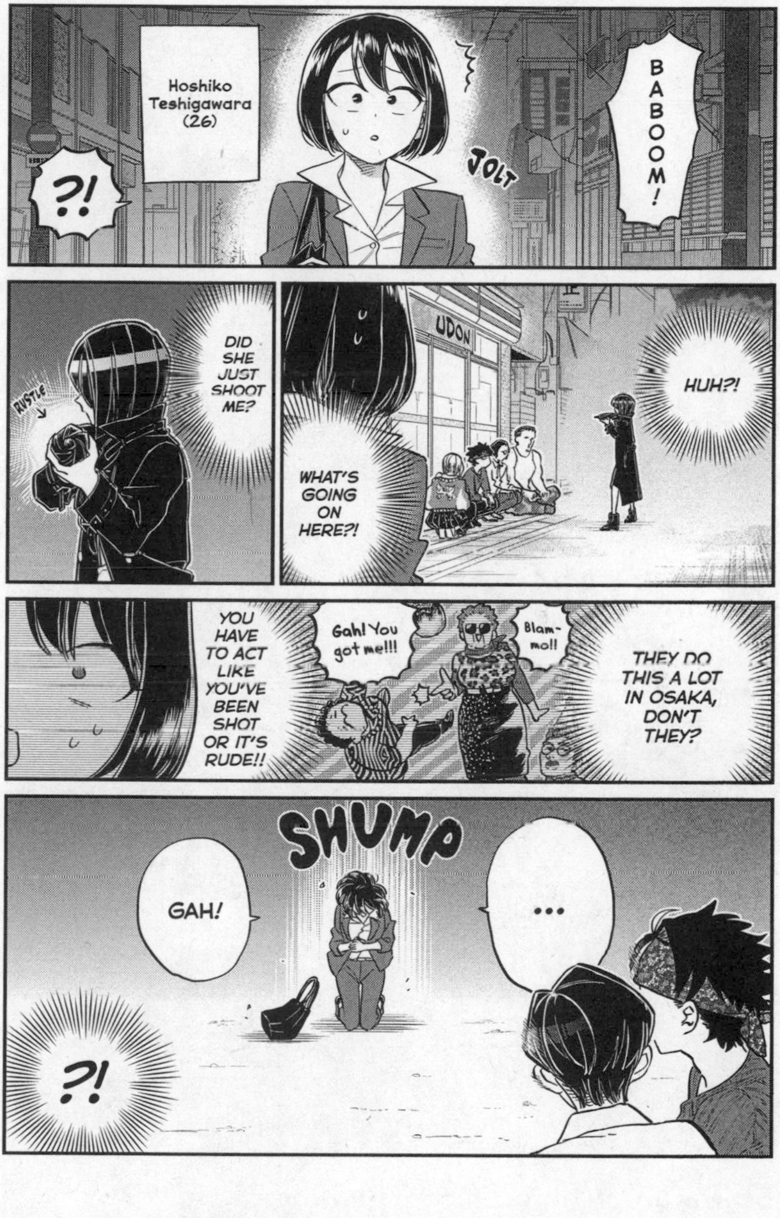
BABOOM!
JOLT
Hoshiko Teshigawara (26)
?!
HUH?!
WHAT'S GOING ON HERE?!
DID SHE JUST SHOOT ME?
RUSTLE
THEY DO THIS A LOT IN OSAKA, DON'T THEY?
Blam-mo!!
Gah! You got me!!!
YOU HAVE TO ACT LIKE YOU'VE BEEN SHOT OR IT'S RUDE!!
SHUMP
...
GAH!
?!

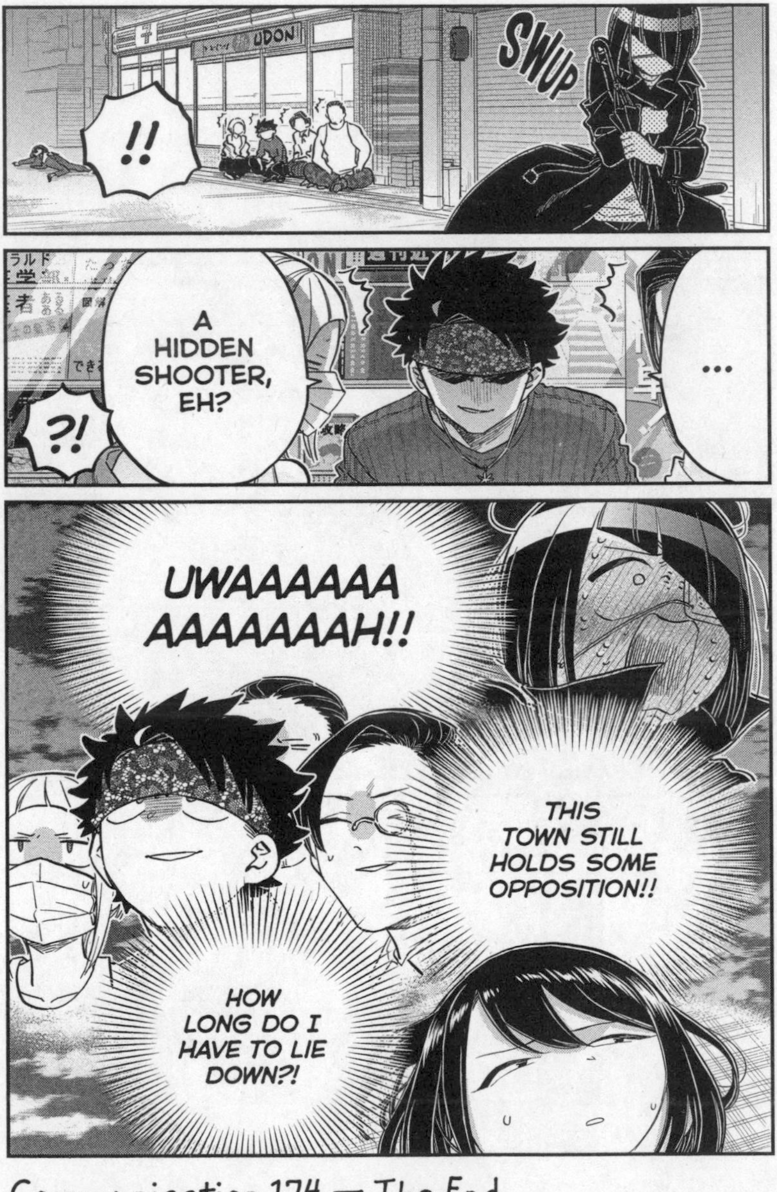
SWUP
UDON
!!
...
A HIDDEN SHOOTER, EH?
?!
UWAAAAAAA AAAAAAAH!!
THIS TOWN STILL HOLDS SOME OPPOSITION!!
HOW LONG DO I HAVE TO LIE DOWN?!

Communication 174 — The End

Komi Can't Communicate

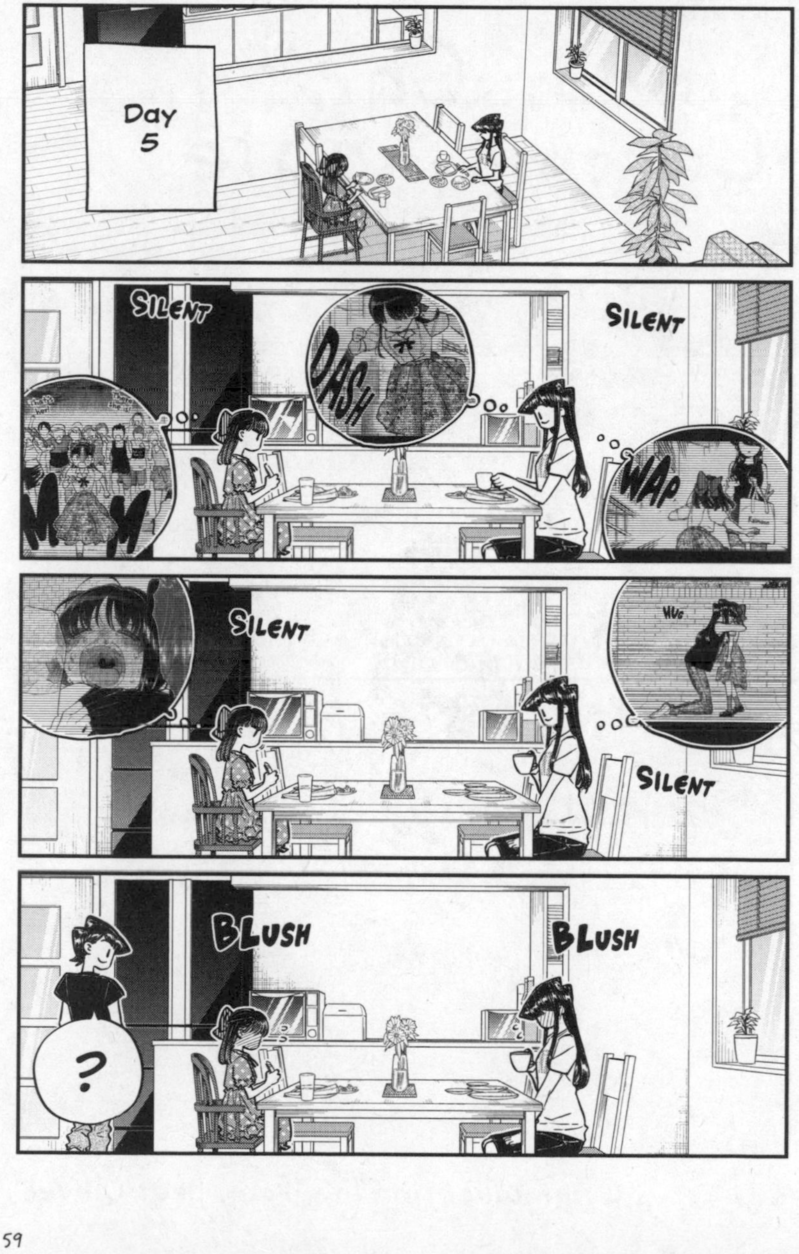
Day 5
SILENT
WAP
DASH
SILENT
HUG
SILENT
SILENT
BLUSH
BLUSH
?

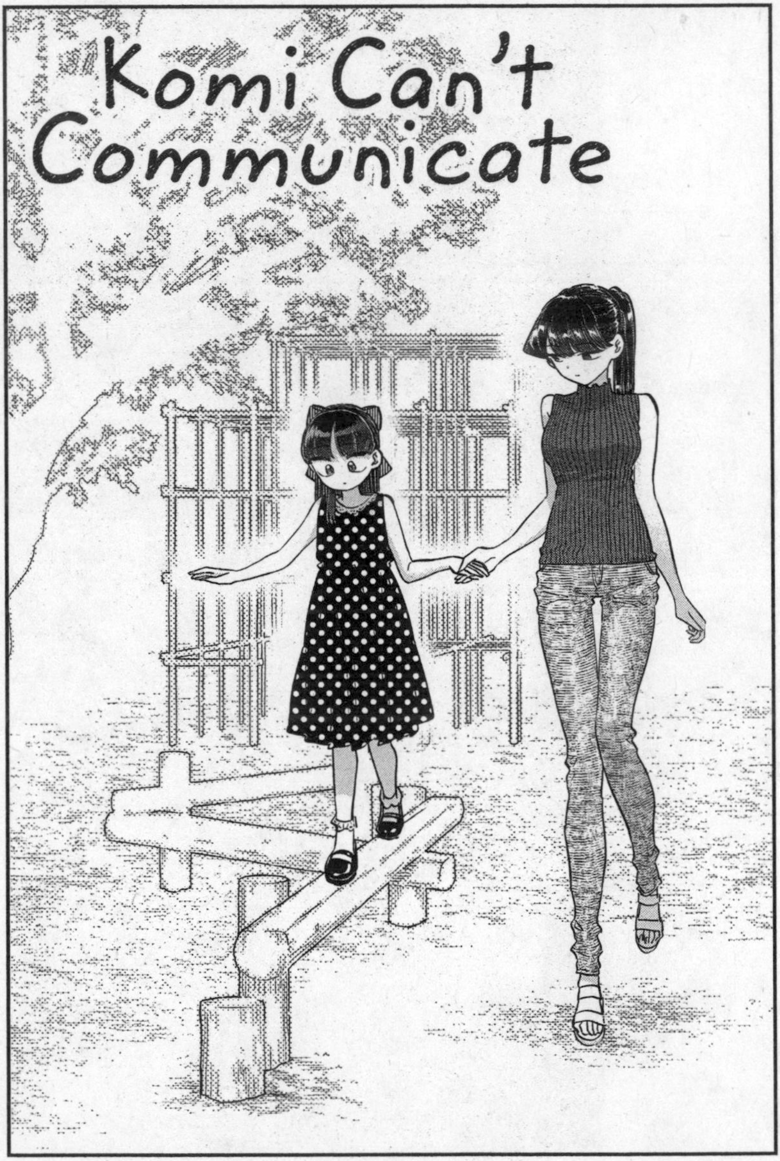
Komi Can't Communicate

Communication 175: Four-Leaf Clover

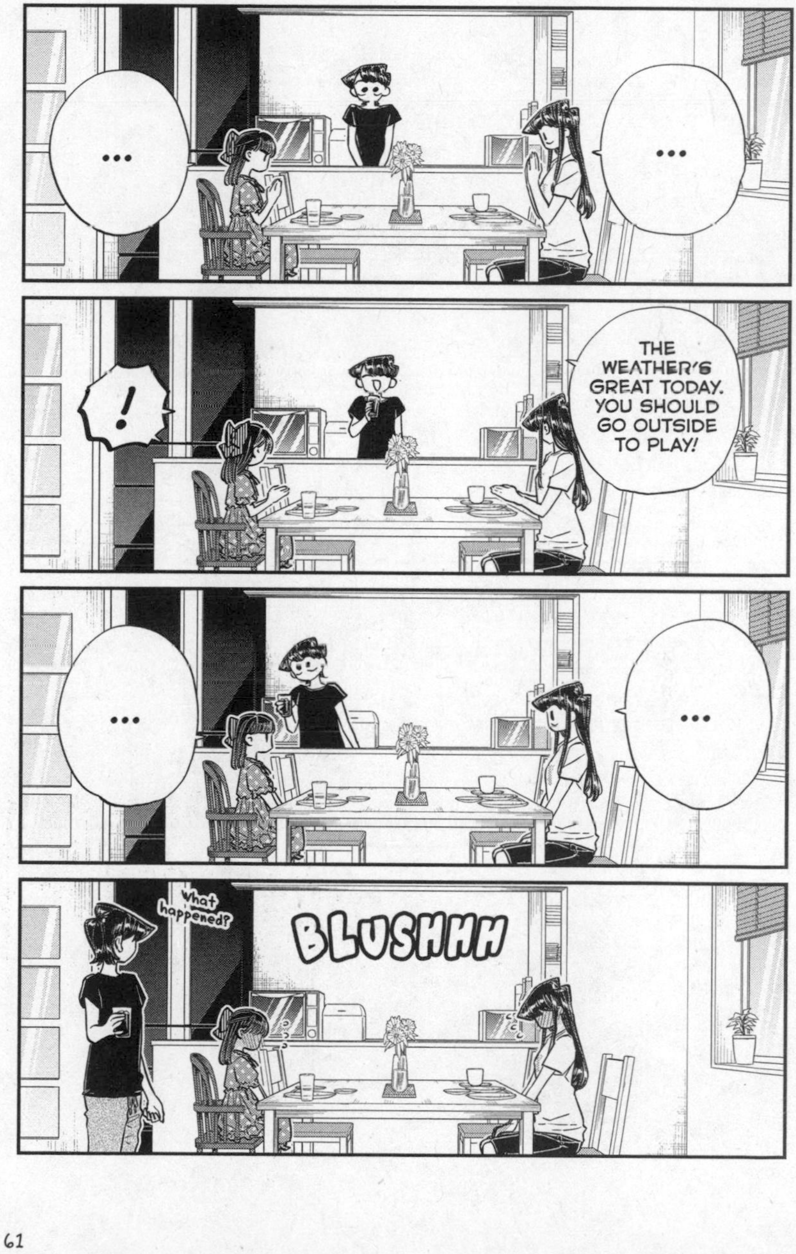
...
...
THE WEATHER'S GREAT TODAY. YOU SHOULD GO OUTSIDE TO PLAY!
!
...
...
BLUSHHH
What happened?

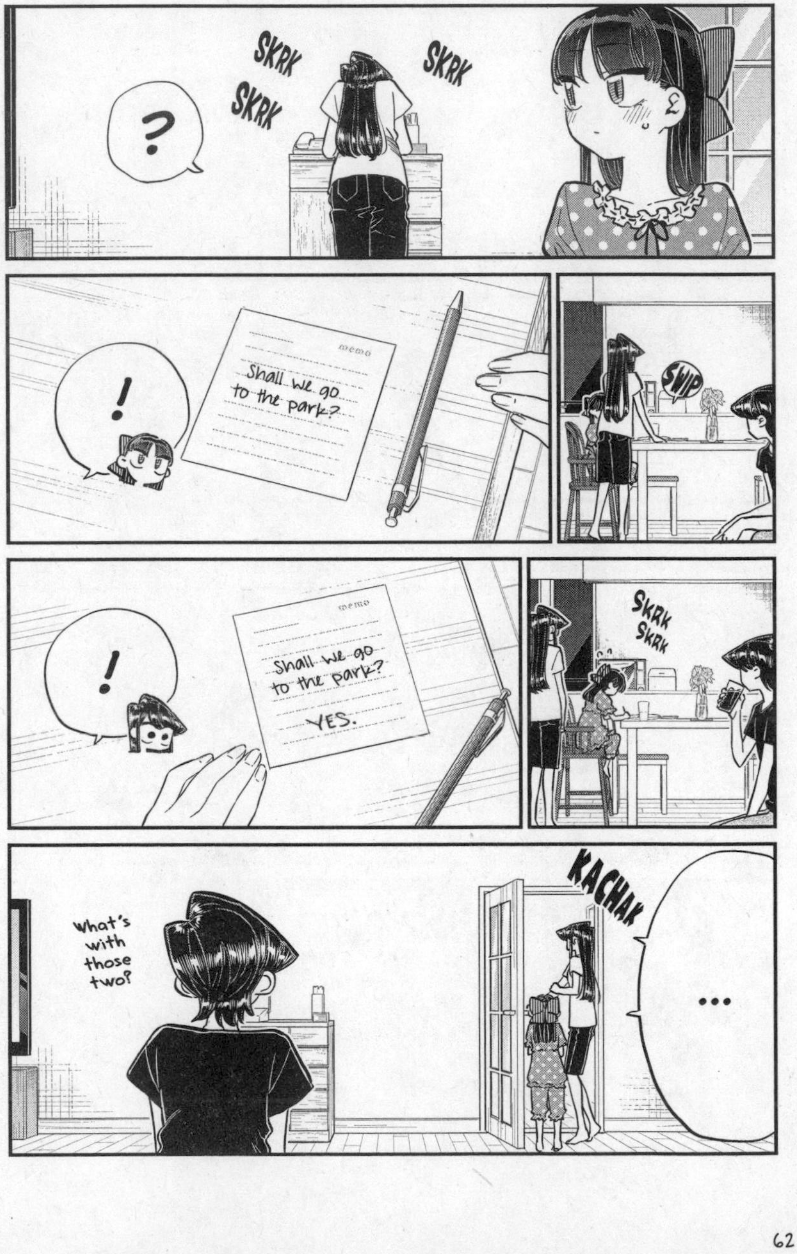
SKRK
SKRK
SKRK
?
SWIP
memo
Shall we go to the park?
!
SKRK SKRK
memo
Shall we go to the park?
YES.
!
KACHAK
...
What's with those two?

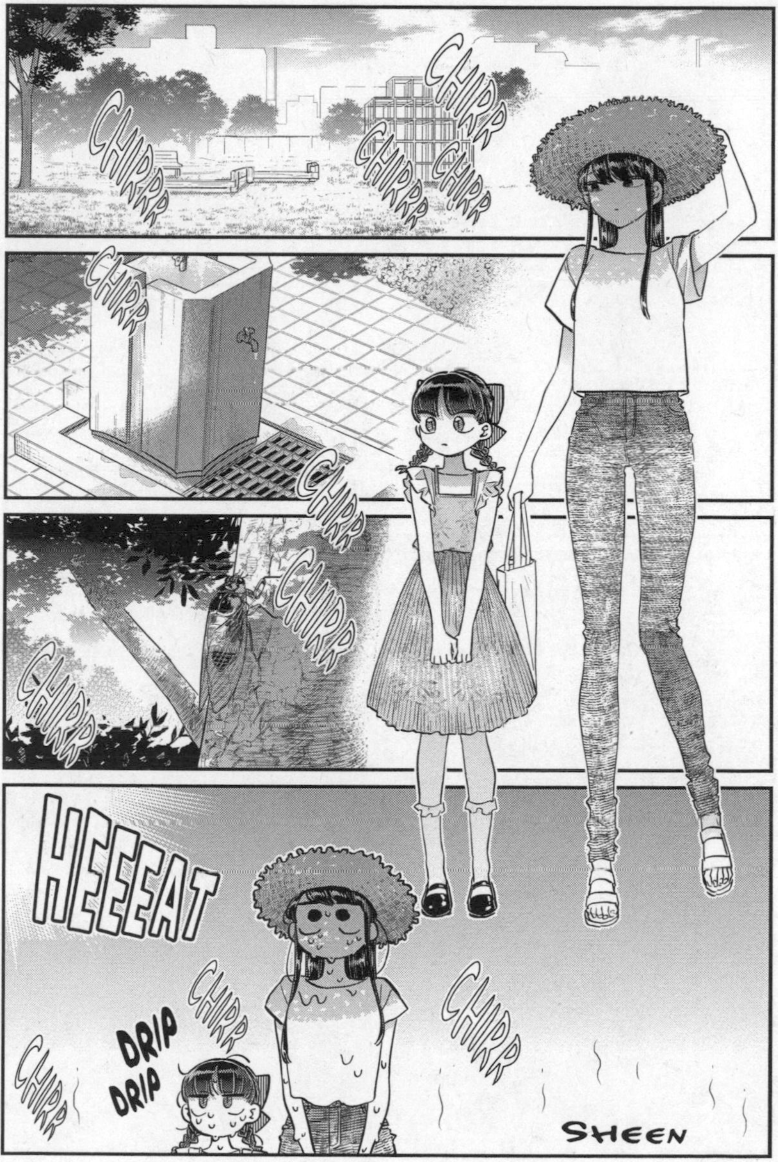
CHIRR
CHIRR
CHIRRR
CHIRRR
CHIRR
CHIRR
CHIRR
CHIRR
HEEEAT
CHIRR
SHEEN
CHIRR
DRIP
DRIP
CHIRR

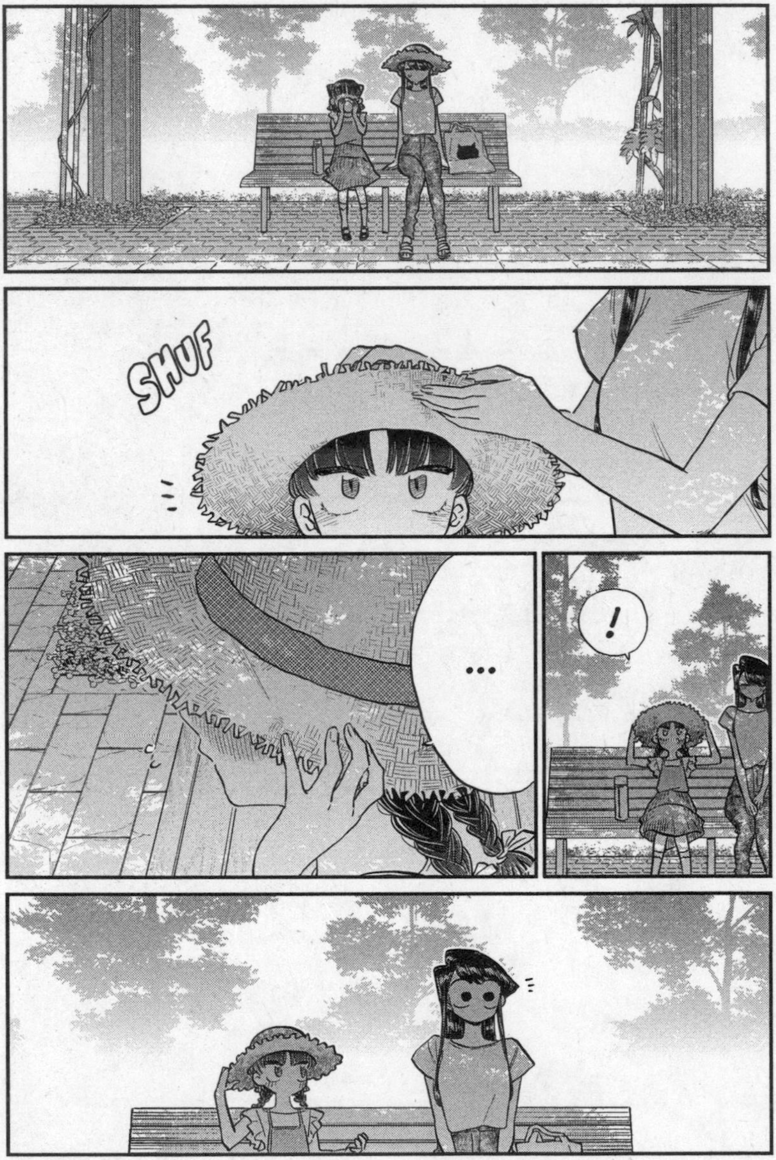
SHUF
...
!

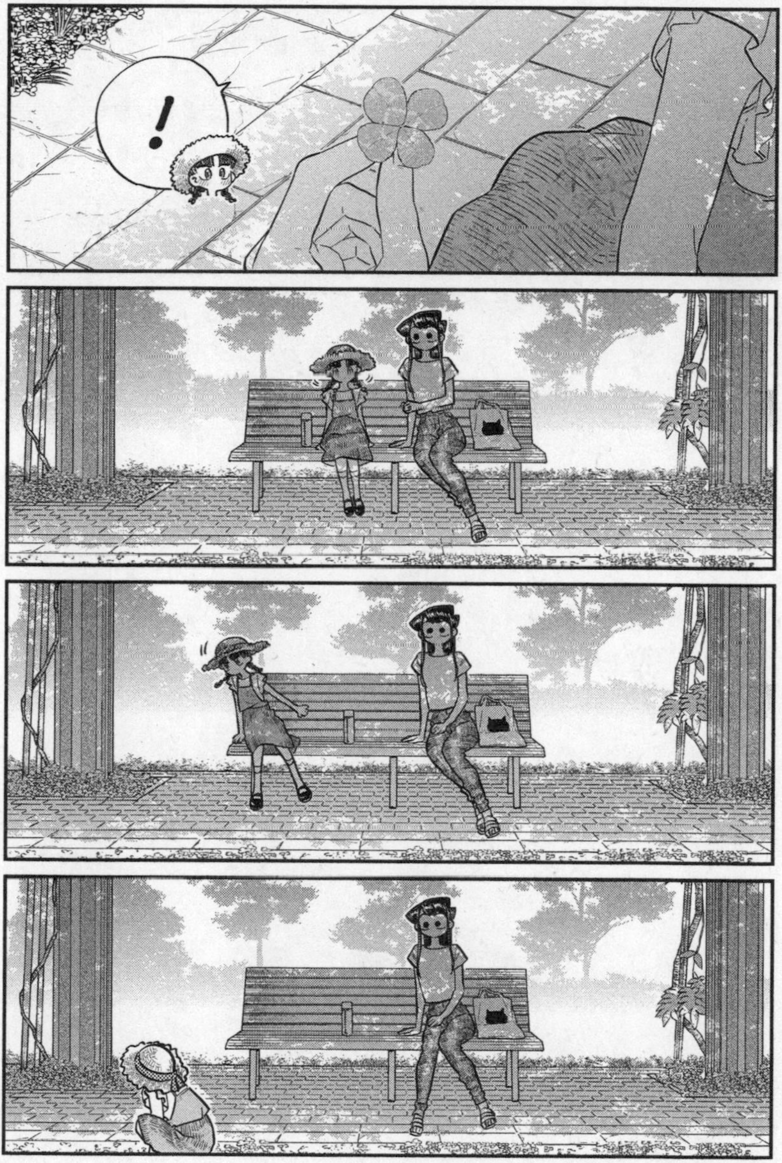
!

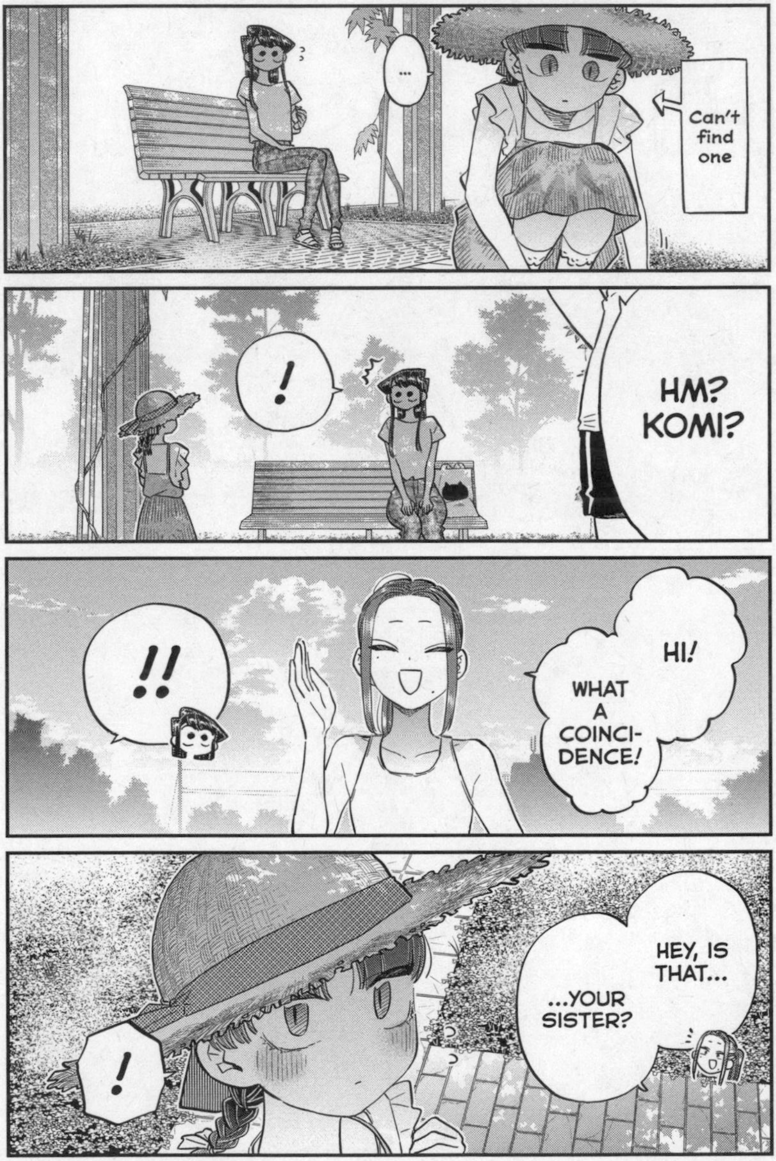

Can't find one
...
HM? KOMI?
!
HI! WHAT A COINCIDENCE!
!!
HEY, IS THAT... ...YOUR SISTER?
!

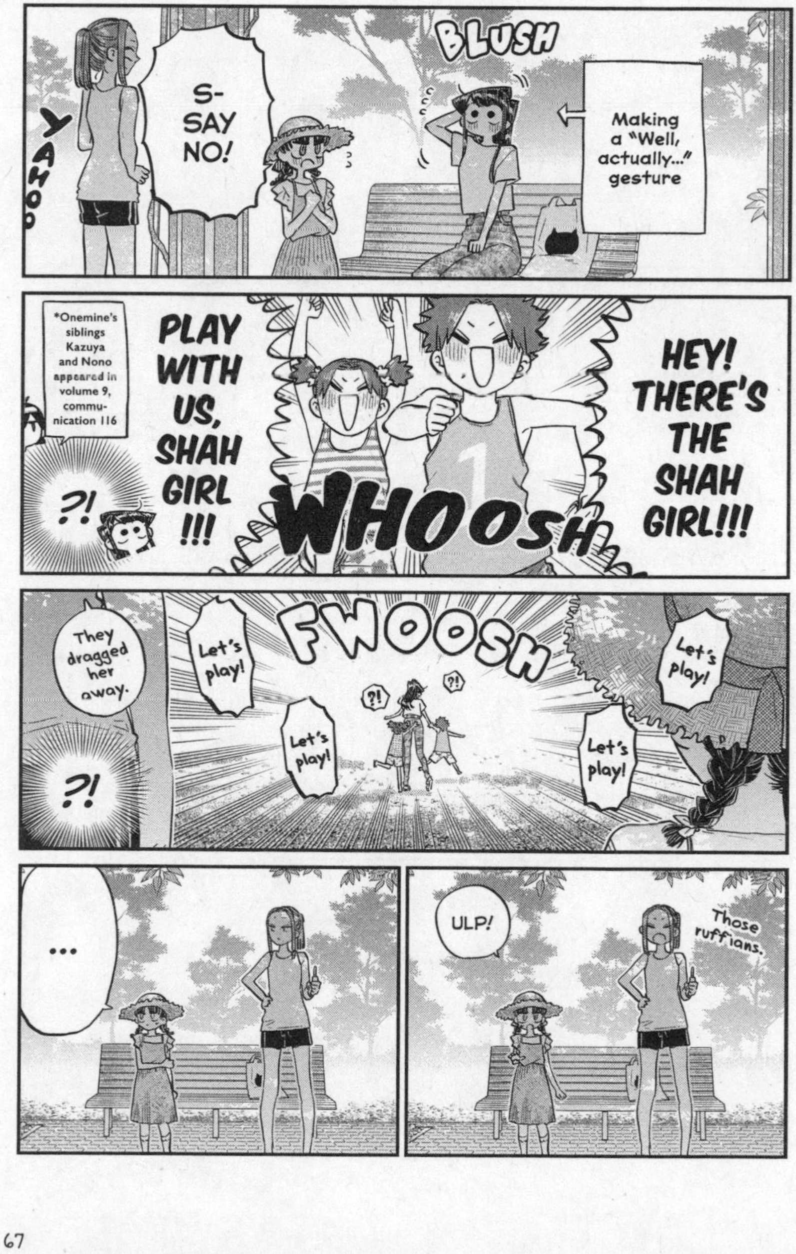
Making a "Well, actually..." gesture
BLUSH
S-SAY NO!
YAHOO
HEY! THERE'S THE SHAH GIRL!!!
PLAY WITH US, SHAH GIRL!!!
*Onemine's siblings Kazuya and Nono appeared in volume 9, communication 116
WHOOSH
?!
Let's play!
Let's play!
FWOOSH
?!
?!
Let's play!
Let's play!
They dragged her away.
?!
Those ruffians.
ULP!
...

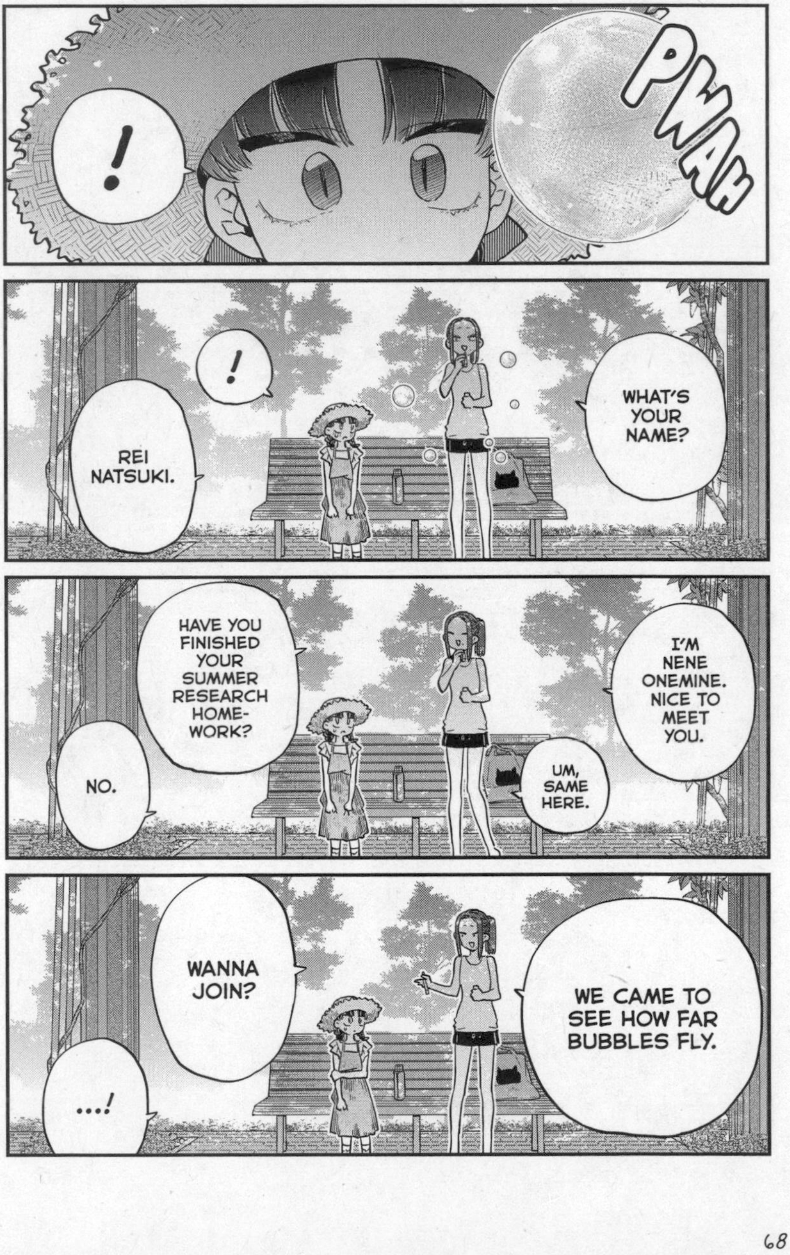
PWAH
!
WHAT'S YOUR NAME?
!
REI NATSUKI.
I'M NENE ONEMINE. NICE TO MEET YOU.
UM, SAME HERE.
HAVE YOU FINISHED YOUR SUMMER RESEARCH HOMEWORK?
NO.
WE CAME TO SEE HOW FAR BUBBLES FLY.
WANNA JOIN?
...!

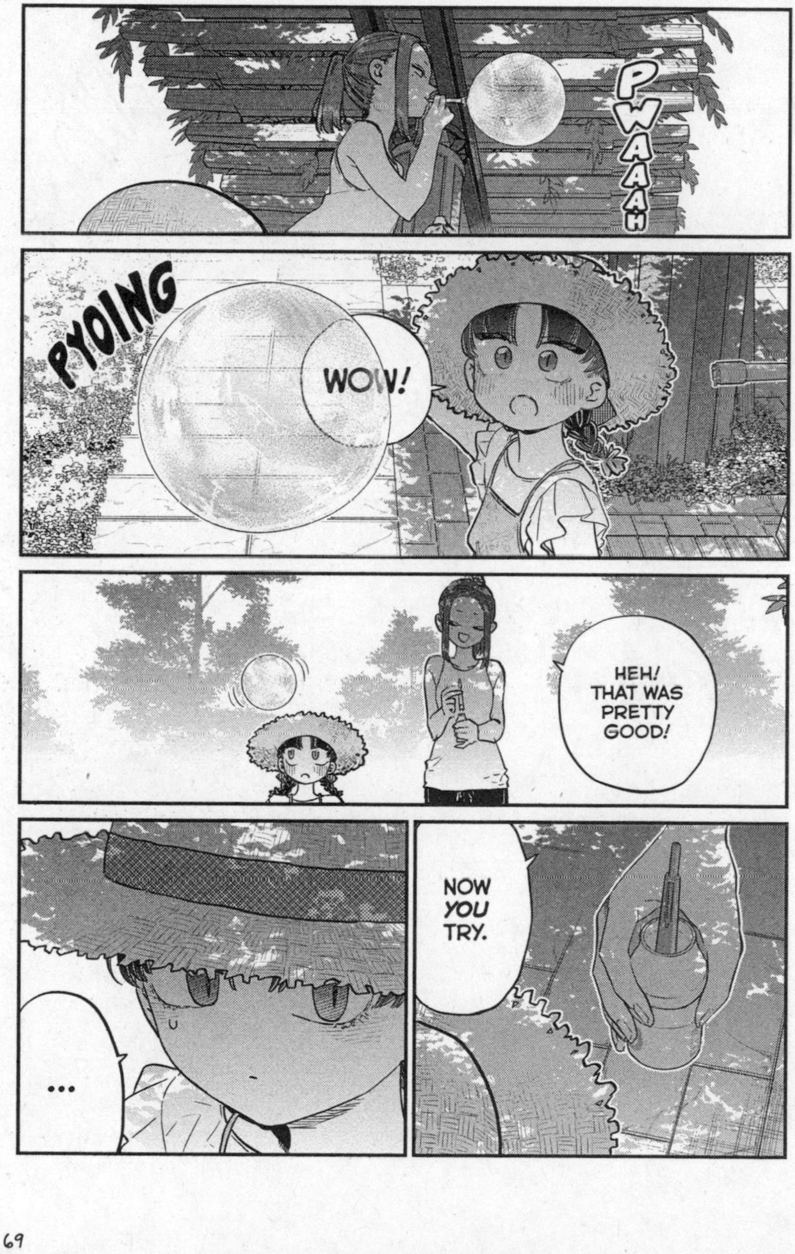
PWAAAH
PYOING
WOW!
HEH! THAT WAS PRETTY GOOD!
NOW *YOU* TRY.
...

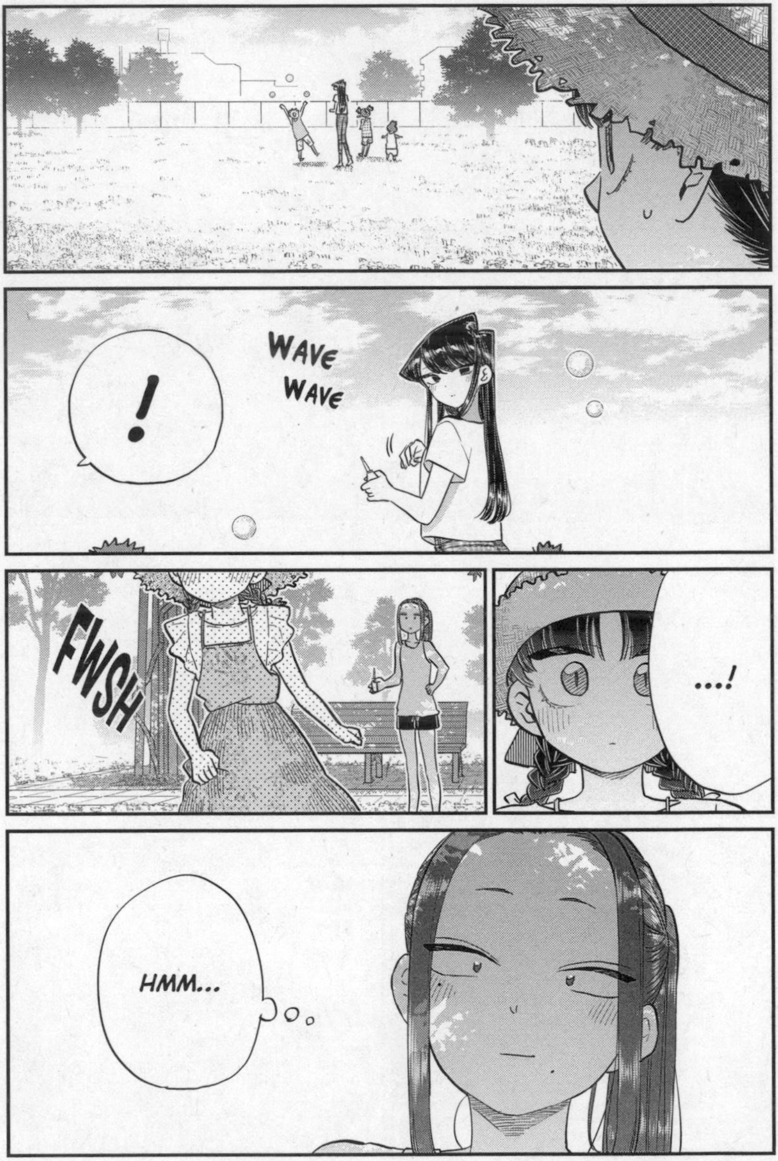
WAVE
WAVE
!
...!
FWSH
HMM...

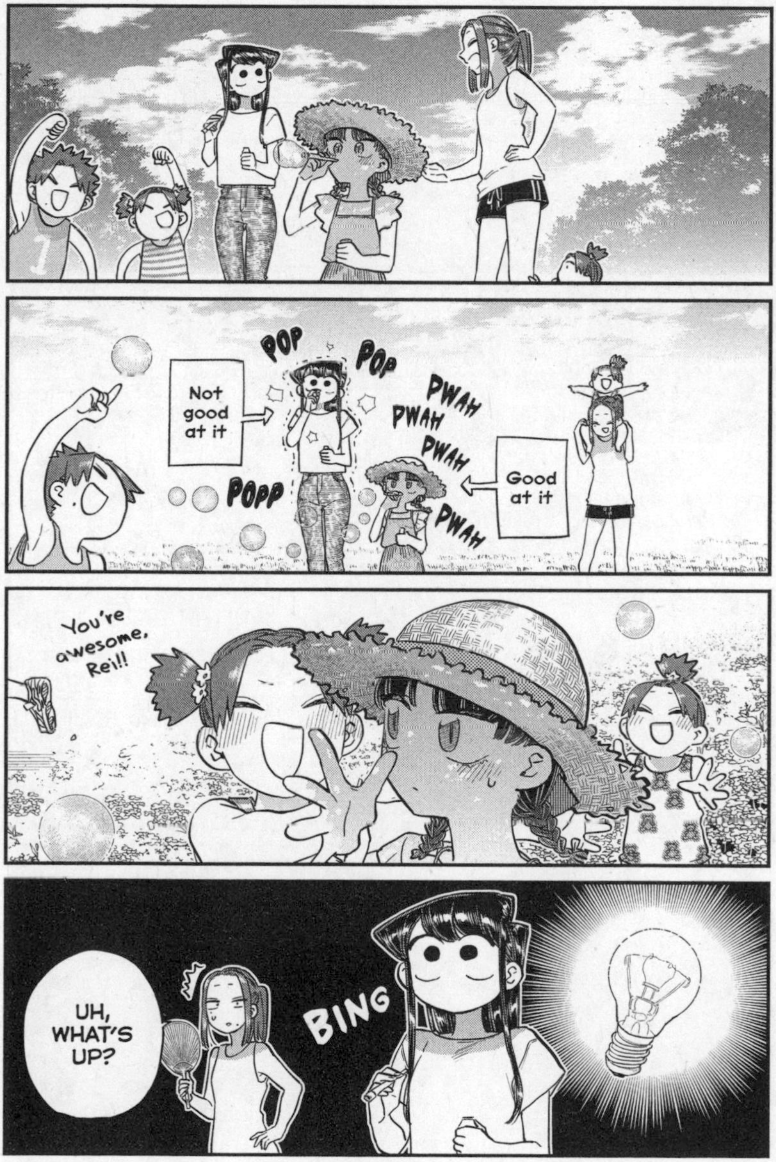
Good at it
PWAH
PWAH
PWAH
PWAH
POP
POP
Not good at it
POPP
You're awesome, Rei!!
BING
UH, WHAT'S UP?

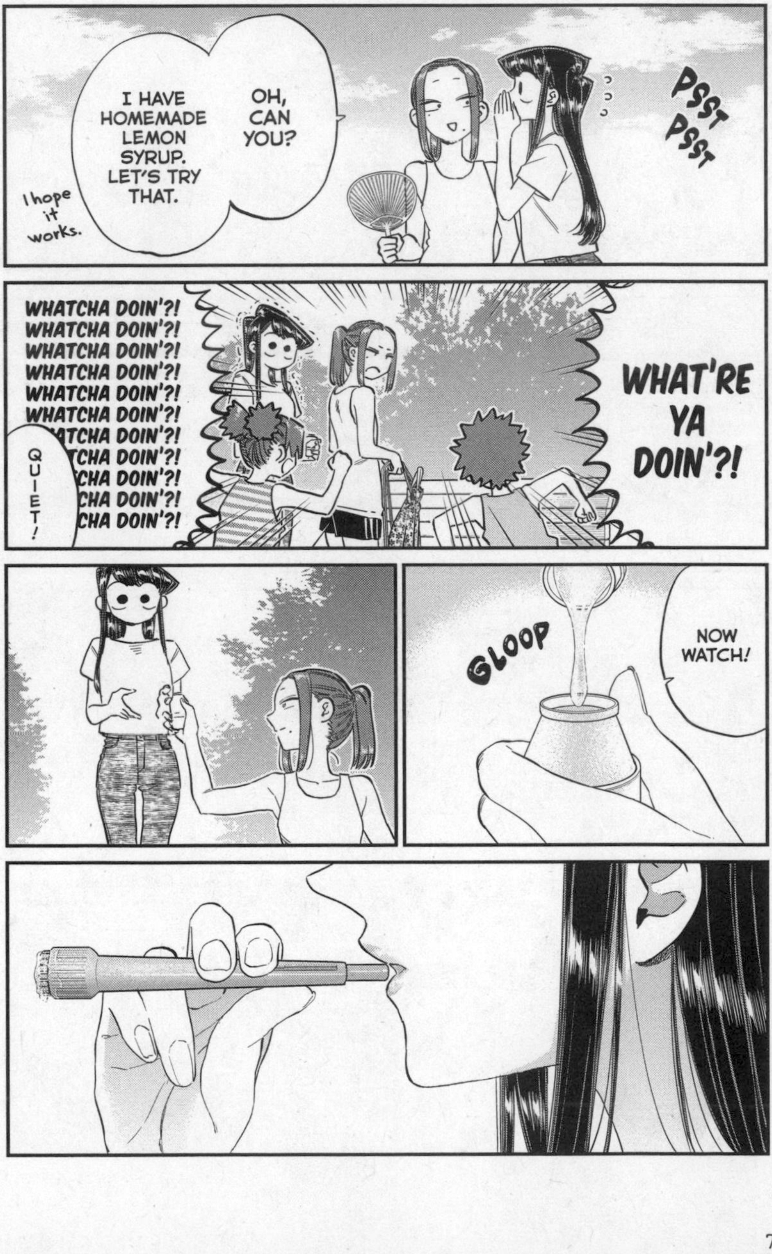
PSST PSST
OH, CAN YOU?
I HAVE HOMEMADE LEMON SYRUP. LET'S TRY THAT.
I hope it works.
WHAT'RE YA DOIN'?!
WHATCHA DOIN'?!
WHATCHA DOIN'?!
WHATCHA DOIN'?!
WHATCHA DOIN'?!
WHATCHA DOIN'?!
WHATCHA DOIN'?!
ATCHA DOIN'?!
TCHA DOIN'?!
CHA DOIN'?!
CHA DOIN'?!
CHA DOIN'?!
QUIET!
NOW WATCH!
GLOOP

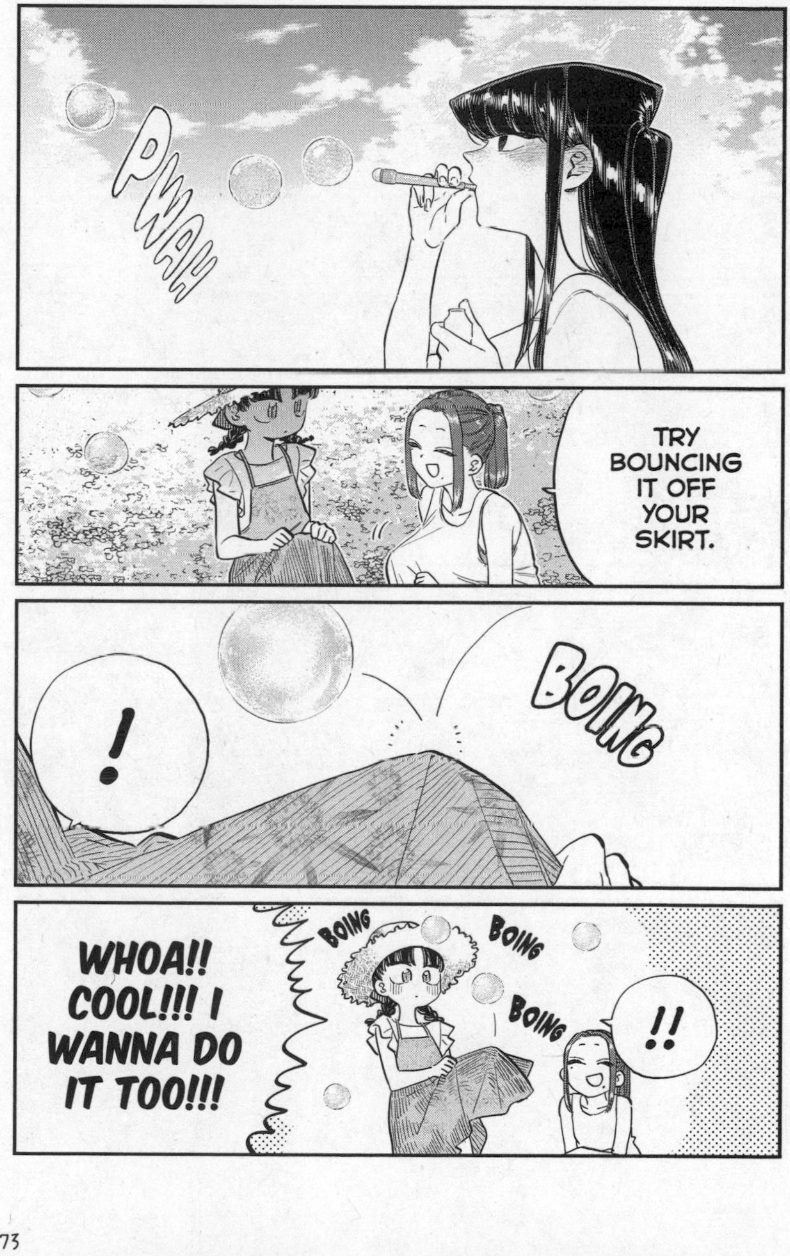
PWAH
TRY BOUNCING IT OFF YOUR SKIRT.
BOING
!
!!
BOING
BOING
BOING
WHOA!! COOL!!! I WANNA DO IT TOO!!!

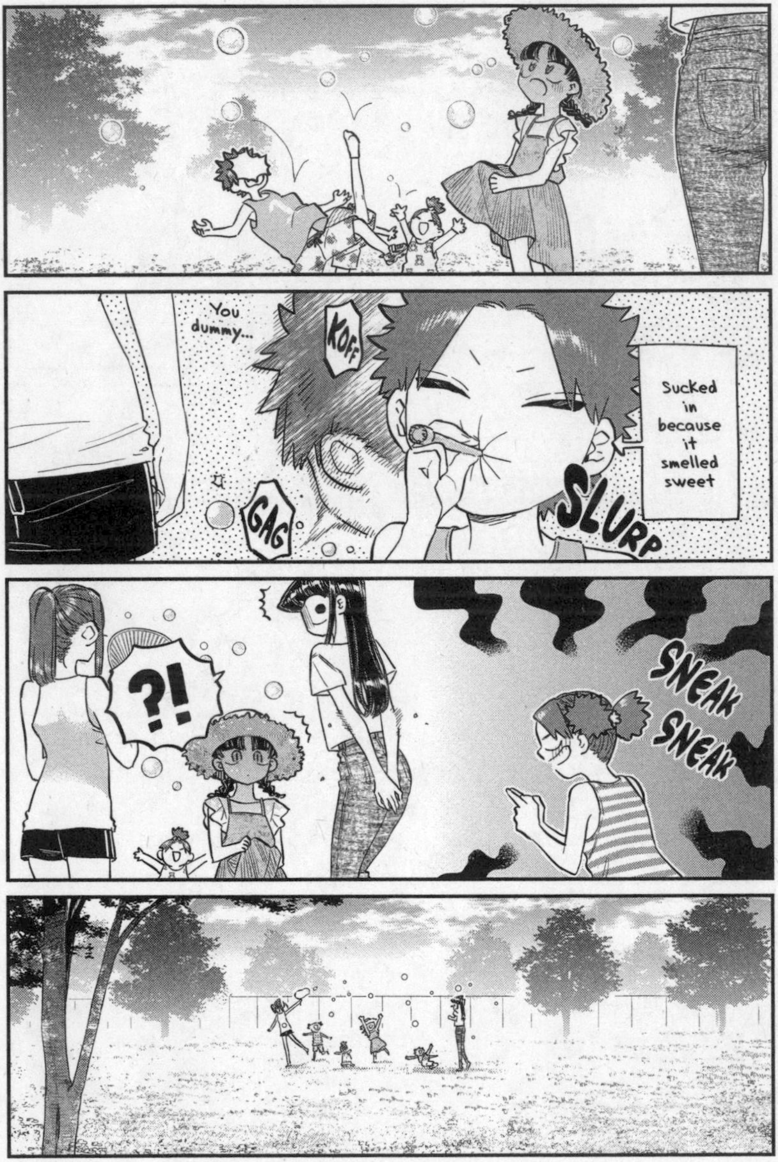
Sucked in because it smelled sweet
SLURP
KOFF
You dummy...
GAG
SNEAK SNEAK
?!

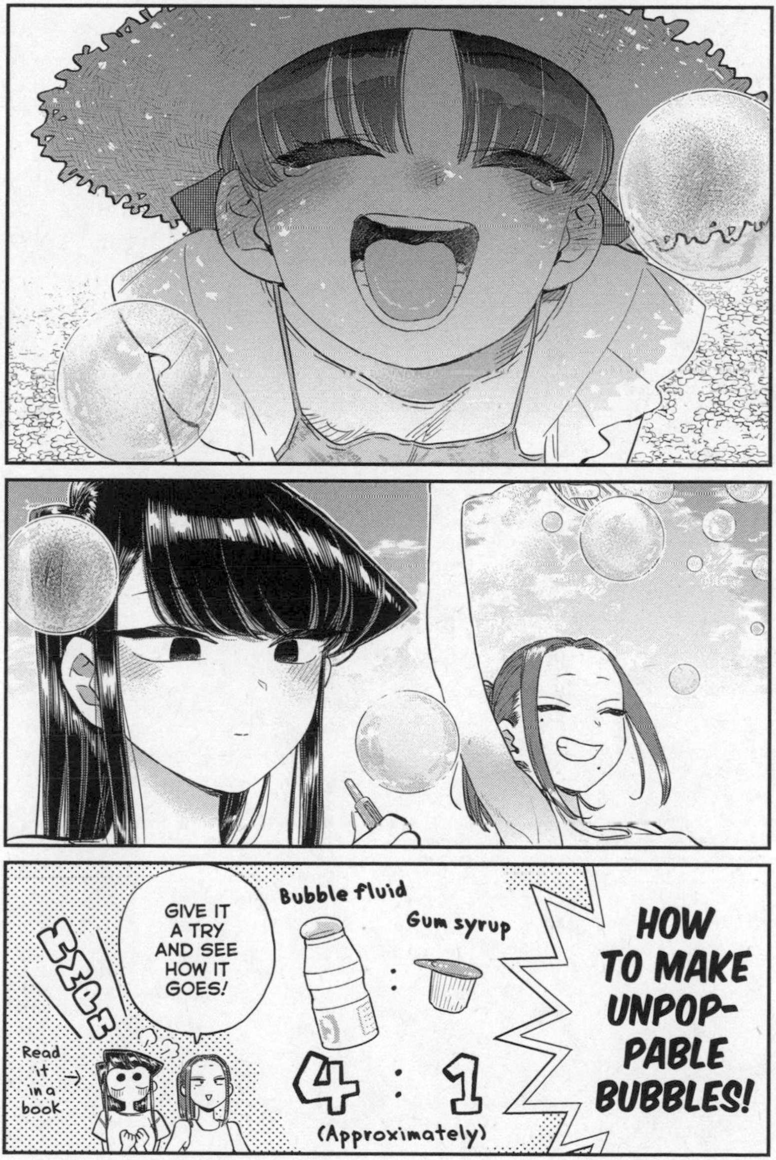
HOW TO MAKE UNPOP-PABLE BUBBLES!
Bubble fluid
Gum syrup
4 : 1
(Approximately)
GIVE IT A TRY AND SEE HOW IT GOES!
HMPH
Read it in a book

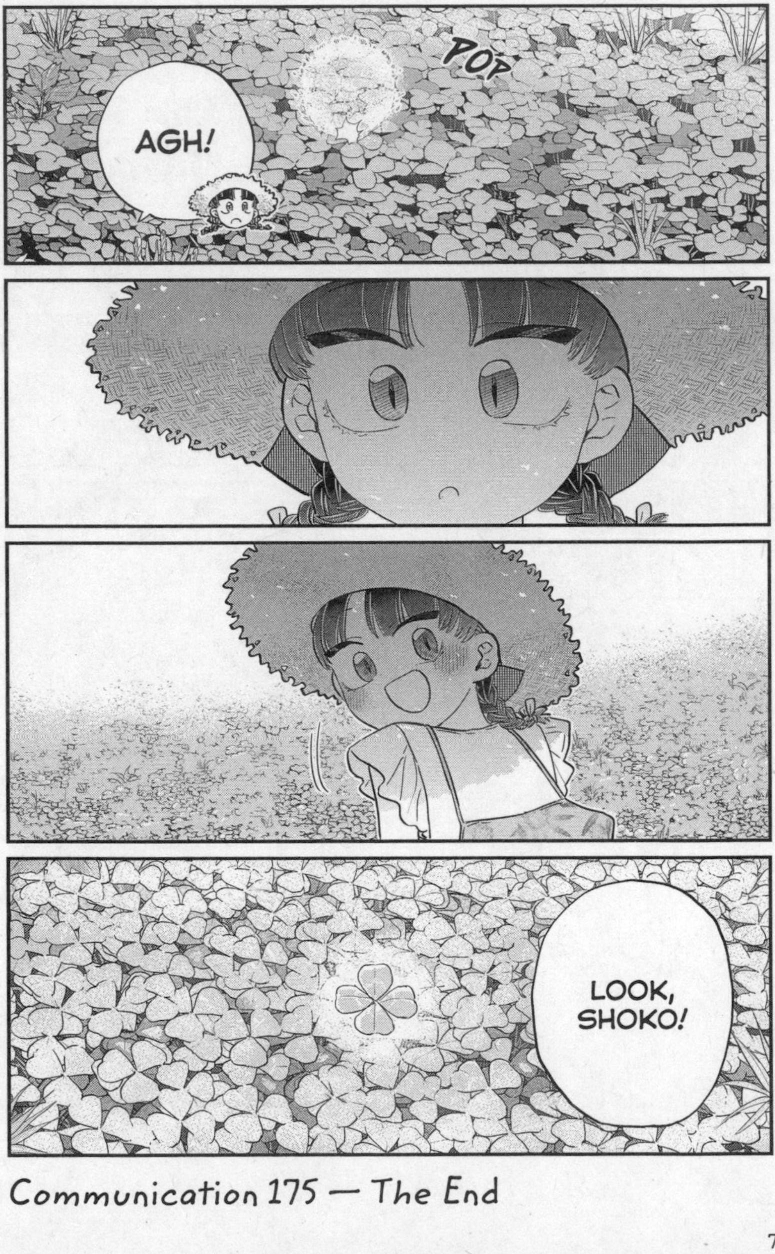
POP
AGH!
LOOK, SHOKO!

Communication 175 — The End

Komi Can't Communicate

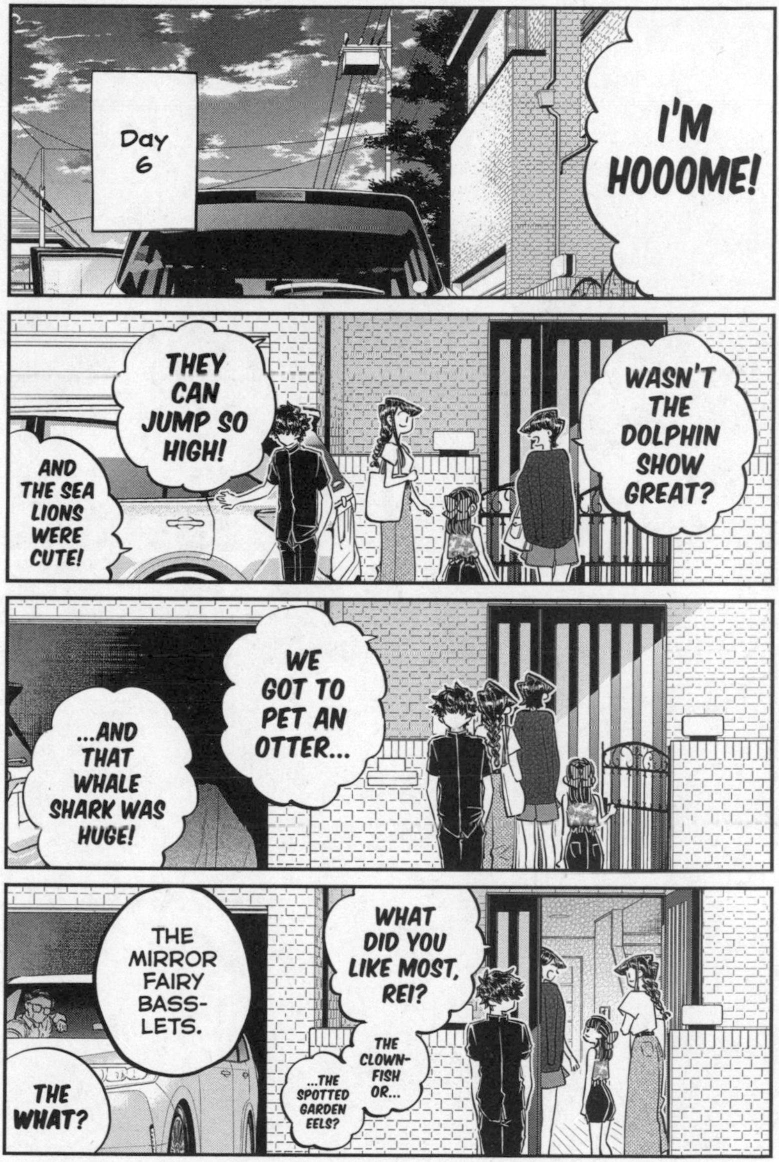
I'M HOOOME!
Day 6
WASN'T THE DOLPHIN SHOW GREAT?
THEY CAN JUMP SO HIGH!
AND THE SEA LIONS WERE CUTE!
WE GOT TO PET AN OTTER...
...AND THAT WHALE SHARK WAS HUGE!
WHAT DID YOU LIKE MOST, REI?
THE CLOWN-FISH OR...
...THE SPOTTED GARDEN EELS?
THE MIRROR FAIRY BASS-LETS.
THE WHAT?

Communication 176: A Bath with Rei

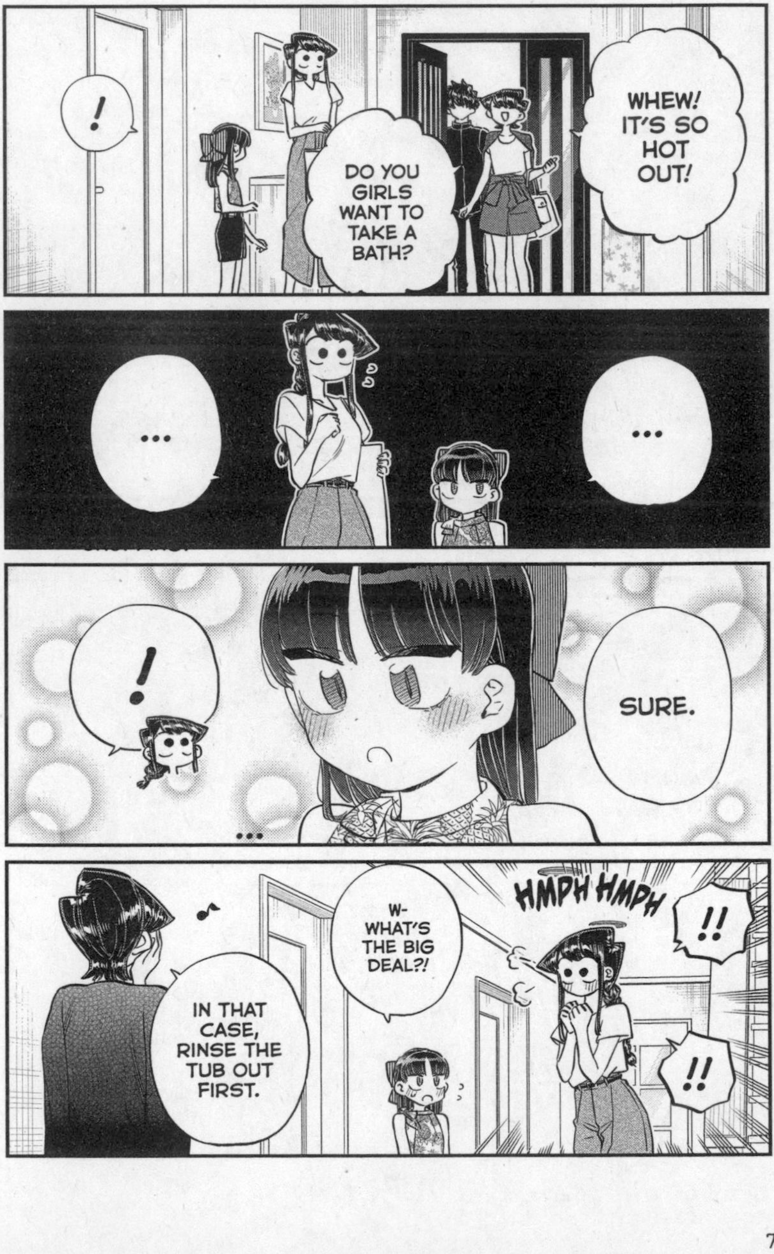
WHEW! IT'S SO HOT OUT!
DO YOU GIRLS WANT TO TAKE A BATH?
!
...
...
SURE.
!
...
!!
!!
HMPH HMPH
W- WHAT'S THE BIG DEAL?!
IN THAT CASE, RINSE THE TUB OUT FIRST.

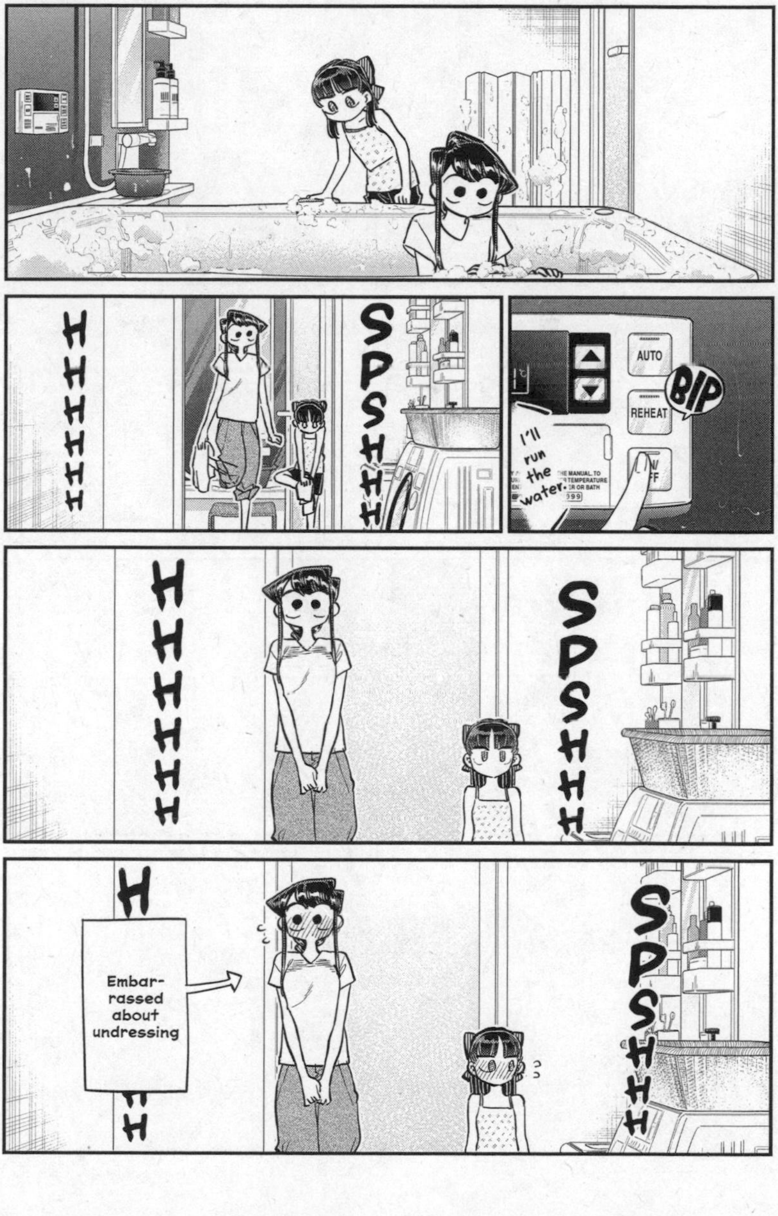
AUTO
REHEAT
BIP
I'll run the water.
SPSHHH
HHHHHHH
SPSHHH
HHHHHHH
SPSHHH
Embar-rassed about undressing
H
H

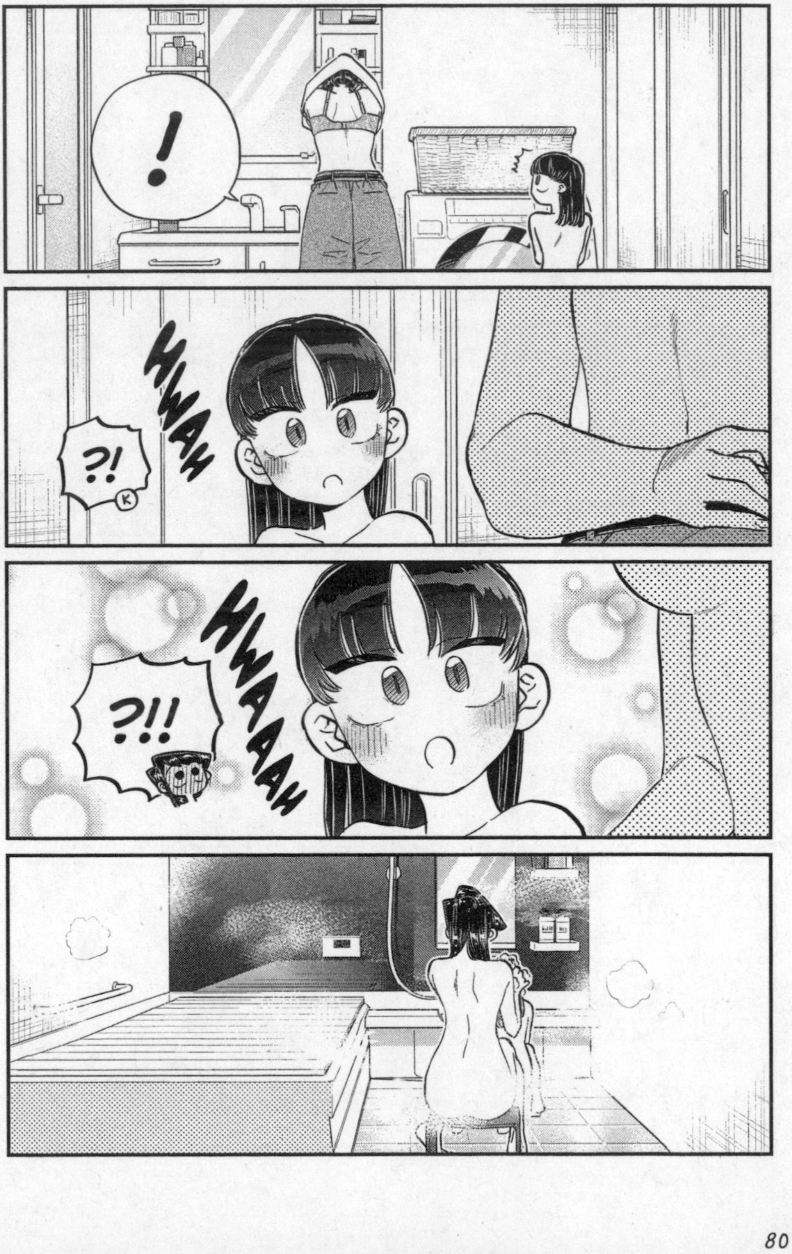
!
HWAH
?!
HWAAAAH
?!!

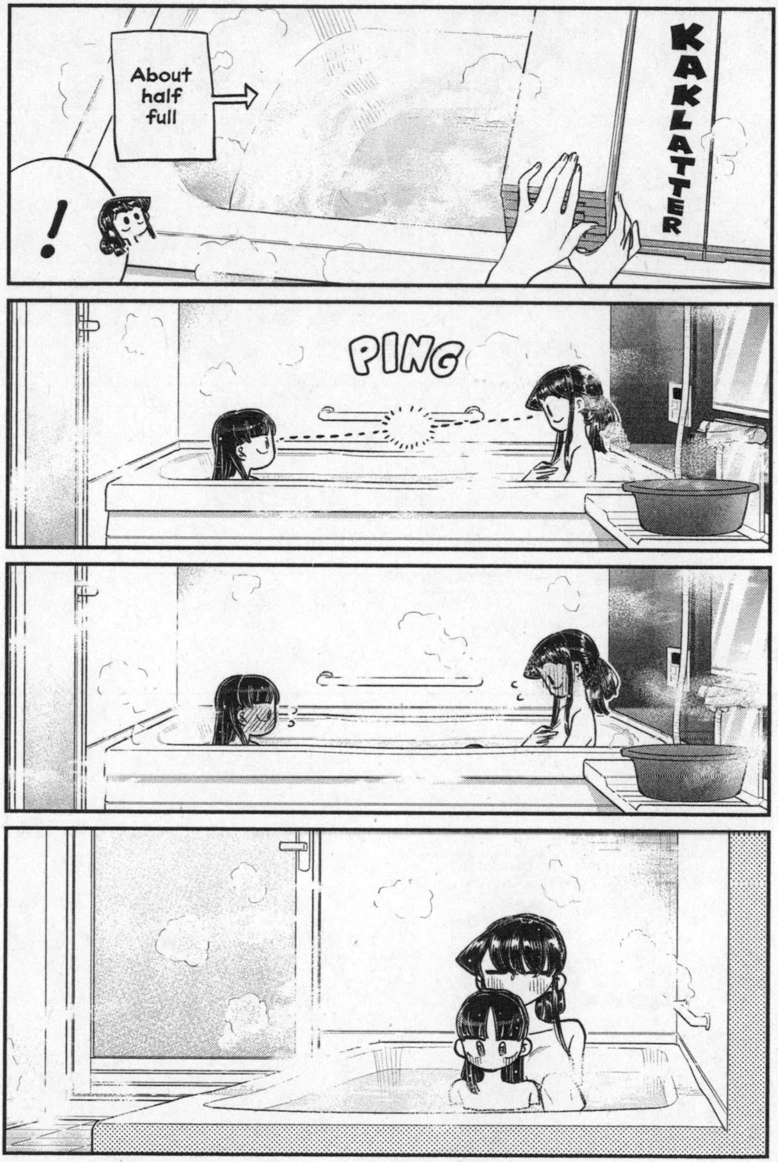
KAKLATTER
About half full
!
PING

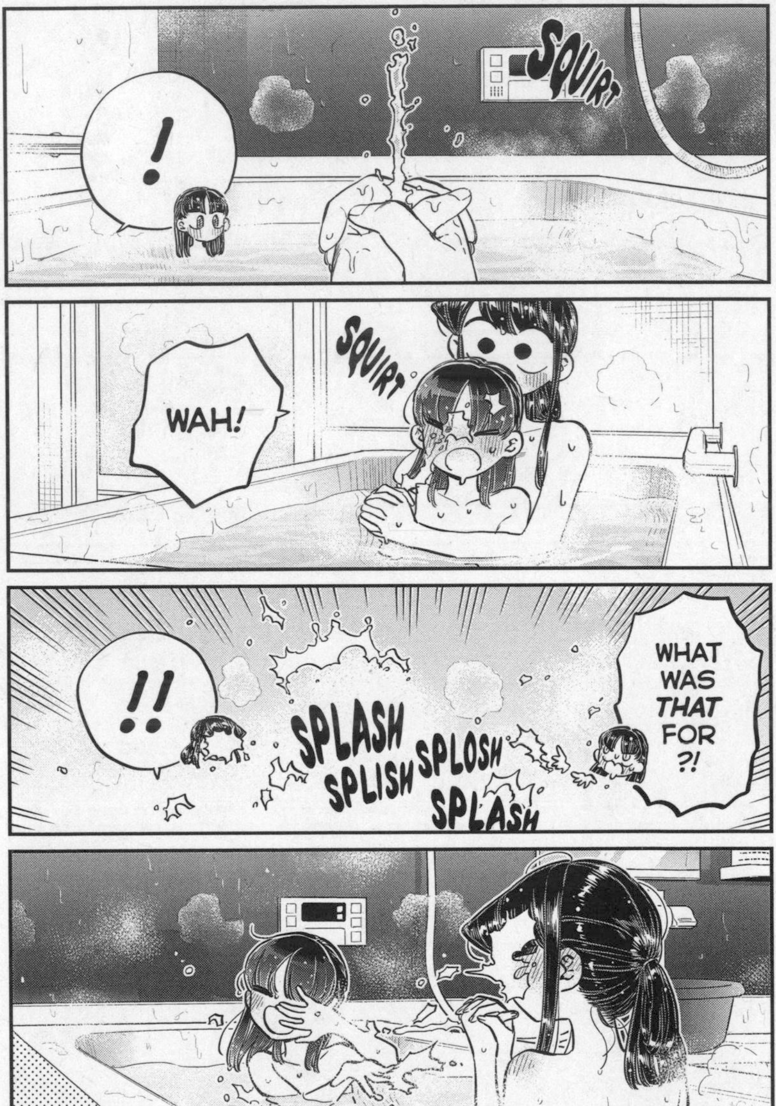
SQUIRT
!
SQUIRT
WAH!
WHAT WAS THAT FOR?!
SPLOSH
SPLASH
SPLASH
SPLISH
!!

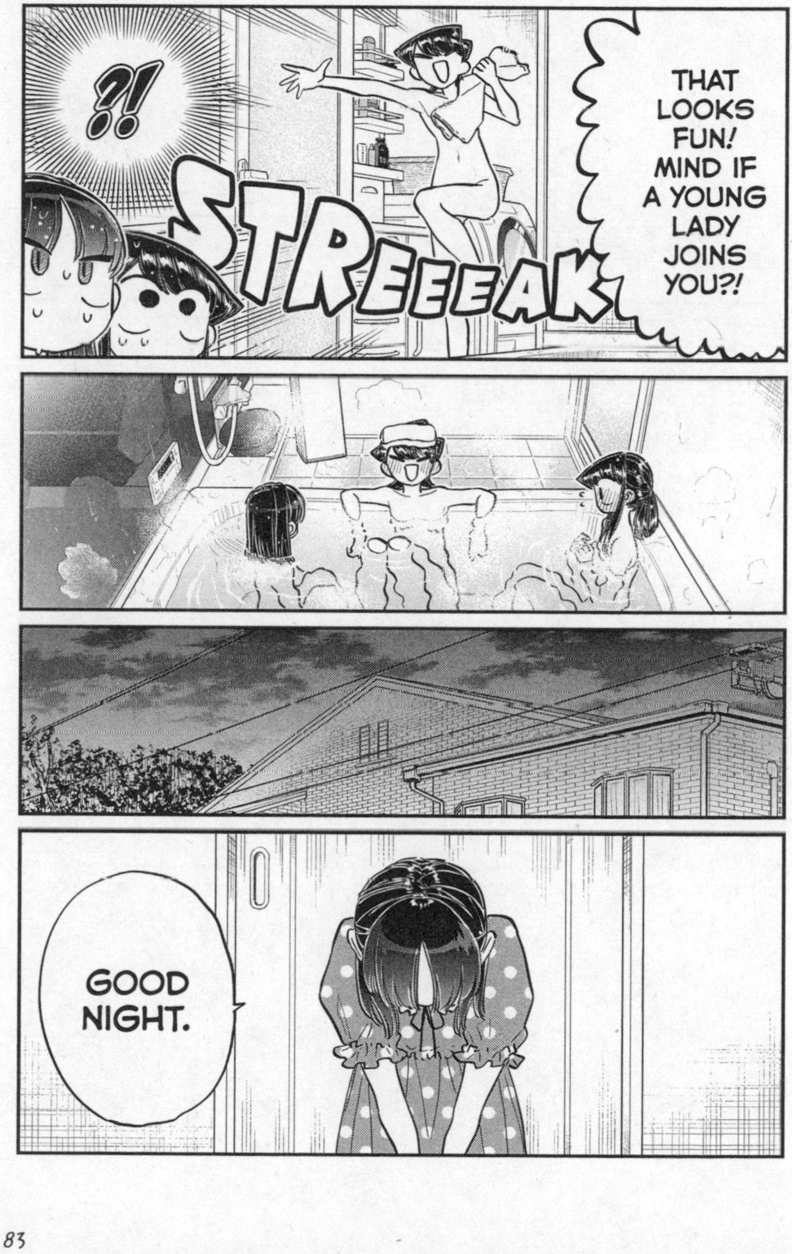
THAT LOOKS FUN! MIND IF A YOUNG LADY JOINS YOU?!
STREEEAK
?!
GOOD NIGHT.

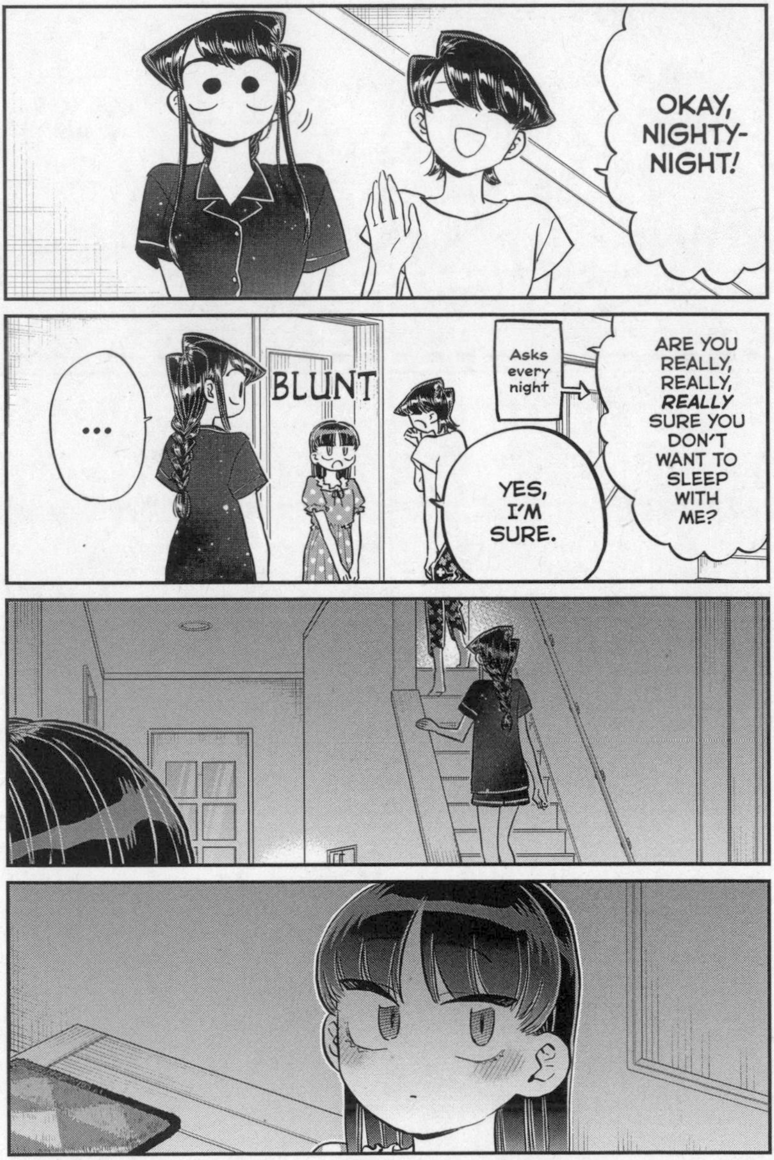
OKAY, NIGHTY-NIGHT!
ARE YOU REALLY, REALLY, *REALLY* SURE YOU DON'T WANT TO SLEEP WITH ME?
Asks every night
YES, I'M SURE.
BLUNT
...

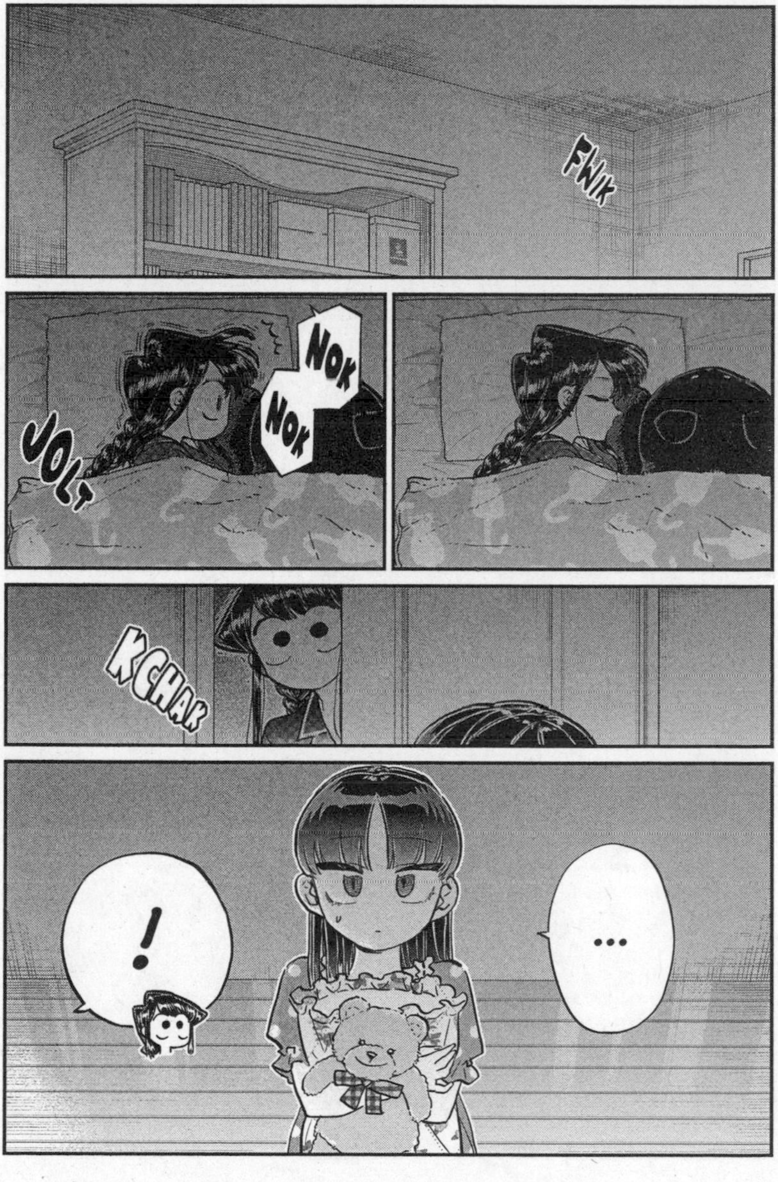
FWIK
NOK NOK
JOLT
KCHAK
...
!

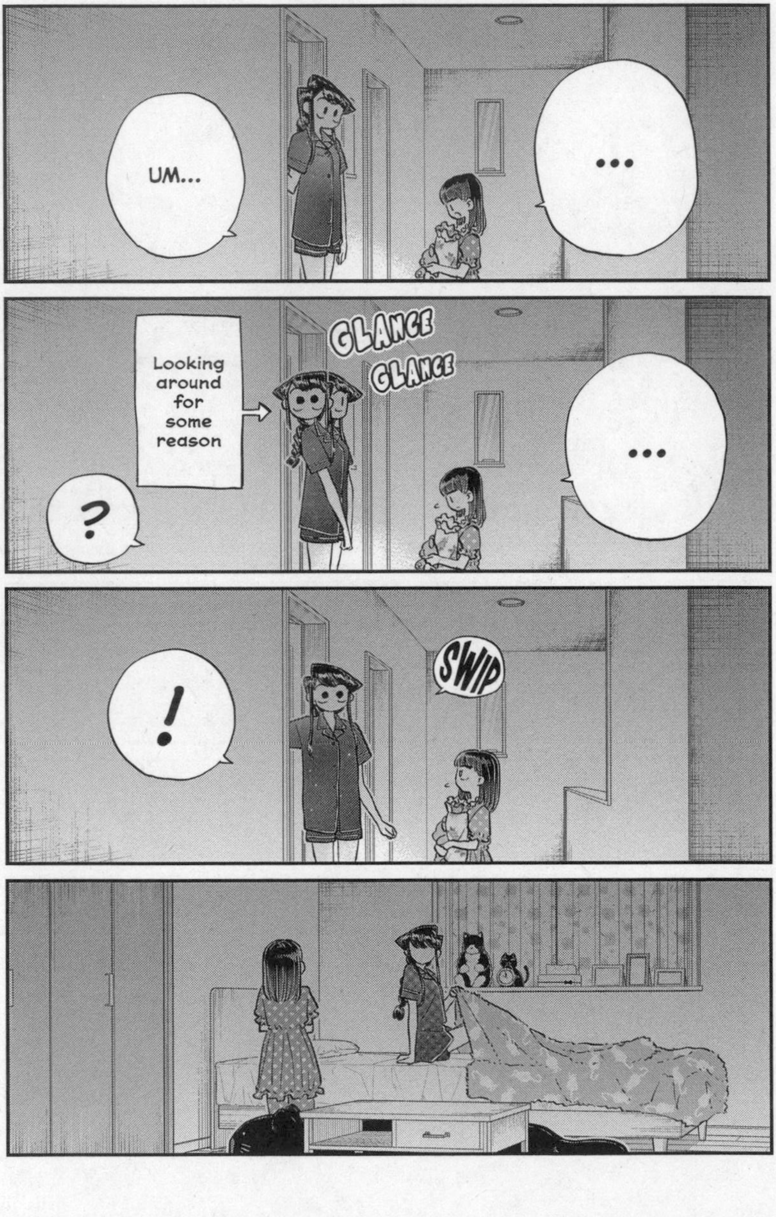
...
UM...
...
GLANCE
GLANCE
Looking around for some reason
?
SWIP
!

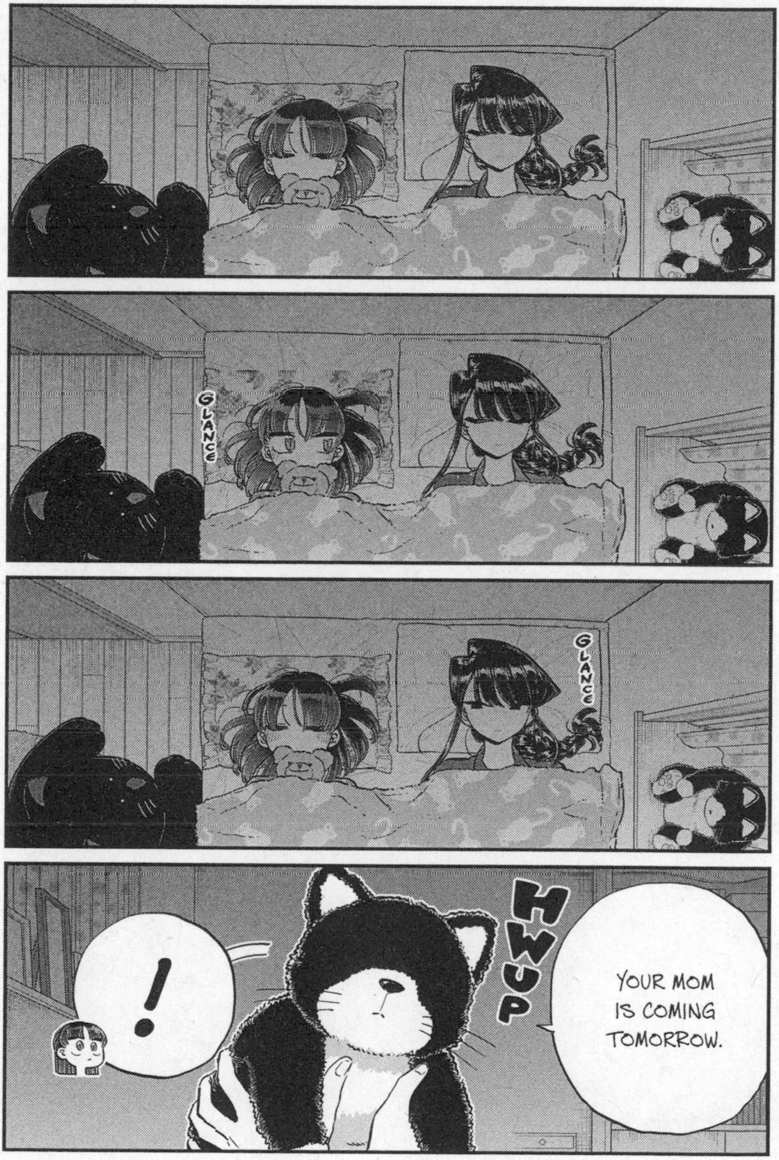
GLANCE
GLANCE
YOUR MOM IS COMING TOMORROW.
HWUP
!

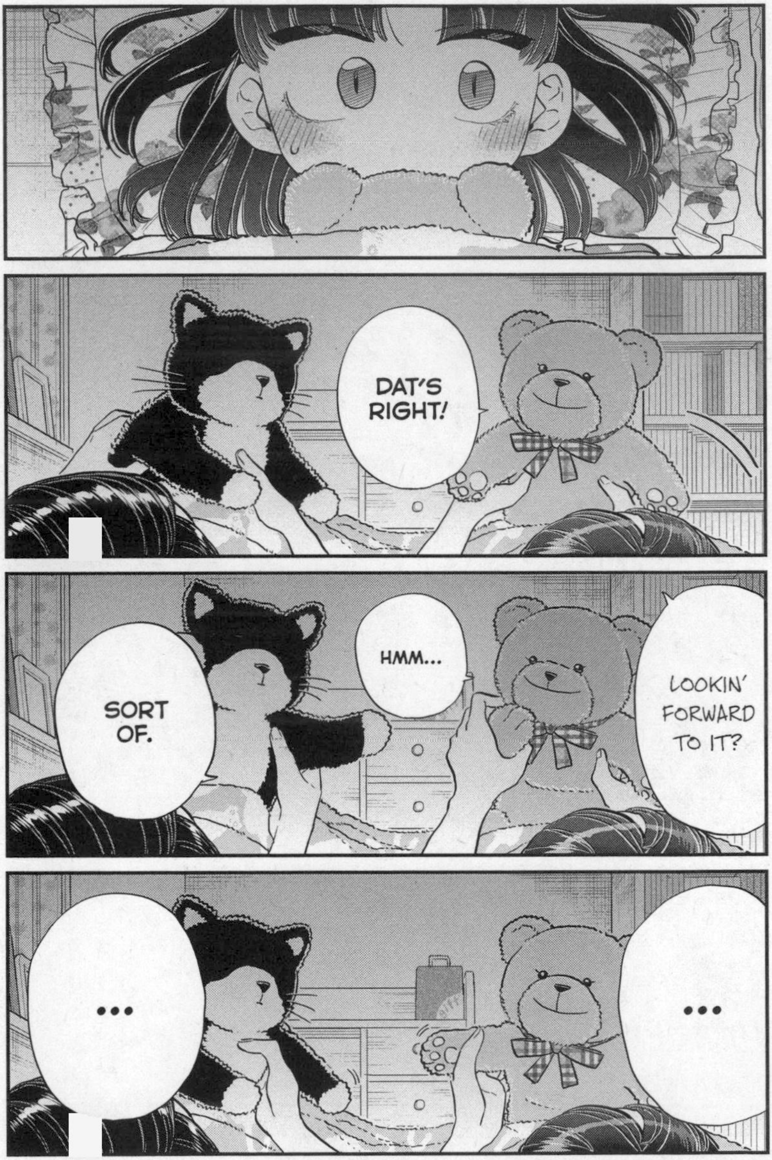
DAT'S RIGHT!
LOOKIN' FORWARD TO IT?
HMM...
SORT OF.
...
...

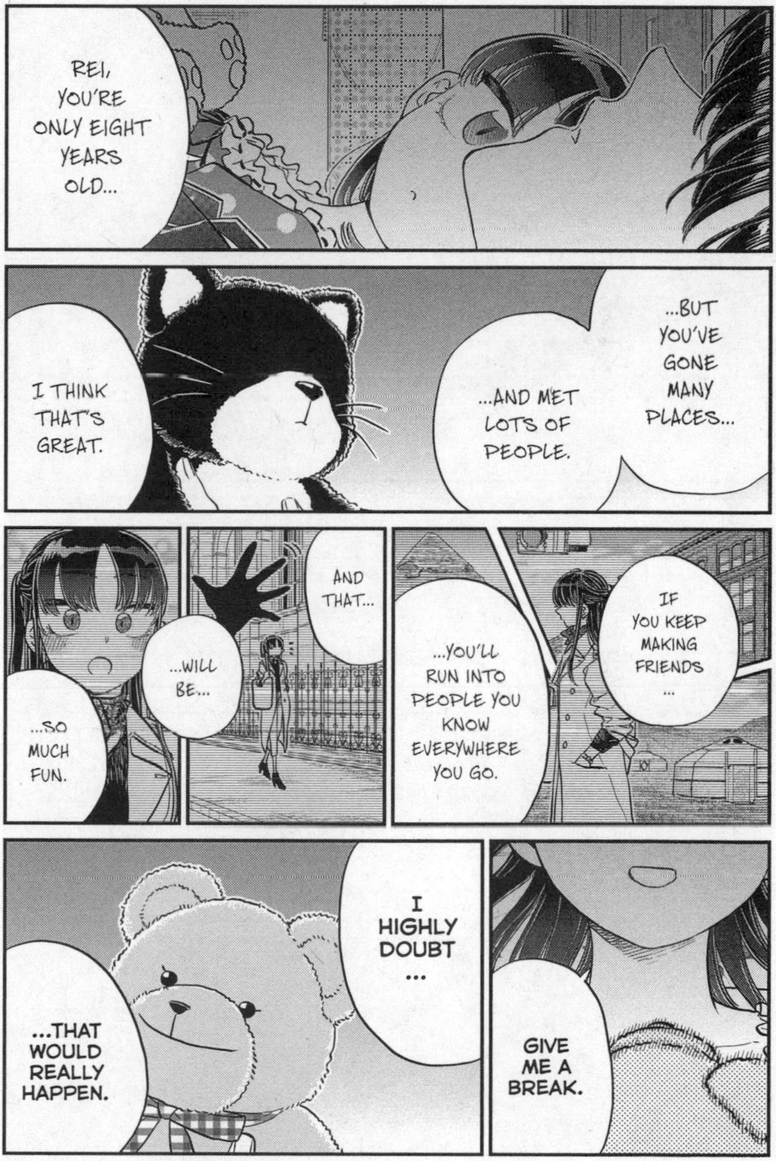
REI, YOU'RE ONLY EIGHT YEARS OLD...
...BUT YOU'VE GONE MANY PLACES...
...AND MET LOTS OF PEOPLE.
I THINK THAT'S GREAT.
IF YOU KEEP MAKING FRIENDS ...
...YOU'LL RUN INTO PEOPLE YOU KNOW EVERYWHERE YOU GO.
AND THAT...
...WILL BE...
...SO MUCH FUN.
GIVE ME A BREAK.
I HIGHLY DOUBT ...
...THAT WOULD REALLY HAPPEN.

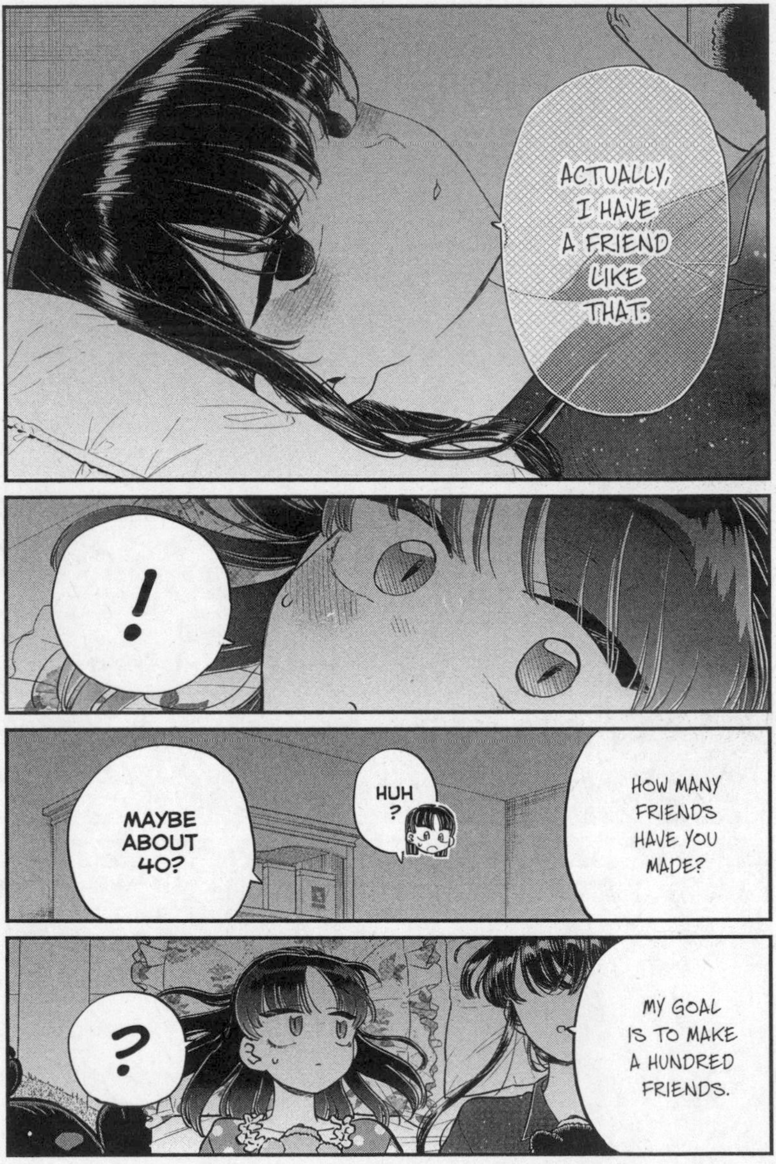
ACTUALLY, I HAVE A FRIEND LIKE THAT.
!
HOW MANY FRIENDS HAVE YOU MADE?
HUH?
MAYBE ABOUT 40?
MY GOAL IS TO MAKE A HUNDRED FRIENDS.
?

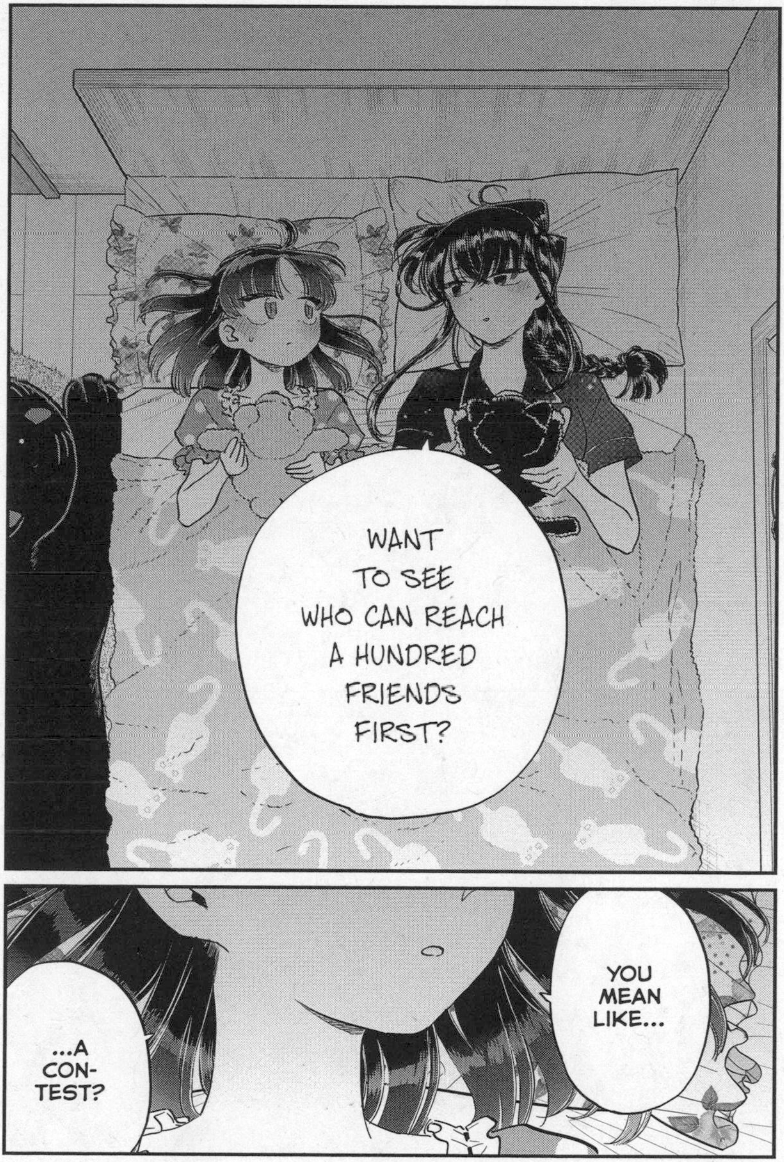
WANT TO SEE WHO CAN REACH A HUNDRED FRIENDS FIRST?
YOU MEAN LIKE...
...A CON-TEST?

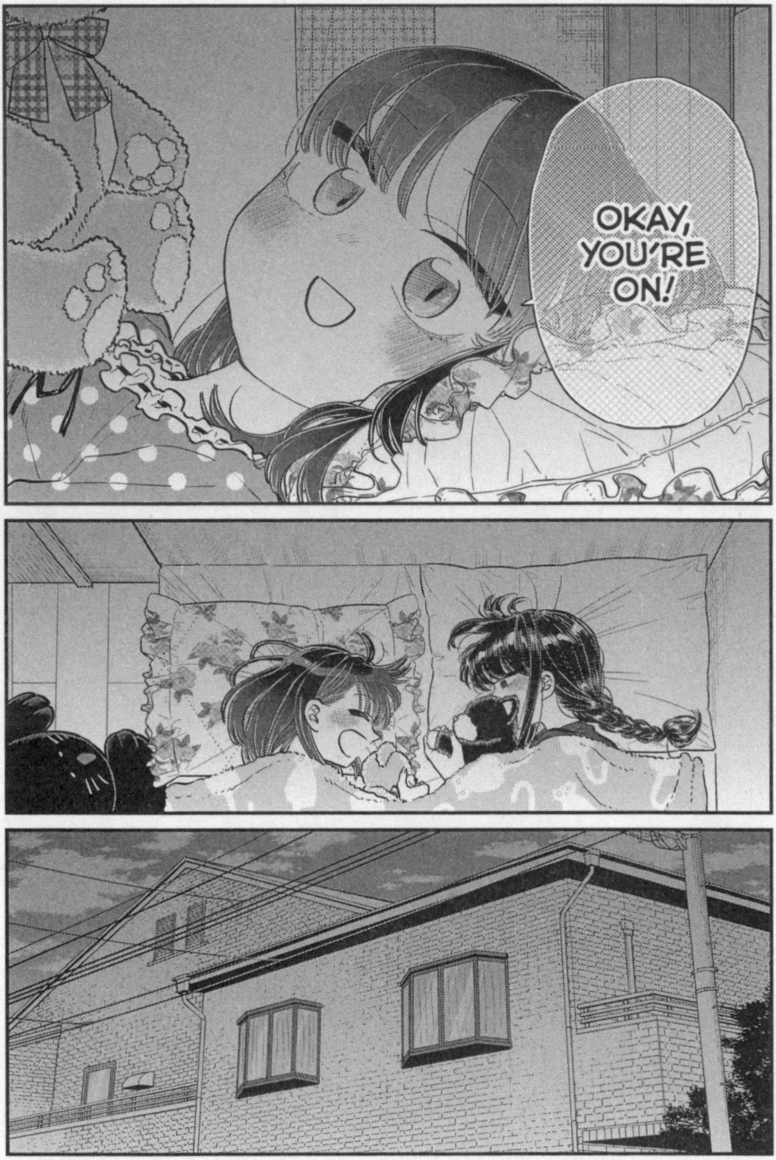
OKAY, YOU'RE ON!

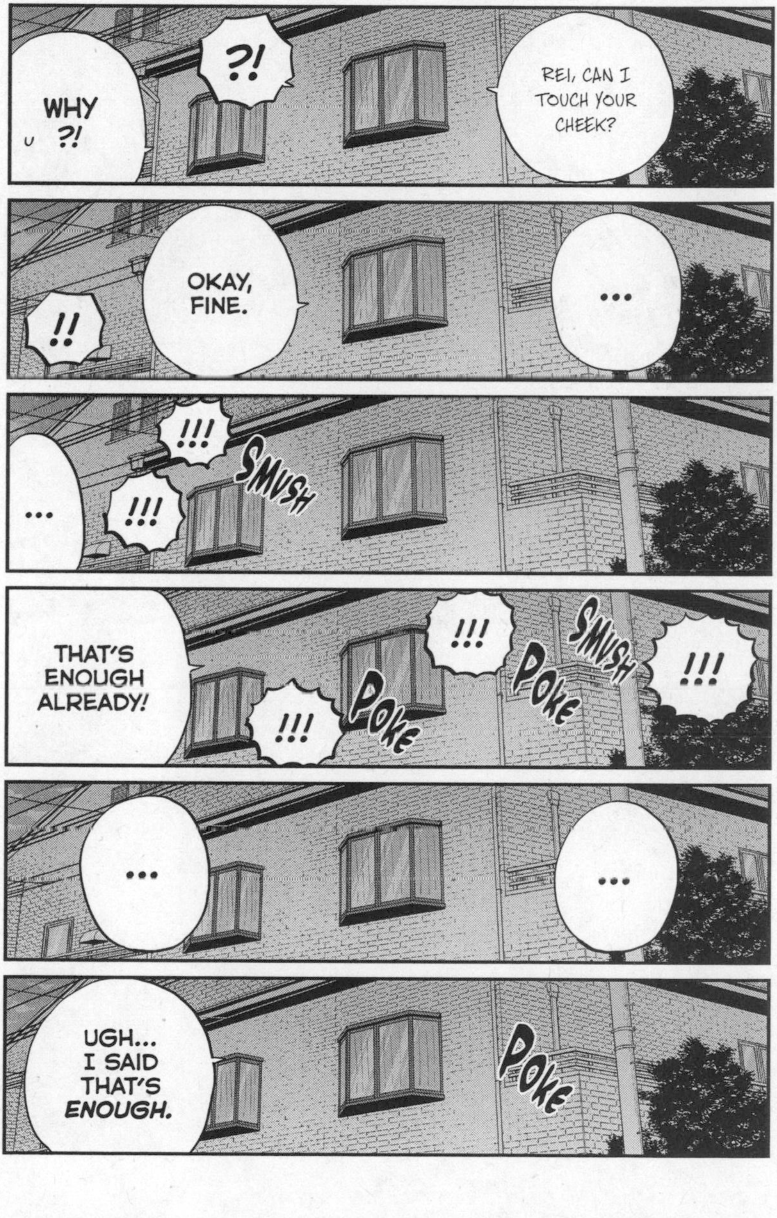
REI, CAN I TOUCH YOUR CHEEK?
?!
WHY ?!
...
OKAY, FINE.
!!
SMUSH
!!!
!!!
...
!!!
SMUSH
POKE
!!!
POKE
!!!
THAT'S ENOUGH ALREADY!
...
...
POKE
UGH... I SAID THAT'S *ENOUGH.*

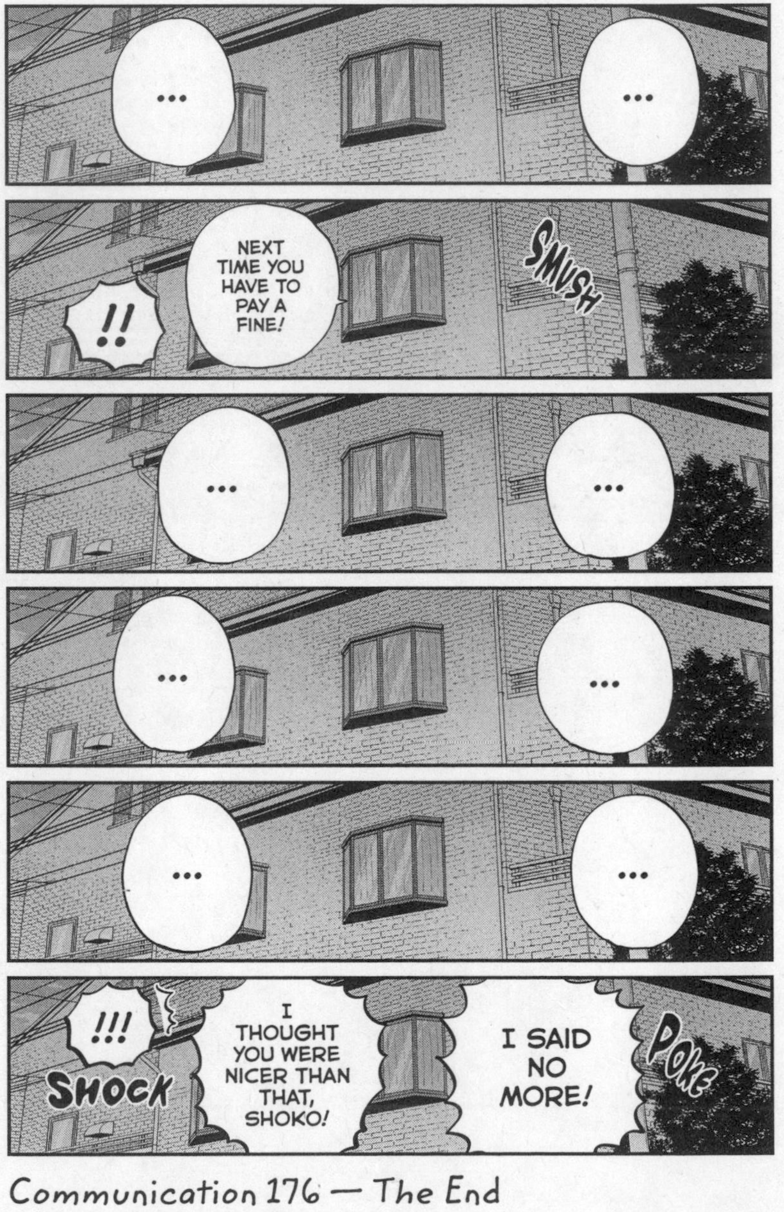
...
...
SMUSH
NEXT TIME YOU HAVE TO PAY A FINE!
!!
...
...
...
...
...
...
POKE
I SAID NO MORE!
I THOUGHT YOU WERE NICER THAN THAT, SHOKO!
!!!
SHOCK

Communication 176 — The End

Komi Can't Communicate

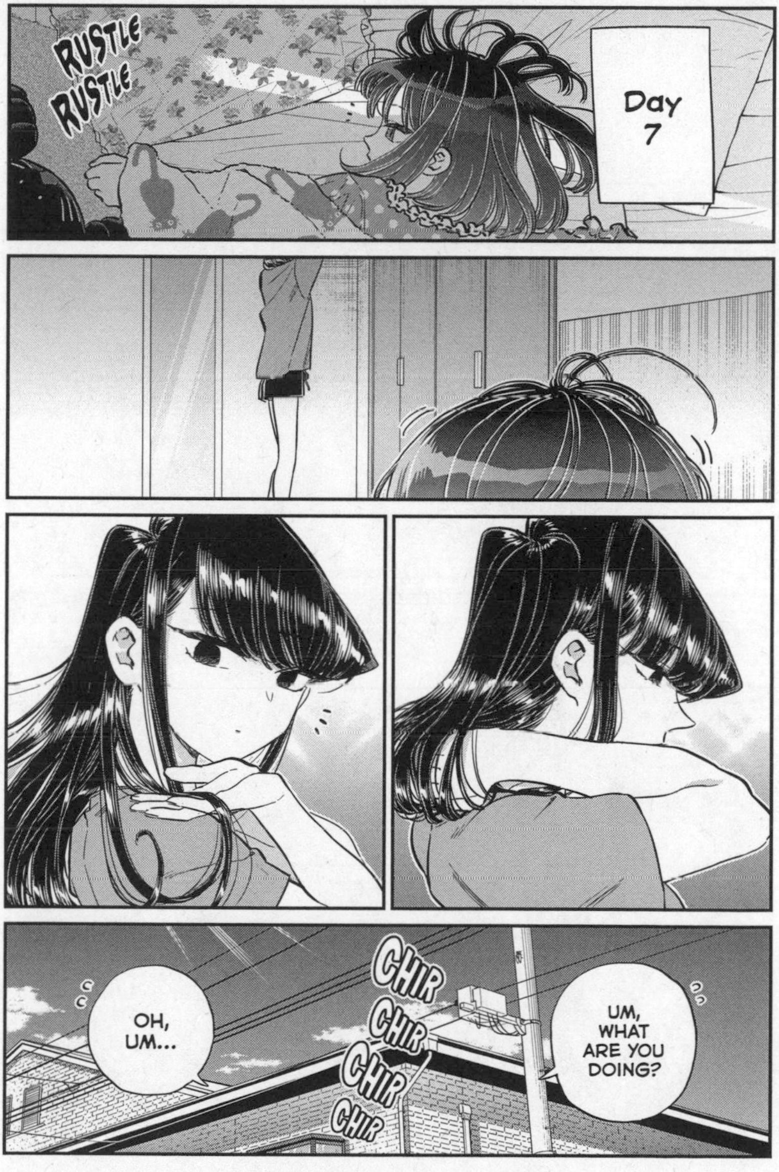
Day 7
RUSTLE RUSTLE
UM, WHAT ARE YOU DOING?
CHIR CHIR CHIR CHIR
OH, UM...

Communication 177: Saying Goodbye to Rei

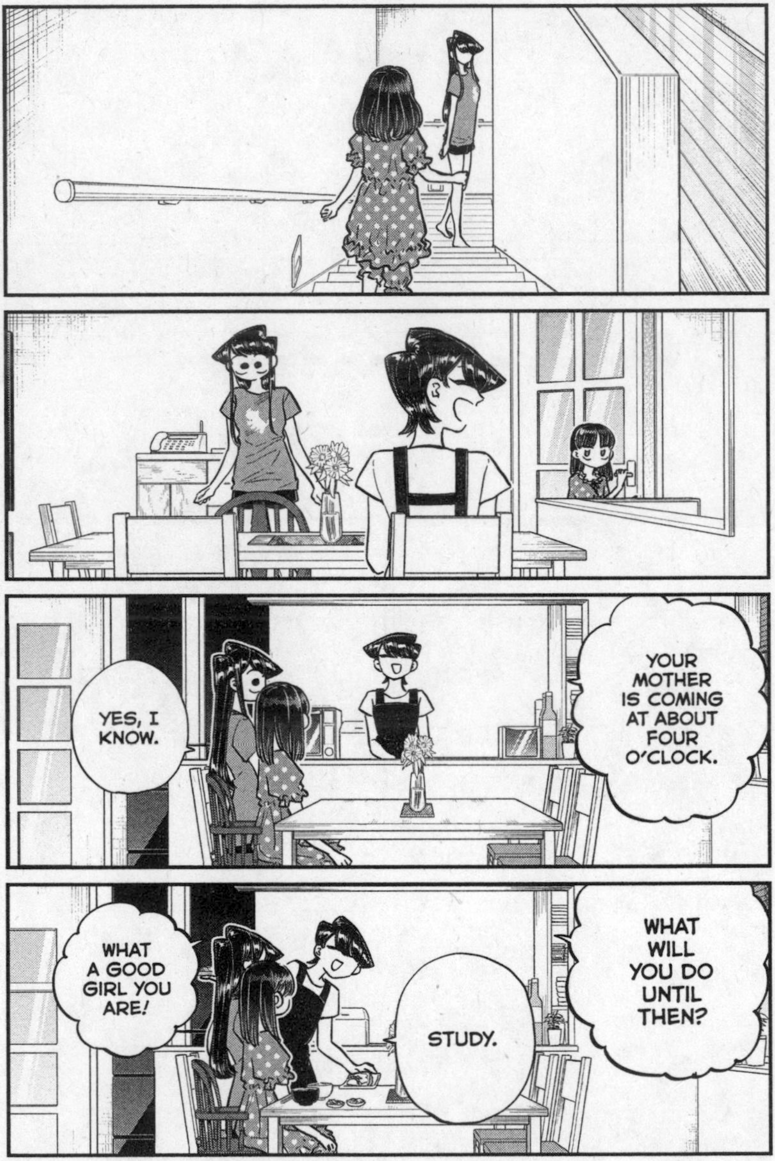
YOUR MOTHER IS COMING AT ABOUT FOUR O'CLOCK.
YES, I KNOW.
WHAT WILL YOU DO UNTIL THEN?
STUDY.
WHAT A GOOD GIRL YOU ARE!

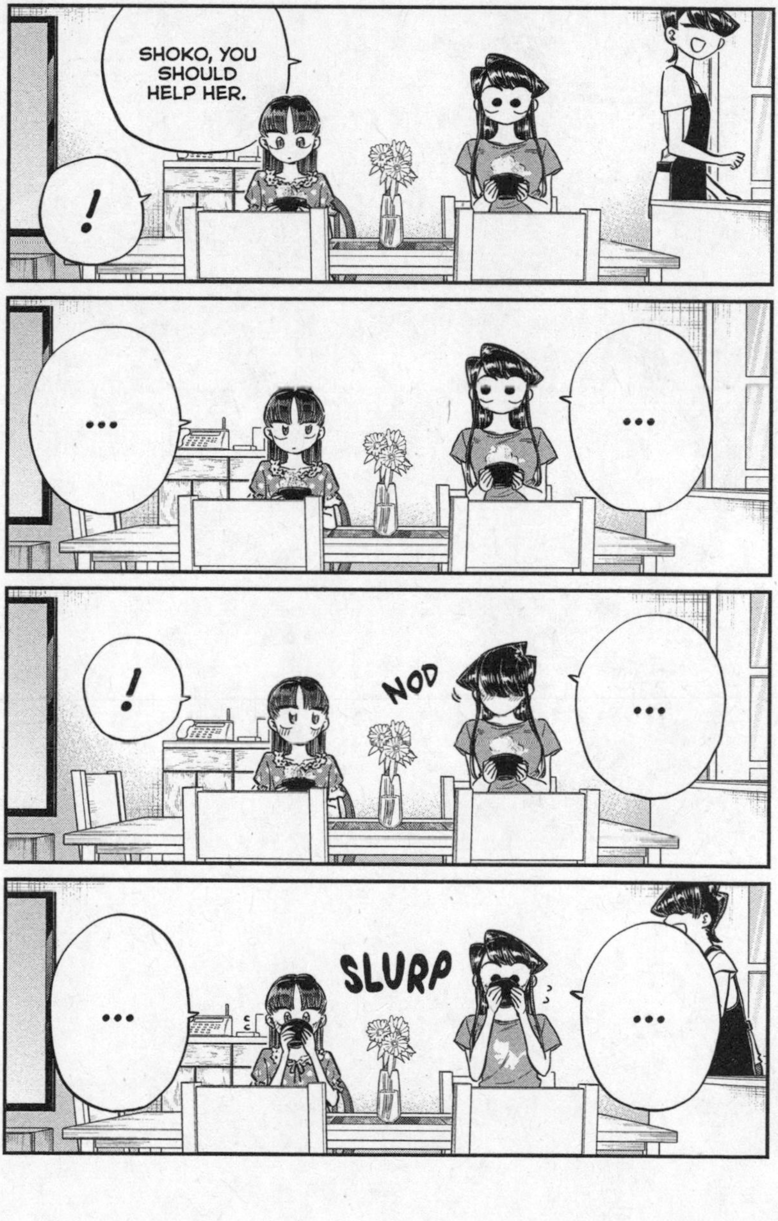
SHOKO, YOU SHOULD HELP HER.
!
...
...
...
NOD
!
...
SLURP
...

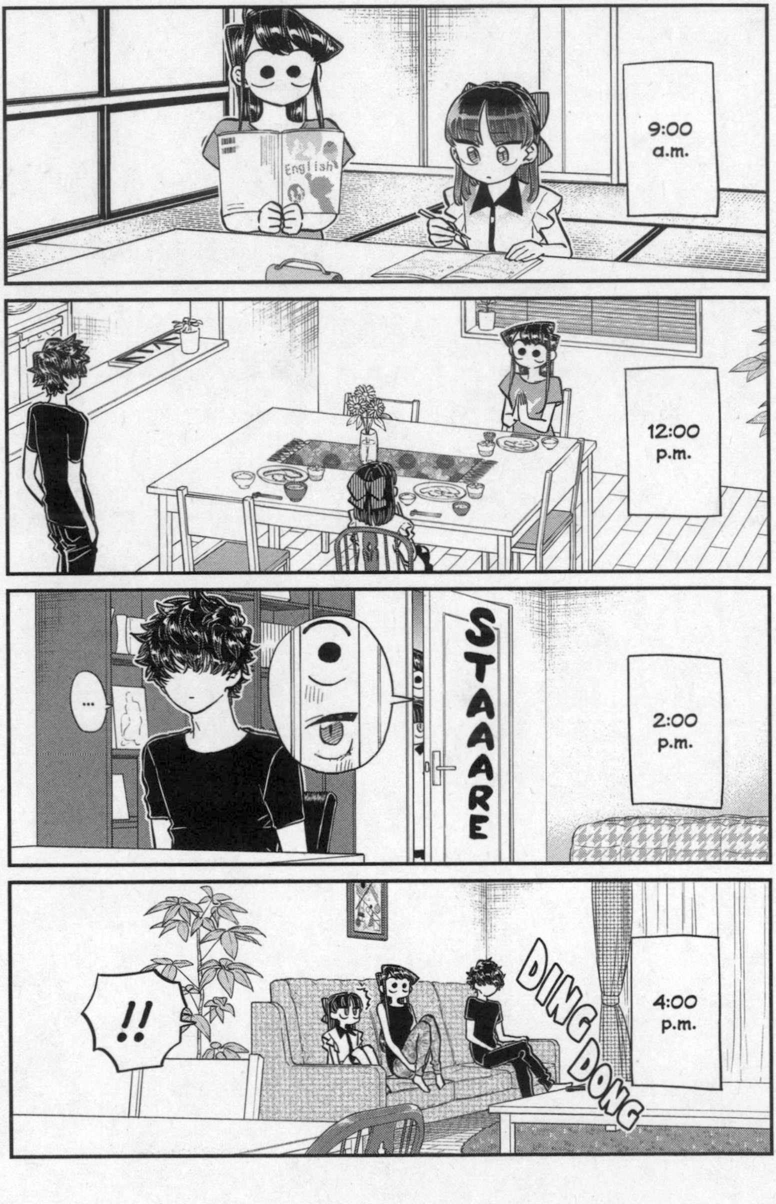
English
9:00 a.m.
12:00 p.m.
2:00 p.m.
STAAARE
...
4:00 p.m.
DING DONG
!!

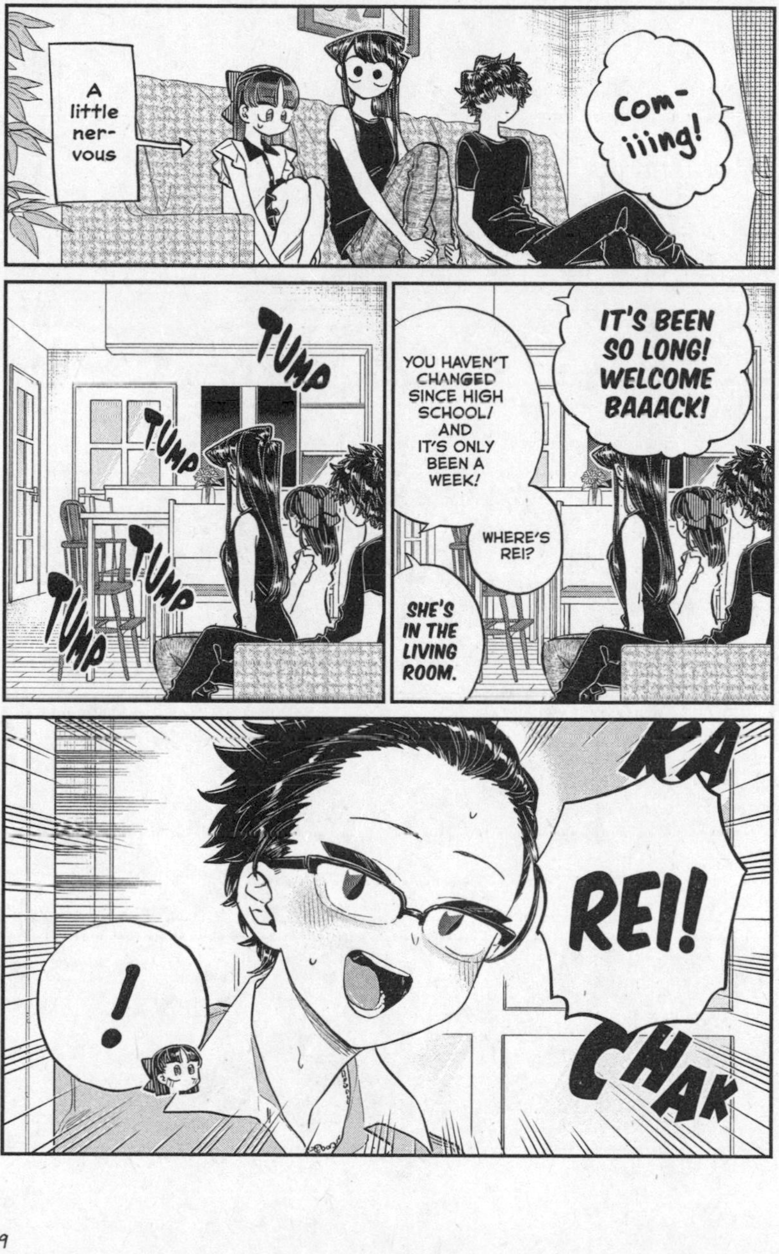
Com-iiing!
A little ner-vous
IT'S BEEN SO LONG! WELCOME BAAACK!
YOU HAVEN'T CHANGED SINCE HIGH SCHOOL! AND IT'S ONLY BEEN A WEEK!
WHERE'S REI?
SHE'S IN THE LIVING ROOM.
TUMP
TUMP
TUMP
TUMP
KA
CHAK
REI!
!

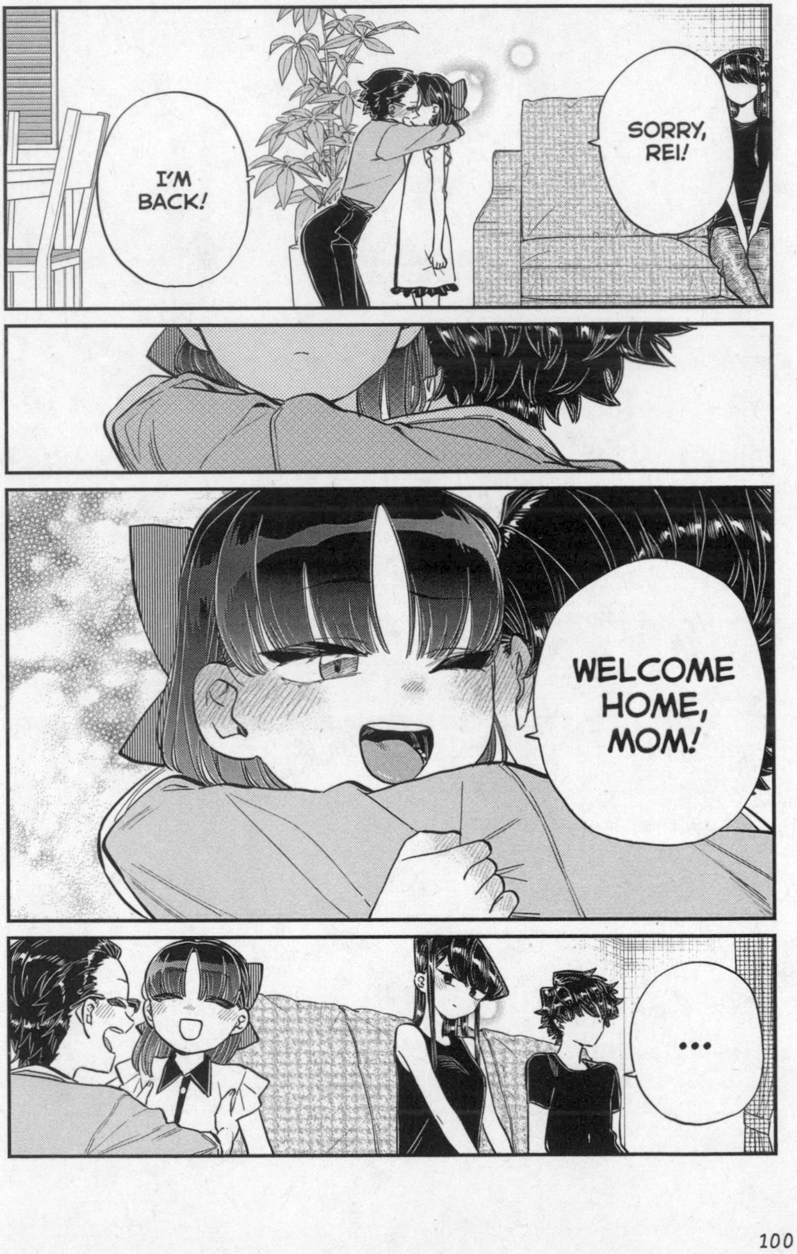
SORRY, REI!
I'M BACK!
WELCOME HOME, MOM!
...

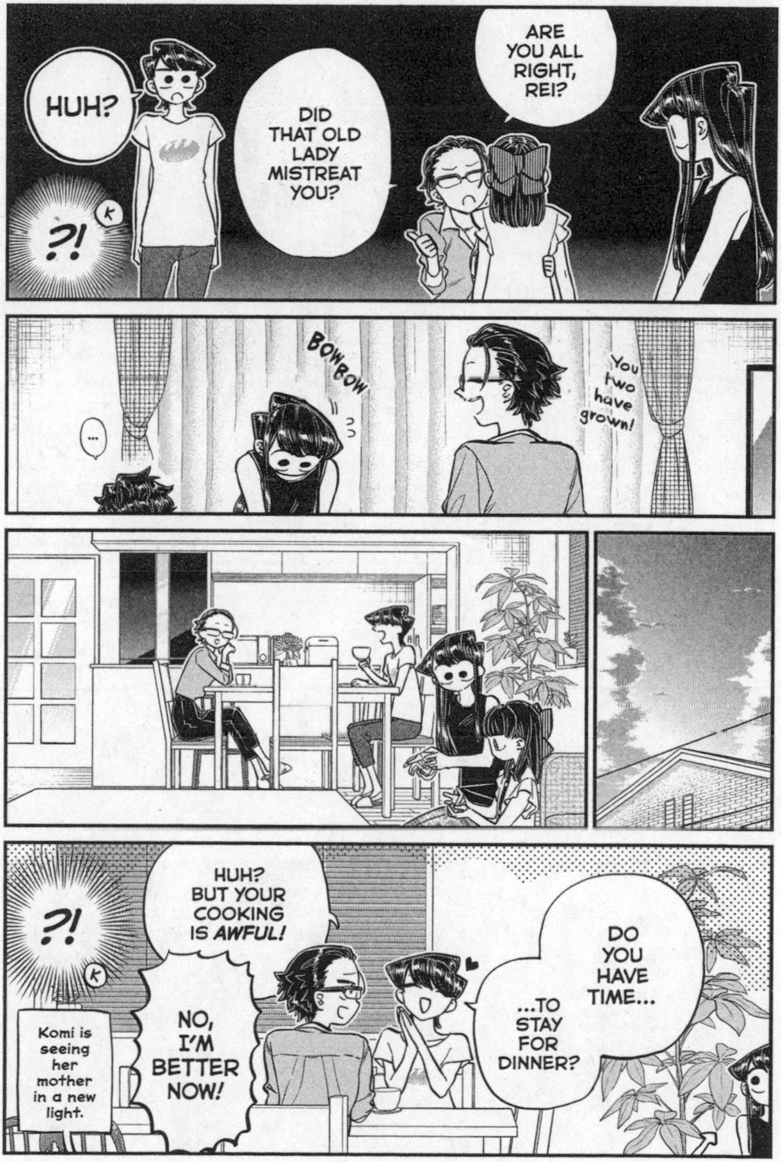
ARE YOU ALL RIGHT, REI?
DID THAT OLD LADY MISTREAT YOU?
HUH?
K
?!
You two have grown!
BOWBOW
...
DO YOU HAVE TIME...
...TO STAY FOR DINNER?
HUH? BUT YOUR COOKING IS *AWFUL!*
NO, I'M BETTER NOW!
K
?!
Komi is seeing her mother in a new light.

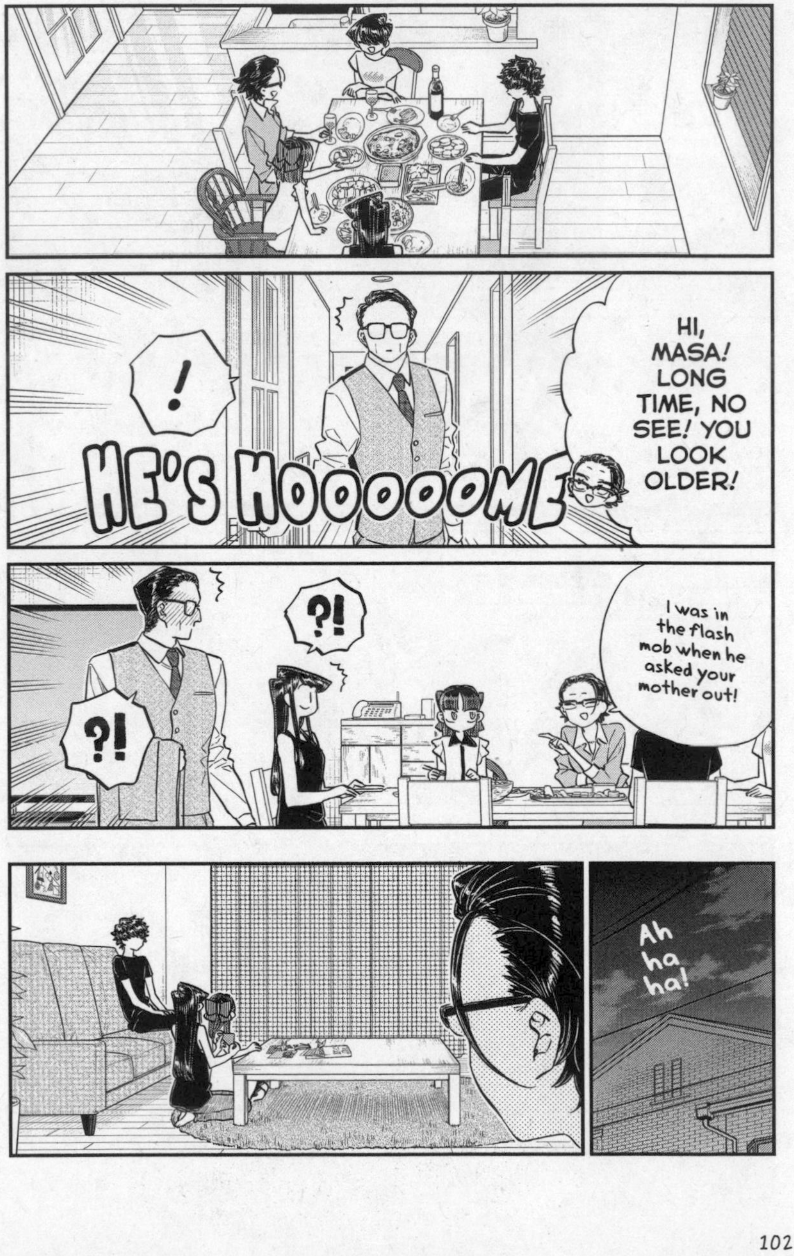
HI, MASA! LONG TIME, NO SEE! YOU LOOK OLDER!
!
HE'S HOOOOOME
I was in the flash mob when he asked your mother out!
?!
?!
Ah ha ha!

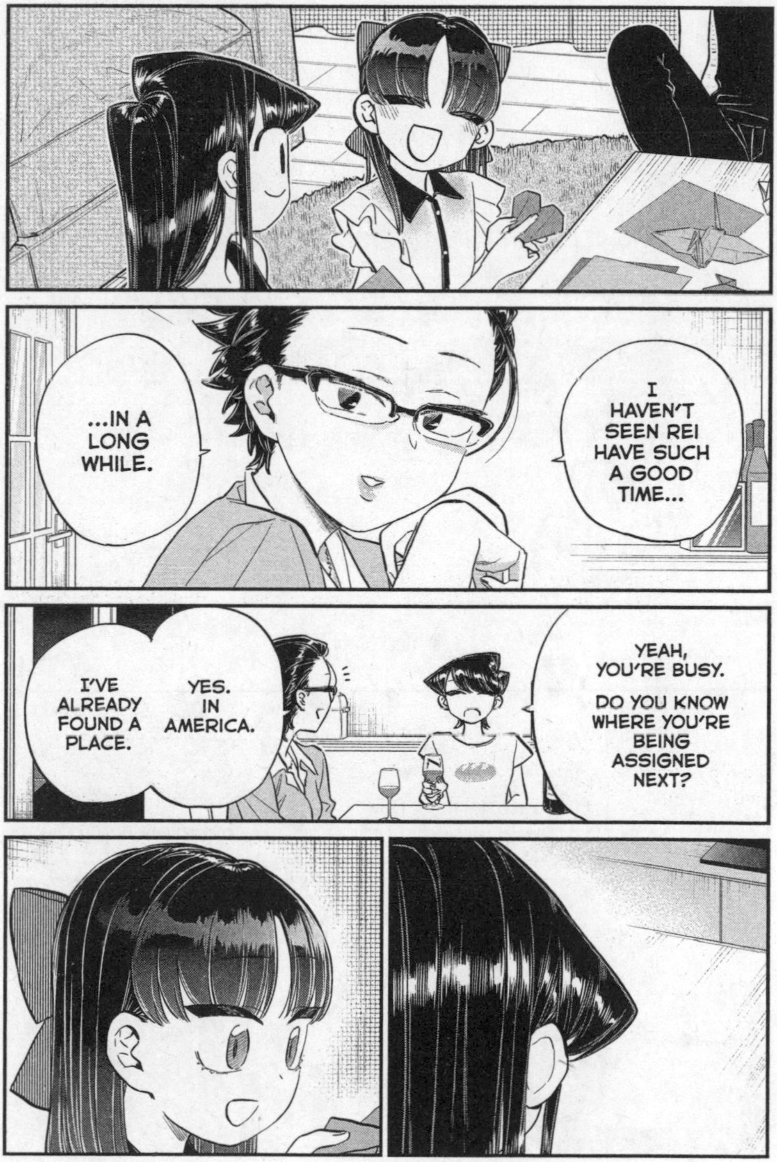
I HAVEN'T SEEN REI HAVE SUCH A GOOD TIME...
...IN A LONG WHILE.
YEAH, YOU'RE BUSY.
DO YOU KNOW WHERE YOU'RE BEING ASSIGNED NEXT?
YES. IN AMERICA.
I'VE ALREADY FOUND A PLACE.

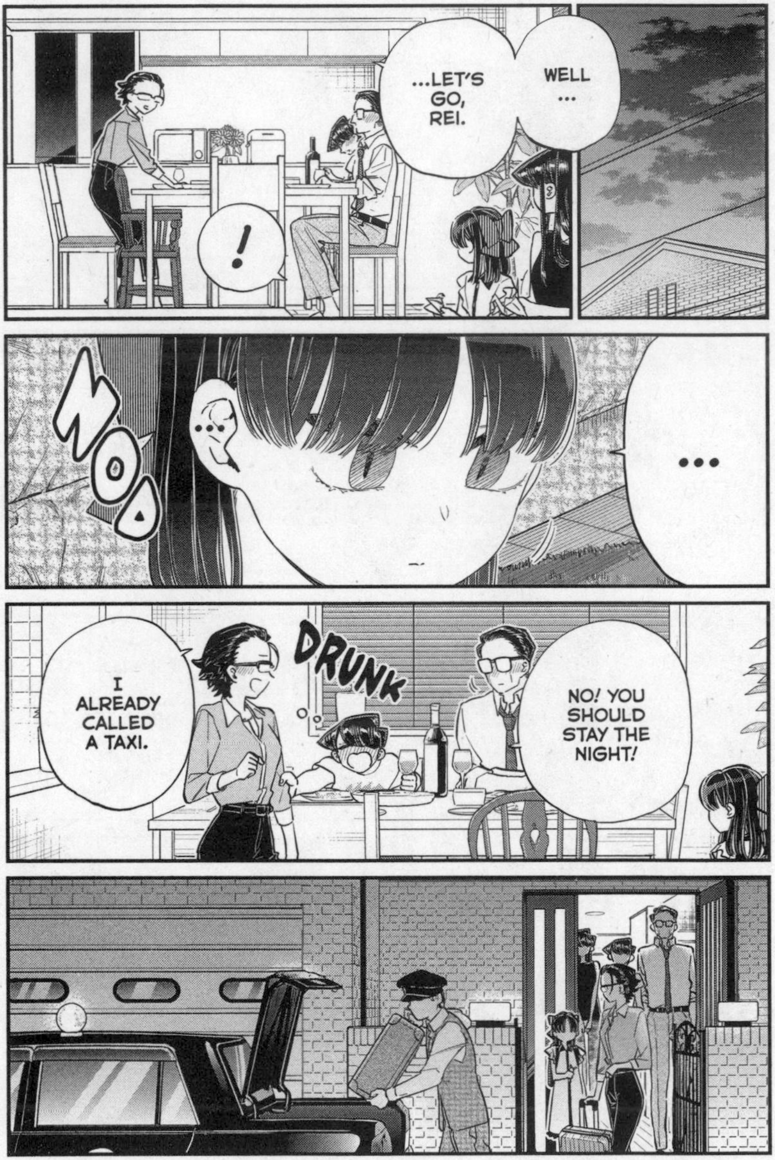
WELL ...
...LET'S GO, REI.
!
...
NOD
...
NO! YOU SHOULD STAY THE NIGHT!
DRUNK
I ALREADY CALLED A TAXI.

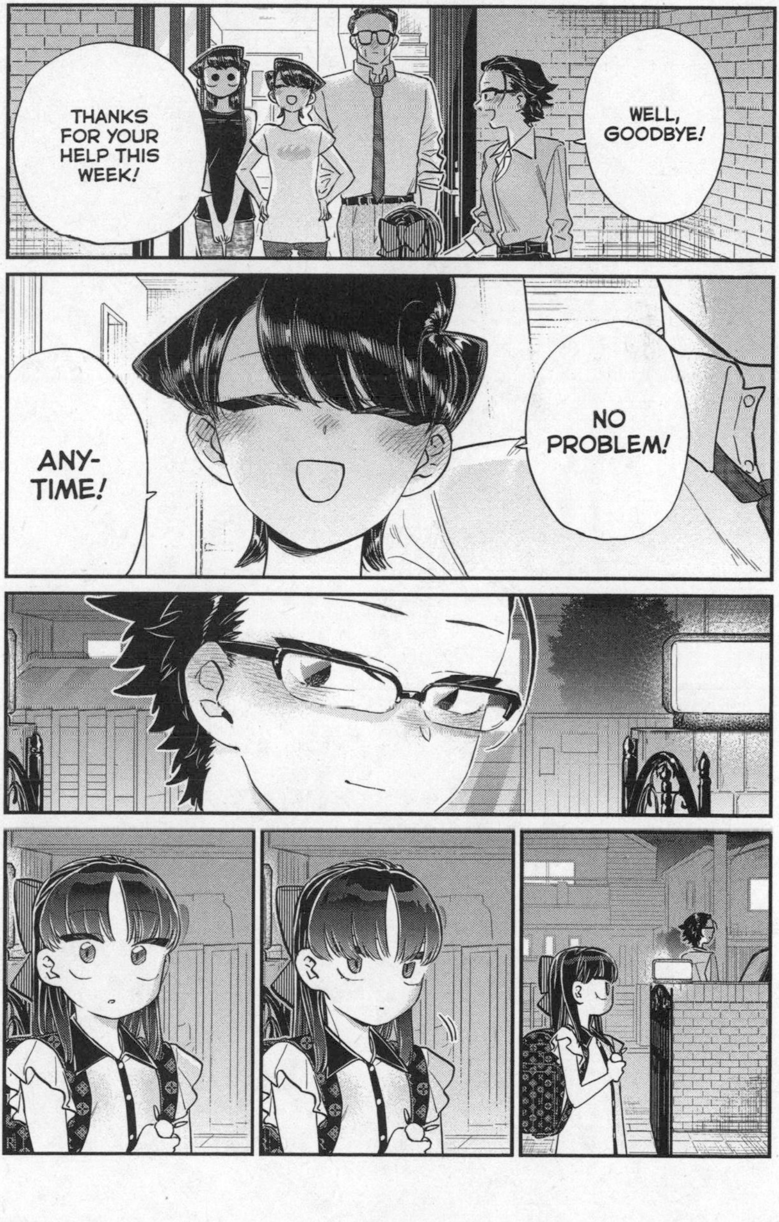
WELL, GOODBYE!
THANKS FOR YOUR HELP THIS WEEK!
NO PROBLEM!
ANY-TIME!

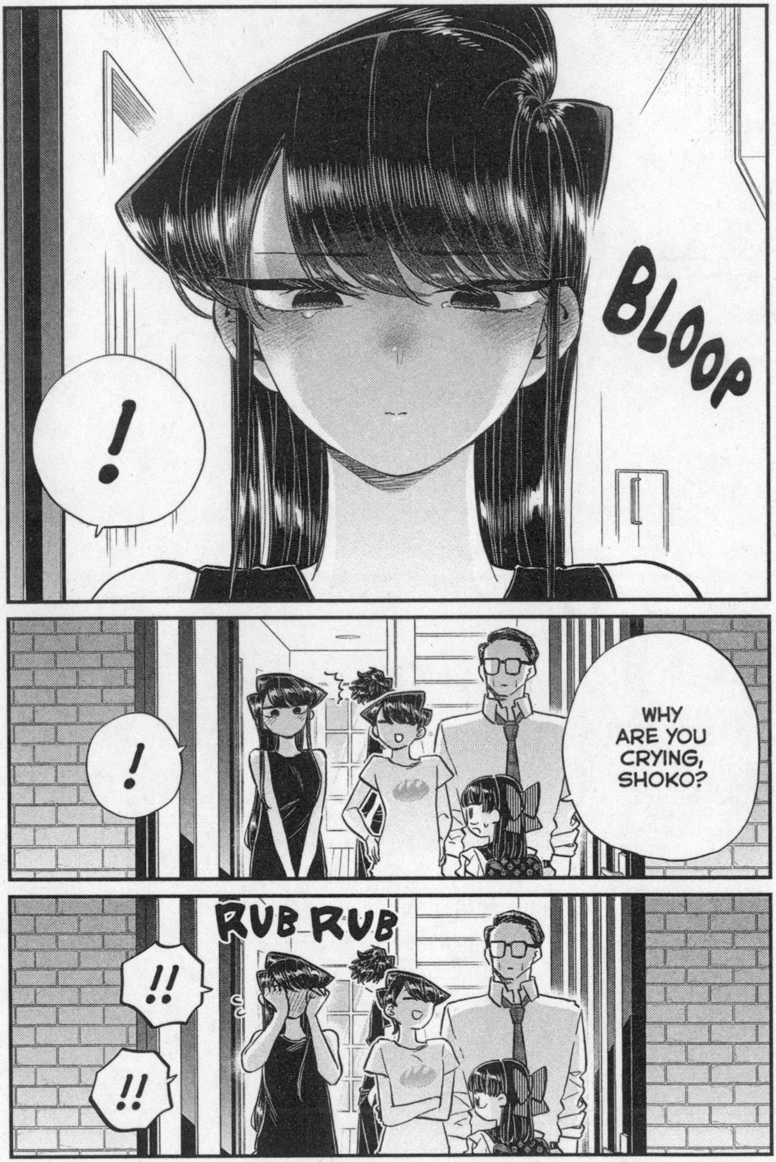
BLOOP
!
WHY ARE YOU CRYING, SHOKO?
!
RUB RUB
!!
!!

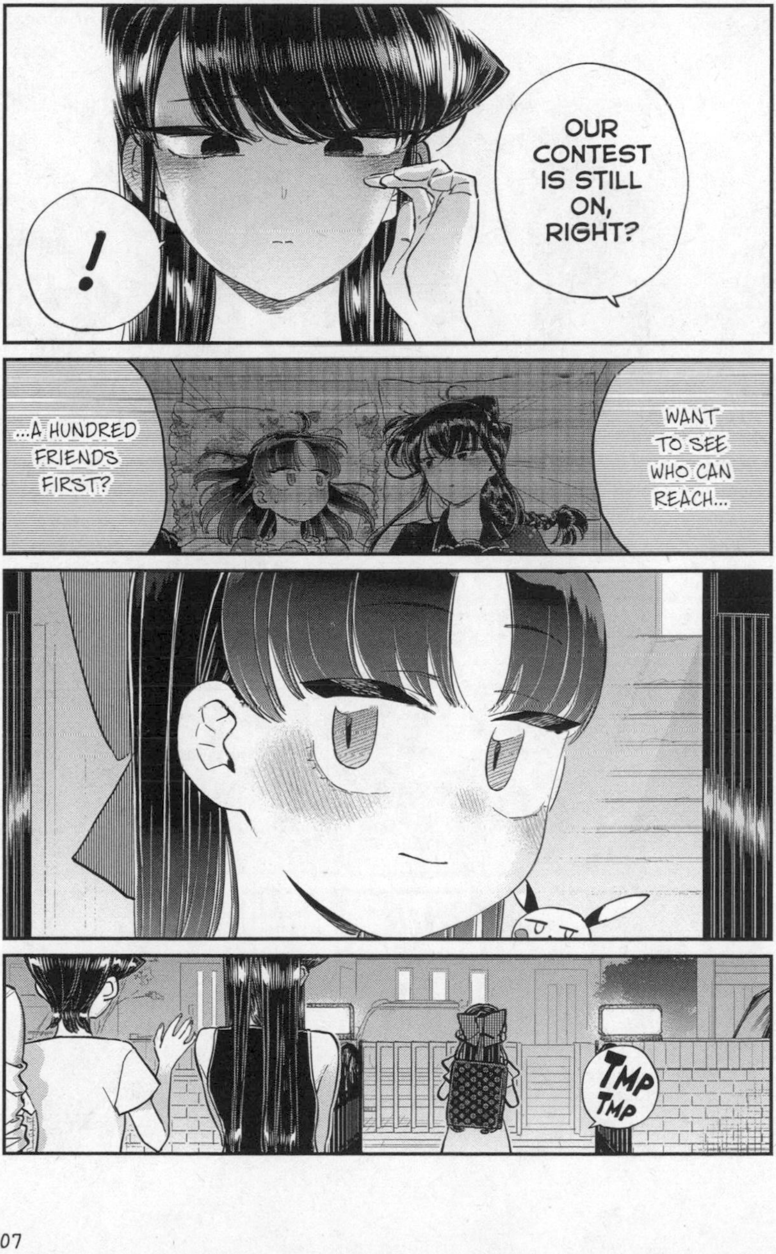
OUR CONTEST IS STILL ON, RIGHT?
!
WANT TO SEE WHO CAN REACH...
...A HUNDRED FRIENDS FIRST?
TMP TMP

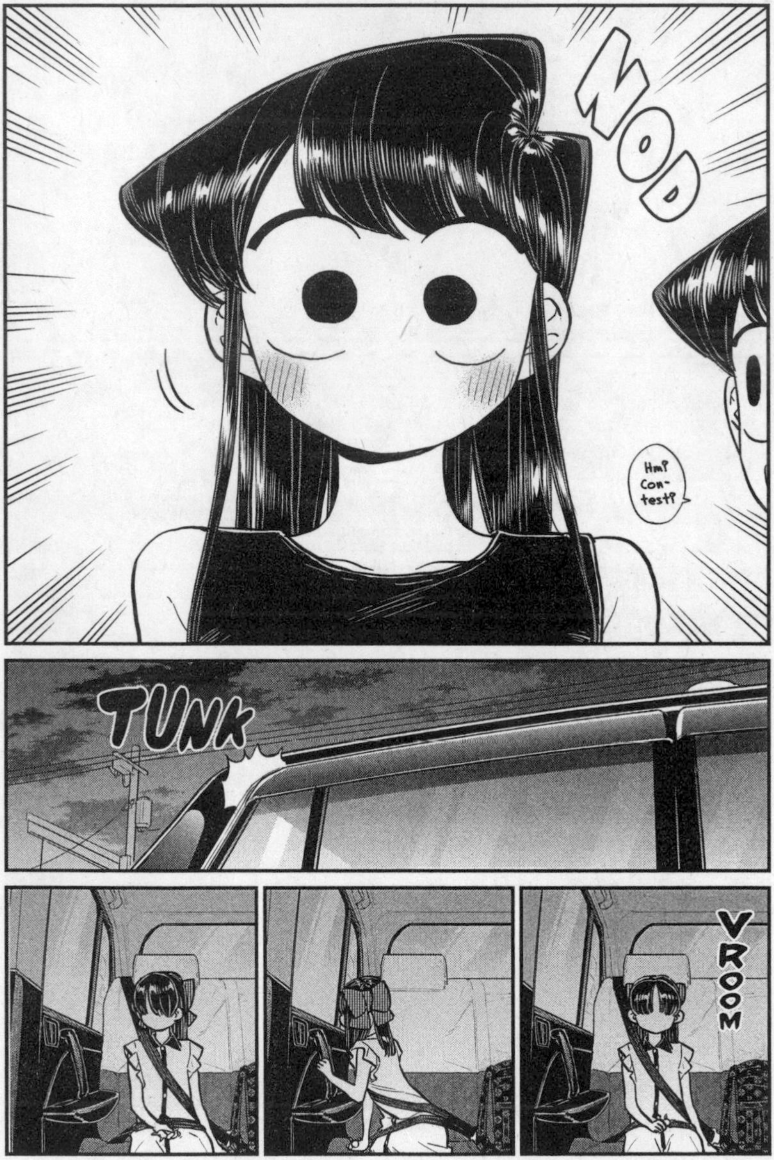
NOD
Hm? Con-test?
TUNK
VROOM

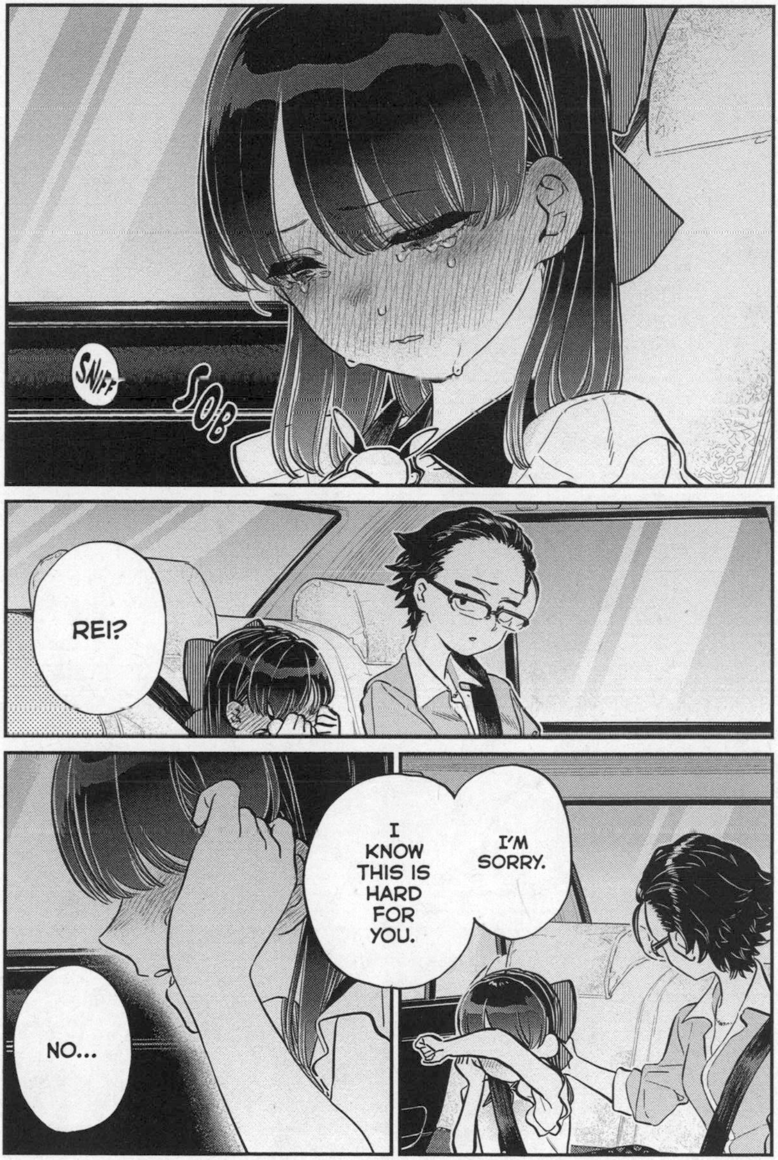
SNIFF
SOB
REI?
I'M SORRY.
I KNOW THIS IS HARD FOR YOU.
NO...

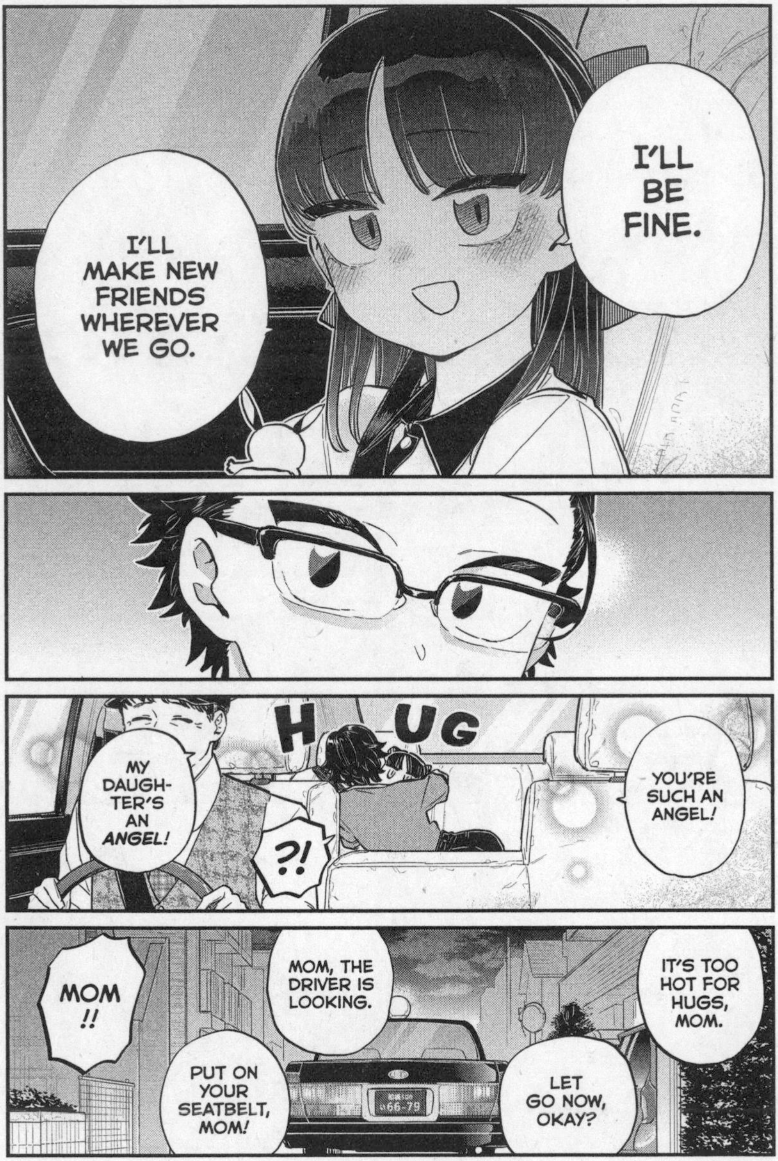
I'LL BE FINE.
I'LL MAKE NEW FRIENDS WHEREVER WE GO.
YOU'RE SUCH AN ANGEL!
HUG
?!
MY DAUGHTER'S AN ANGEL!
IT'S TOO HOT FOR HUGS, MOM.
LET GO NOW, OKAY?
MOM, THE DRIVER IS LOOKING.
PUT ON YOUR SEATBELT, MOM!
MOM !!

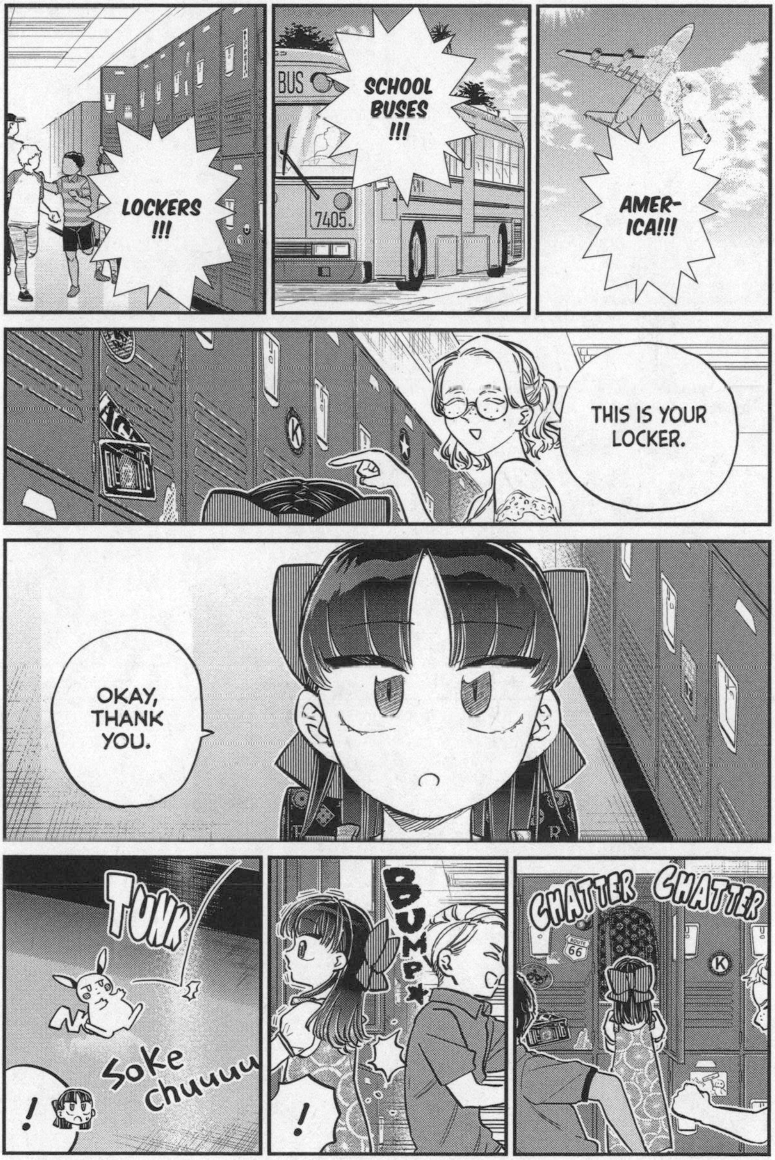
AMER-ICA!!!
SCHOOL BUSES !!!
LOCKERS !!!
THIS IS YOUR LOCKER.
OKAY, THANK YOU.
CHATTER CHATTER
BUMP
!
TUNK
Soke chuuuu
!

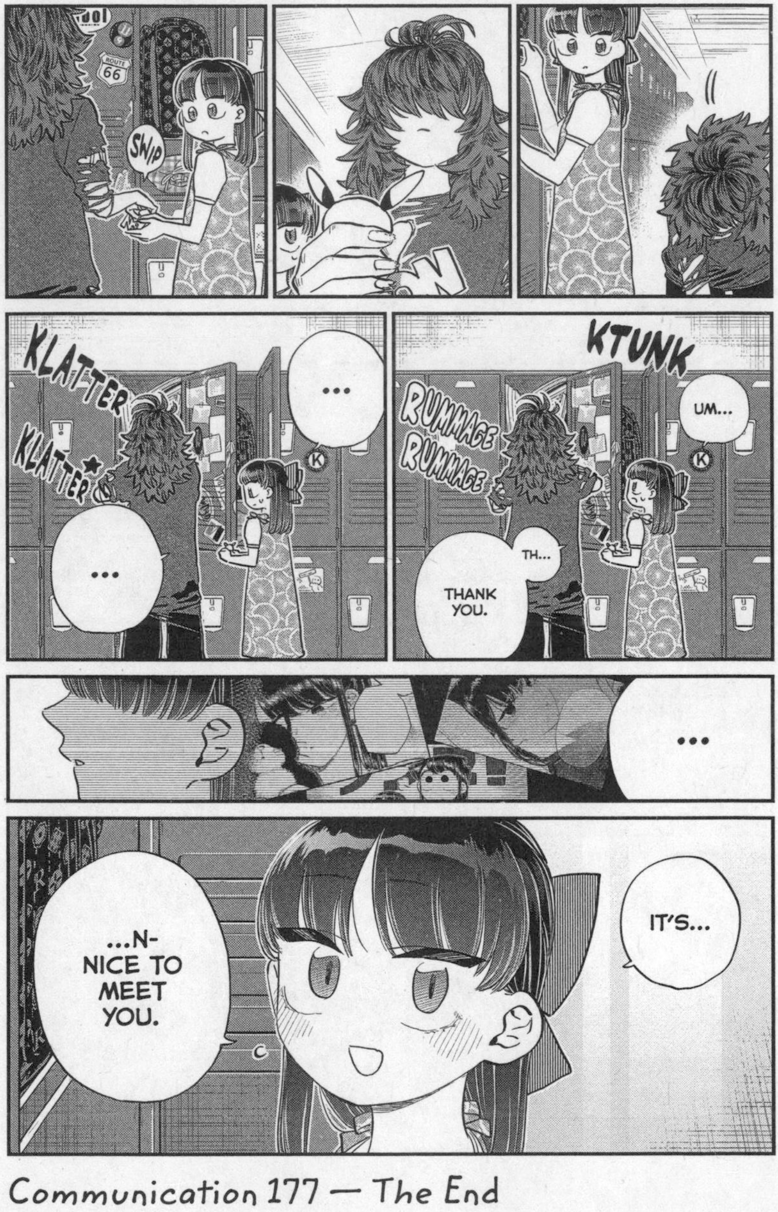
SWIP
UM...
KTUNK
RUMMAGE
RUMMAGE
TH...
THANK YOU.
...
KLATTER
KLATTER
...
...
IT'S...
...N- NICE TO MEET YOU.

Communication 177 — The End

Komi Can't Communicate

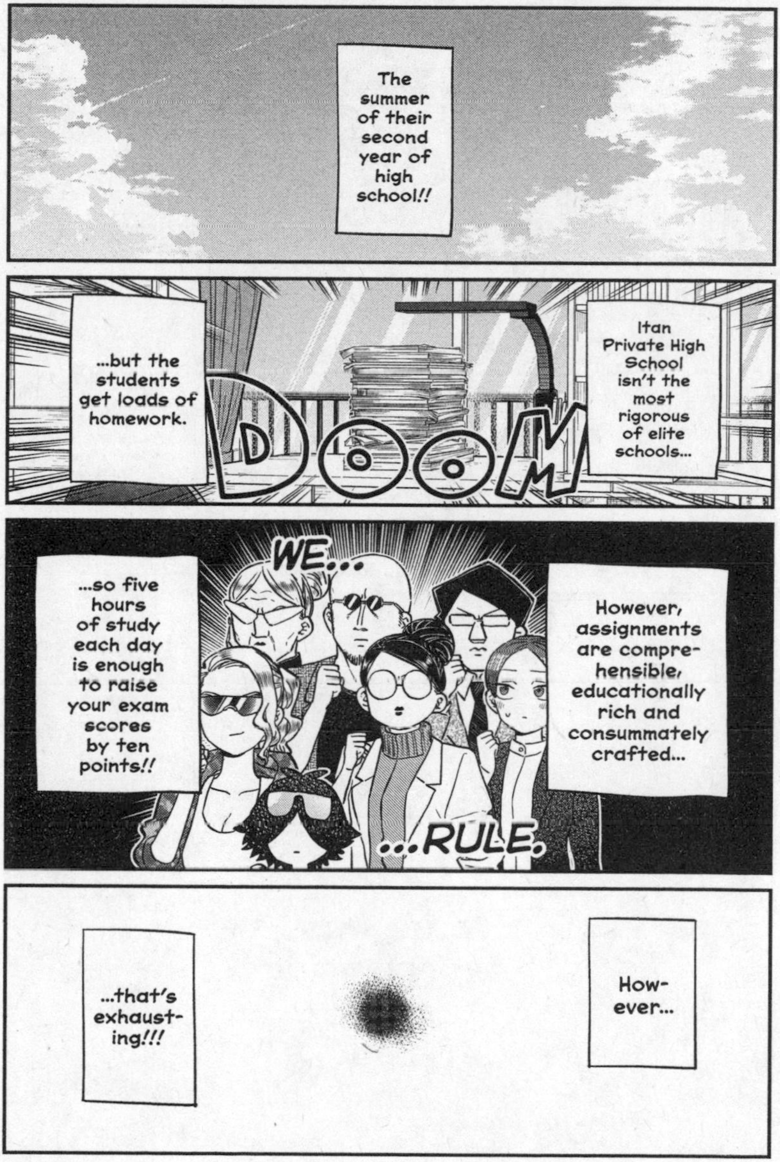
The summer of their second year of high school!!
Itan Private High School isn't the most rigorous of elite schools...
DOOM
...but the students get loads of homework.
However, assignments are comprehensible, educationally rich and consummately crafted...
WE...
...RULE.
...so five hours of study each day is enough to raise your exam scores by ten points!!
However...
...that's exhausting!!!

Communication 178: Summer Rendezvous

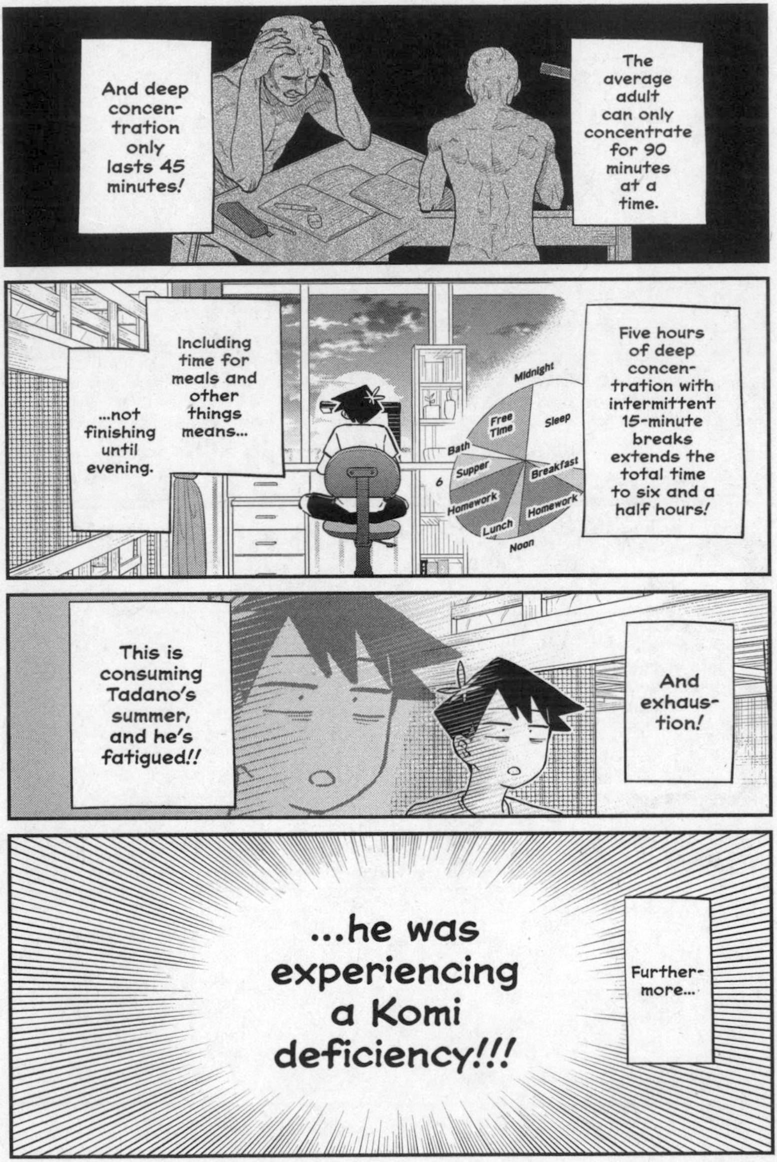
The average adult can only concentrate for 90 minutes at a time.
And deep concentration only lasts 45 minutes!
Five hours of deep concentration with intermittent 15-minute breaks extends the total time to six and a half hours!
Midnight
Sleep
Breakfast
Homework
Noon
Lunch
Homework
6
Supper
Bath
Free Time
Including time for meals and other things means...
...not finishing until evening.
And exhaustion!
This is consuming Tadano's summer, and he's fatigued!!
Furthermore...
...he was experiencing a Komi deficiency!!!

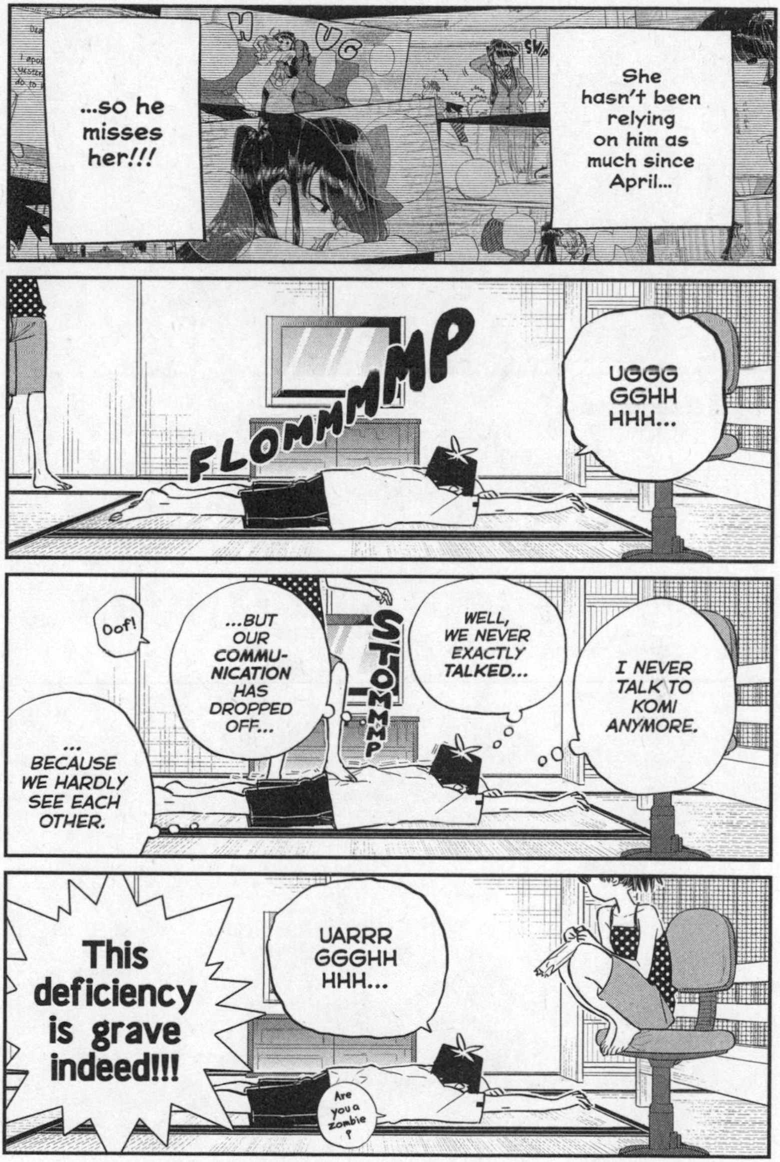
SWIP
She hasn't been relying on him as much since April...
H UG
...so he misses her!!!
UGGG GGHH HHH...
FLOMMMMP
I NEVER TALK TO KOMI ANYMORE.
WELL, WE NEVER EXACTLY TALKED...
STOMMMP
...BUT OUR COMMUNICATION HAS DROPPED OFF...
Oof!
...BECAUSE WE HARDLY SEE EACH OTHER.
UARRR GGGHH HHH...
Are you a zombie?
This deficiency is grave indeed!!!

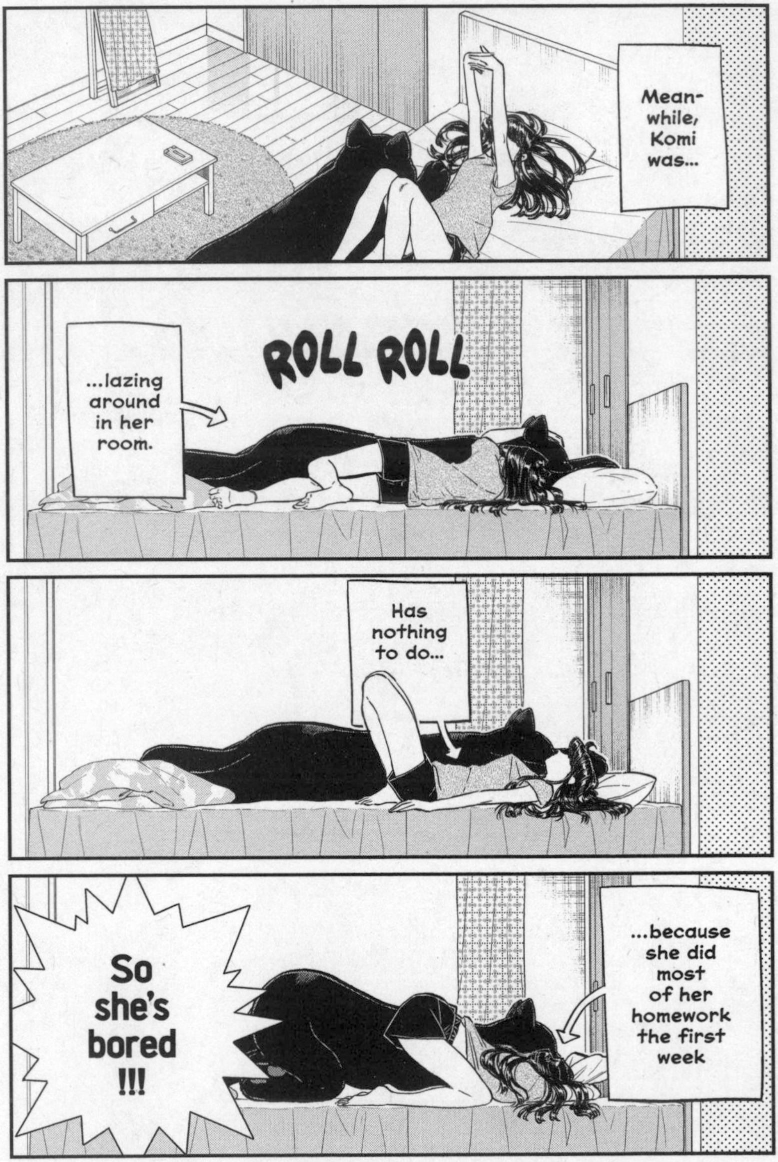
Mean-while, Komi was...
ROLL ROLL
...lazing around in her room.
Has nothing to do...
...because she did most of her homework the first week
So she's bored !!!

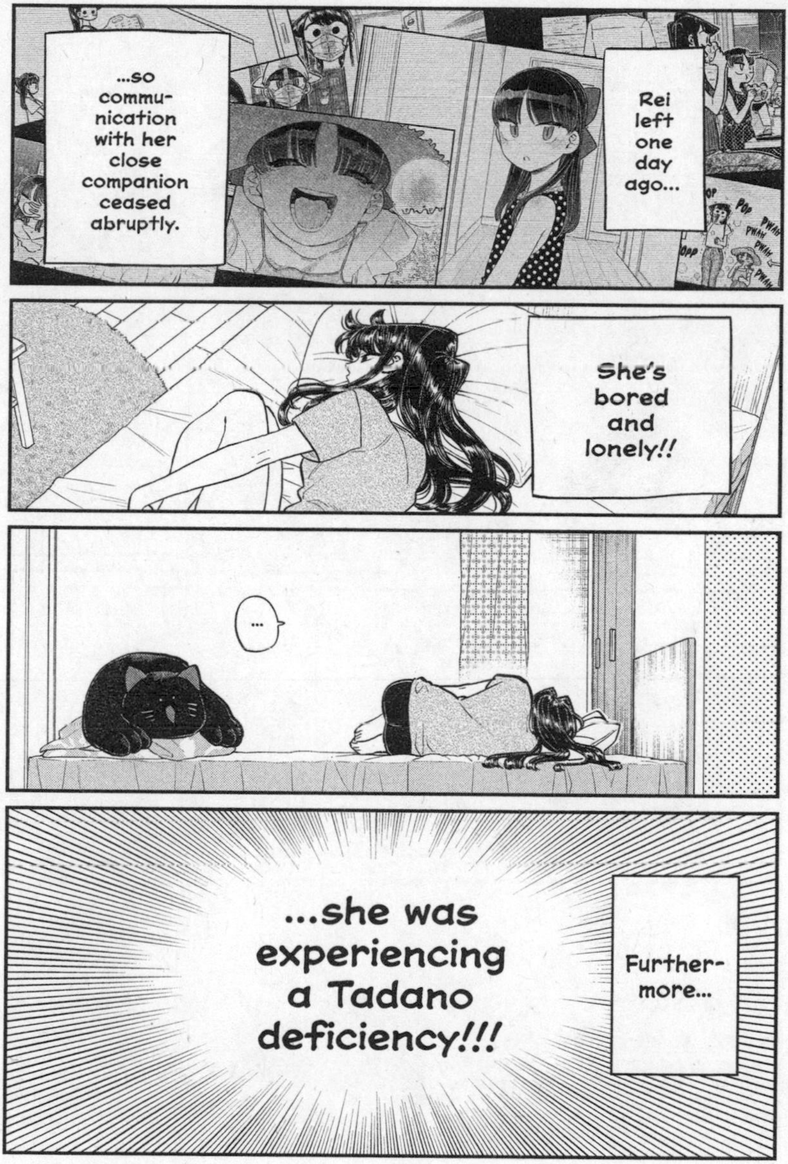
Rei left one day ago...
...so communication with her close companion ceased abruptly.
She's bored and lonely!!
...
Furthermore...
...she was experiencing a Tadano deficiency!!!

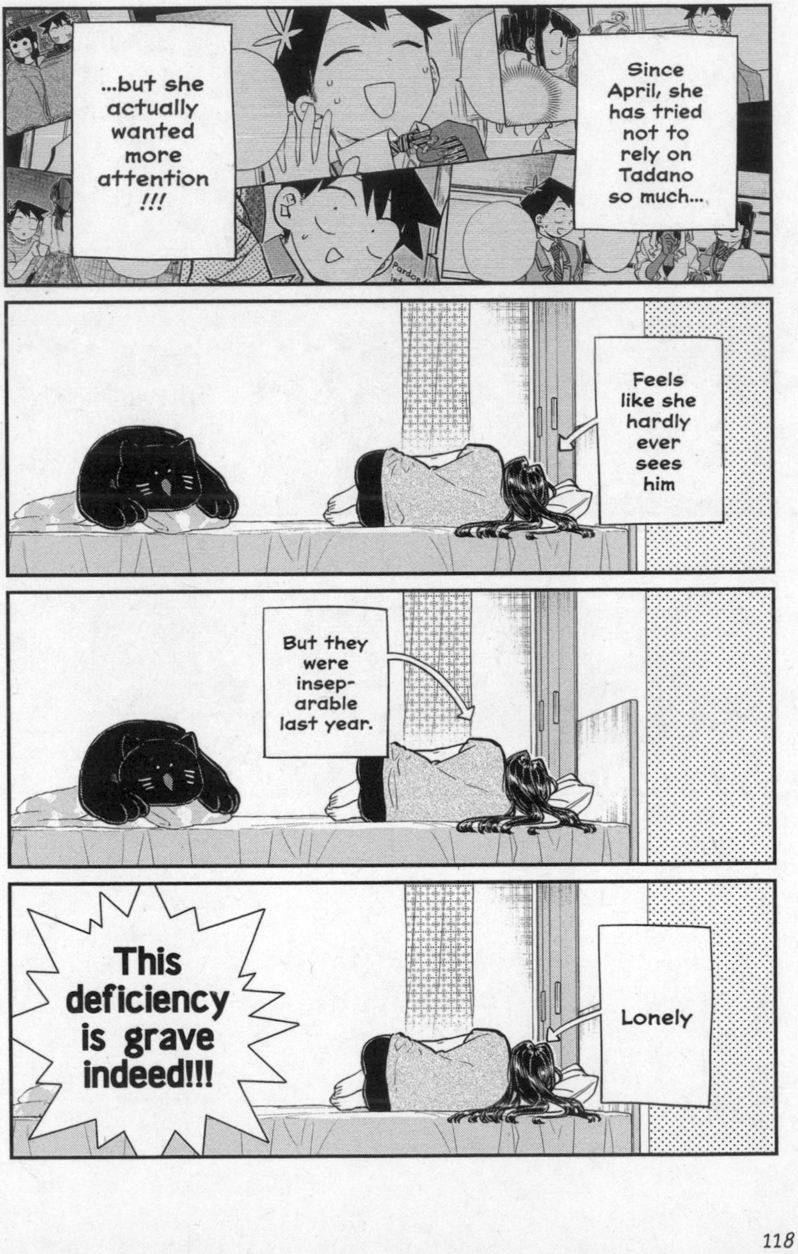
Since April, she has tried not to rely on Tadano so much...
Pardon
...but she actually wanted more attention!!!
Feels like she hardly ever sees him
But they were insep-arable last year.
Lonely
This deficiency is grave indeed!!!

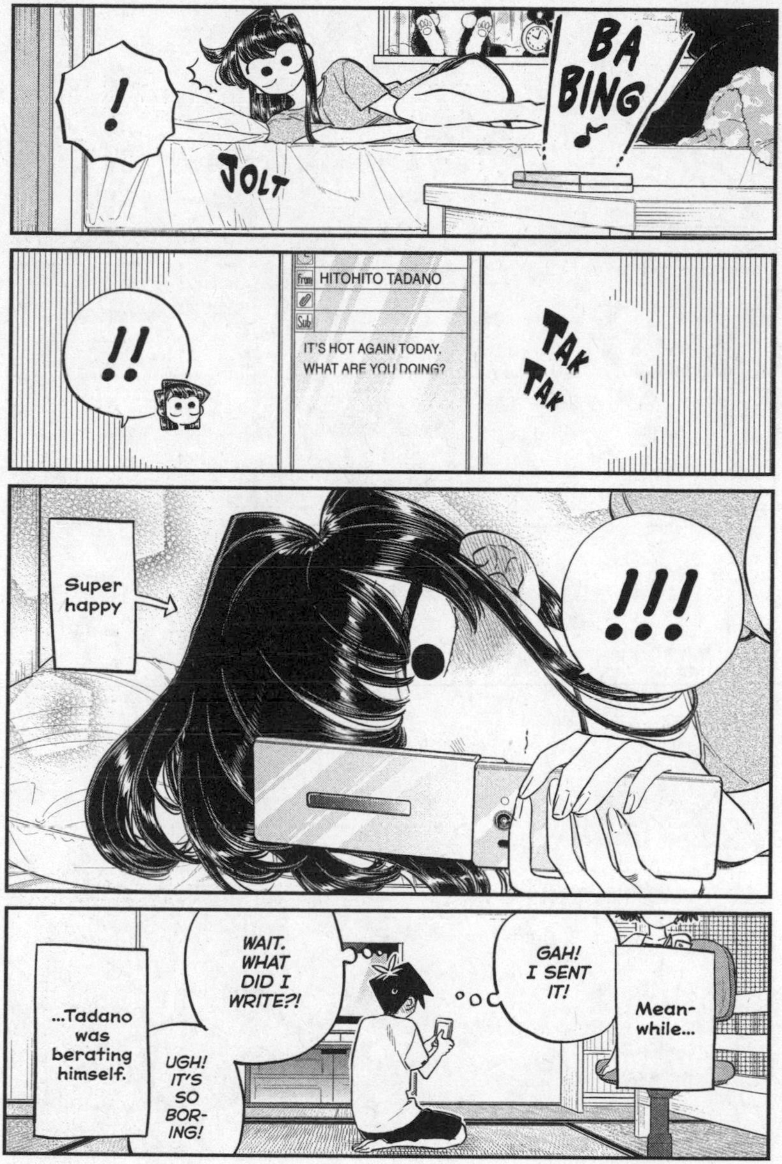
BA BING ♪
!
JOLT
TAK TAK
From HITOHITO TADANO
Sub
IT'S HOT AGAIN TODAY.
WHAT ARE YOU DOING?
!!
!!!
Super happy
Mean-while...
GAH! I SENT IT!
WAIT. WHAT DID I WRITE?!
UGH! IT'S SO BOR-ING!
...Tadano was berating himself.

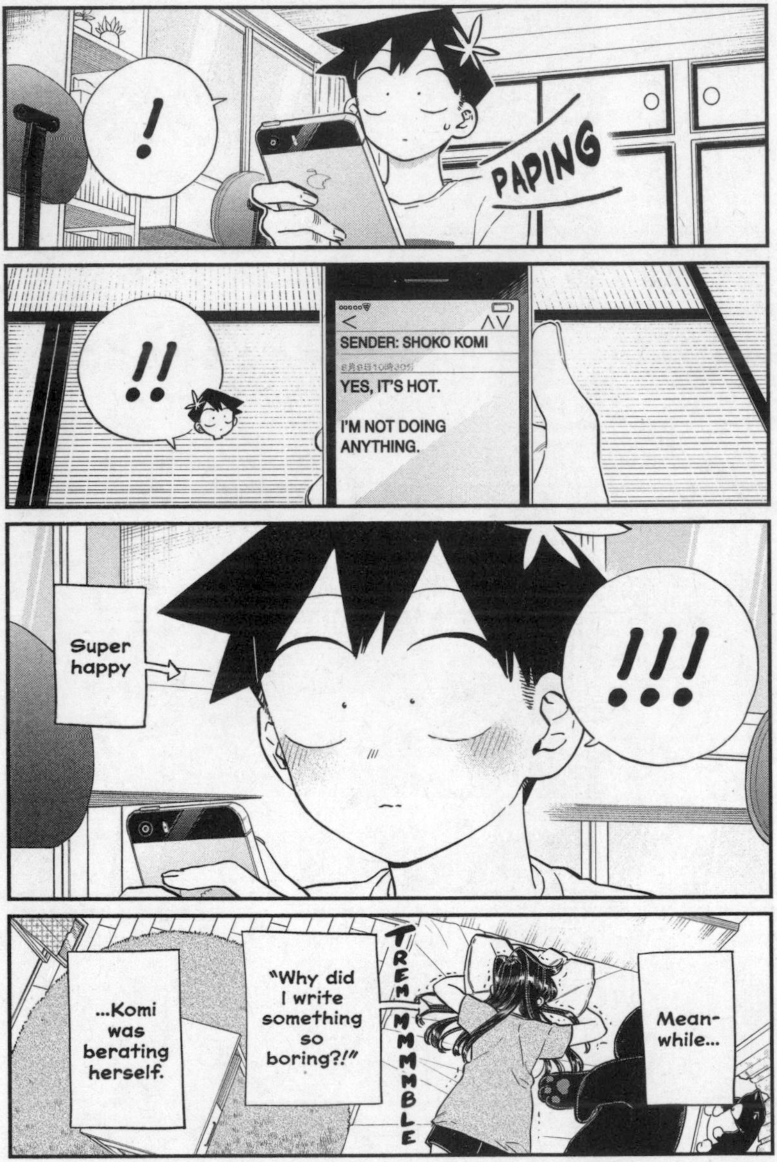
PAPING
!
SENDER: SHOKO KOMI
YES, IT'S HOT.
I'M NOT DOING ANYTHING.
!!
!!!
Super happy
Mean-while...
TREMMMMMBLE
"Why did I write something so boring?!"
...Komi was berating herself.

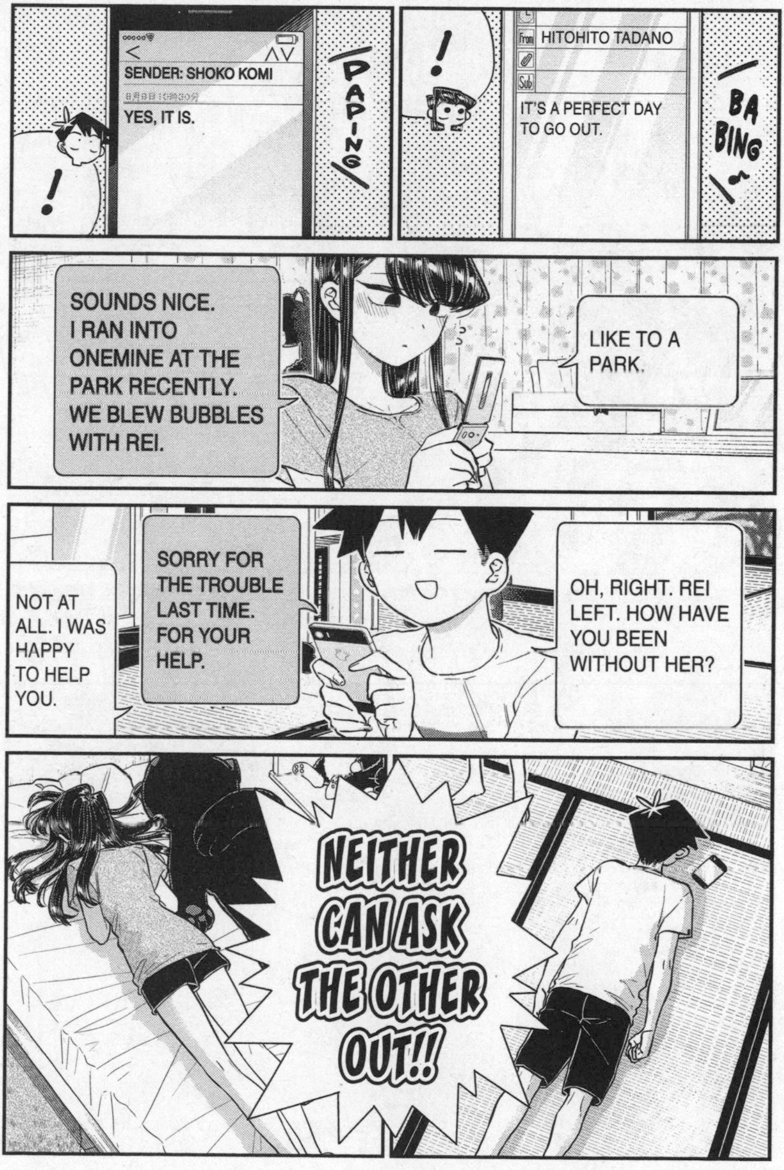
BA BING
From HITOHITO TADANO
Sub
IT'S A PERFECT DAY TO GO OUT.
!
PAPING
SENDER: SHOKO KOMI
YES, IT IS.
!
LIKE TO A PARK.
SOUNDS NICE. I RAN INTO ONEMINE AT THE PARK RECENTLY. WE BLEW BUBBLES WITH REI.
OH, RIGHT. REI LEFT. HOW HAVE YOU BEEN WITHOUT HER?
SORRY FOR THE TROUBLE LAST TIME. FOR YOUR HELP.
NOT AT ALL. I WAS HAPPY TO HELP YOU.
NEITHER CAN ASK THE OTHER OUT!!

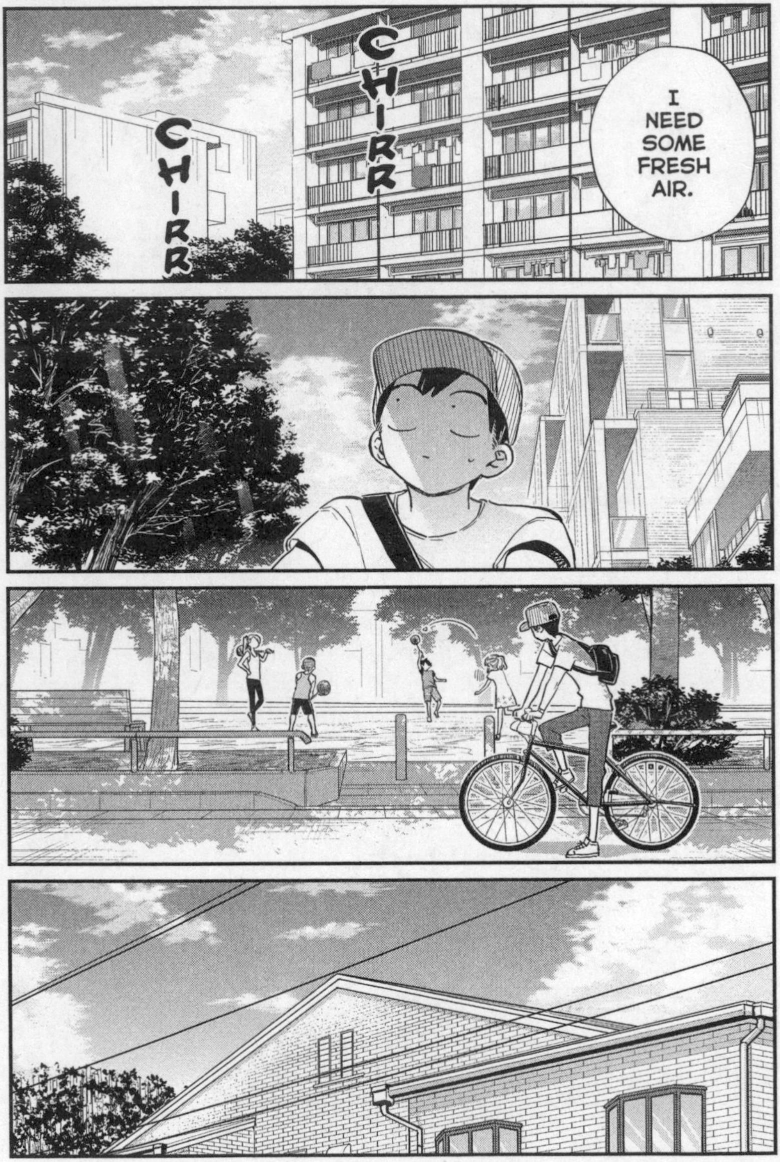
I NEED SOME FRESH AIR.
CHIRR
CHIRR

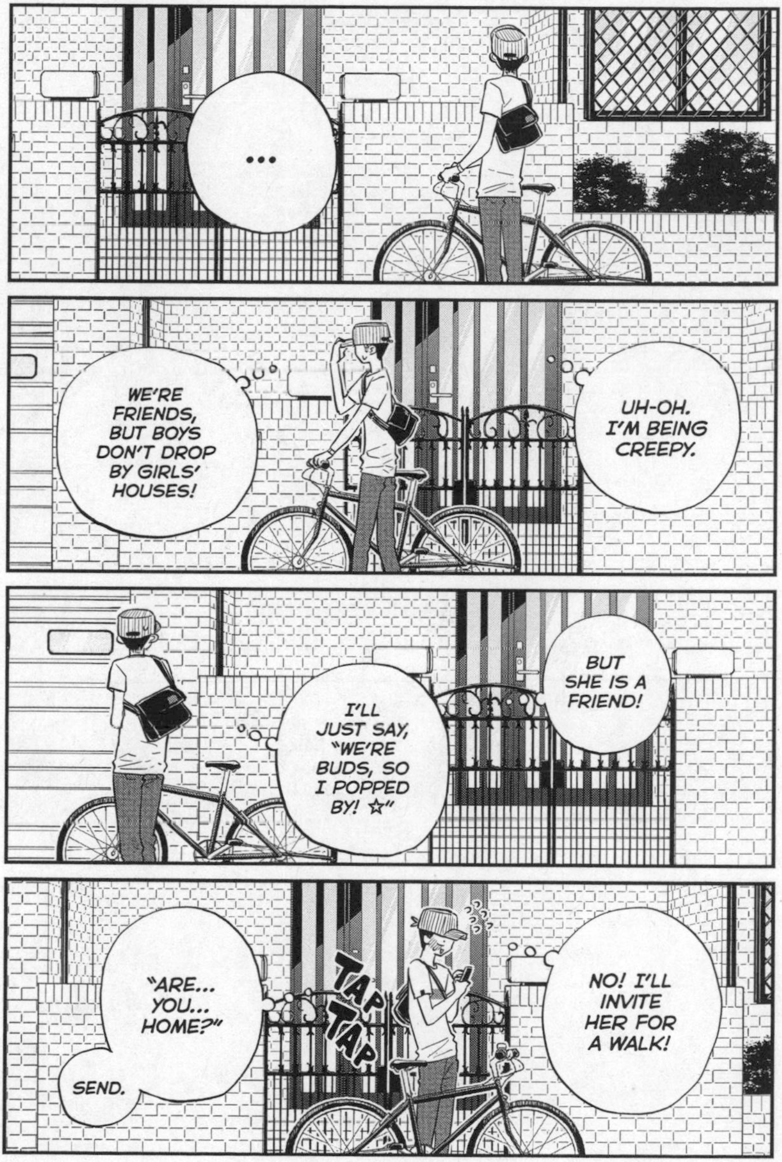
...
UH-OH. I'M BEING CREEPY.
WE'RE FRIENDS, BUT BOYS DON'T DROP BY GIRLS' HOUSES!
BUT SHE IS A FRIEND!
I'LL JUST SAY, "WE'RE BUDS, SO I POPPED BY! ☆"
NO! I'LL INVITE HER FOR A WALK!
TAP TAP
"ARE... YOU... HOME?"
SEND.

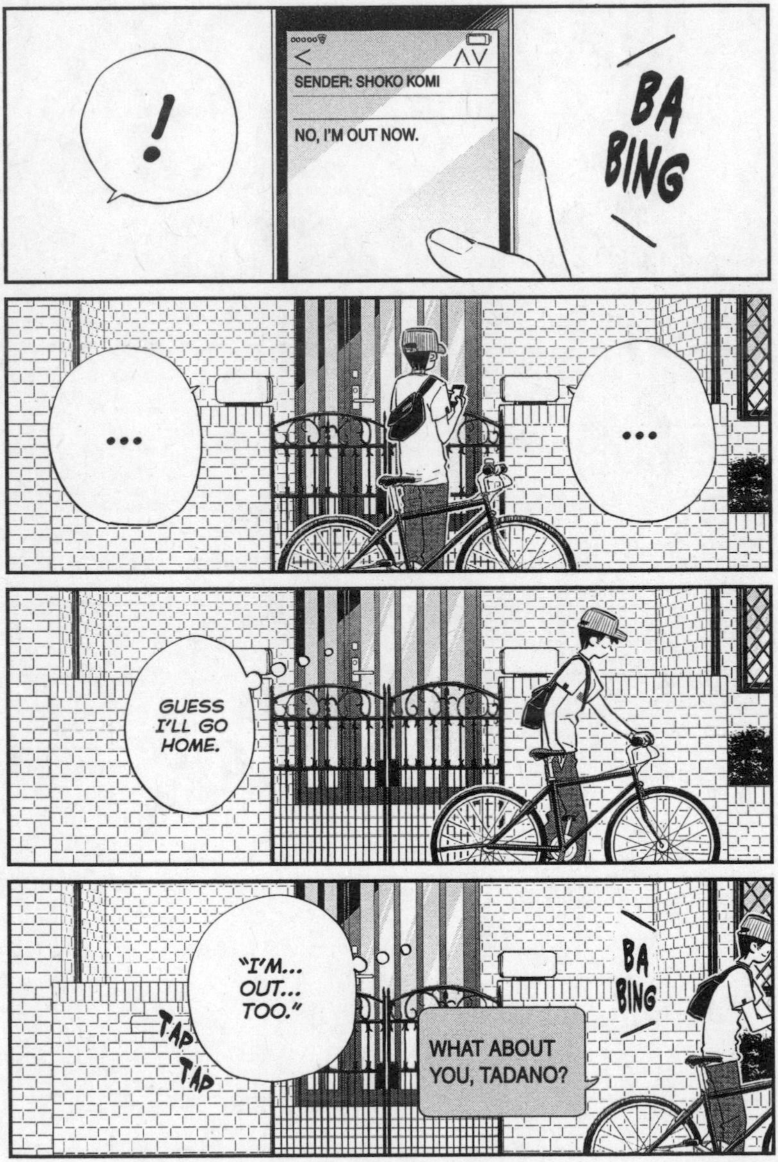

BA BING
SENDER: SHOKO KOMI
NO, I'M OUT NOW.
!
...
...
GUESS I'LL GO HOME.
BA BING
WHAT ABOUT YOU, TADANO?
"I'M... OUT... TOO."
TAP TAP

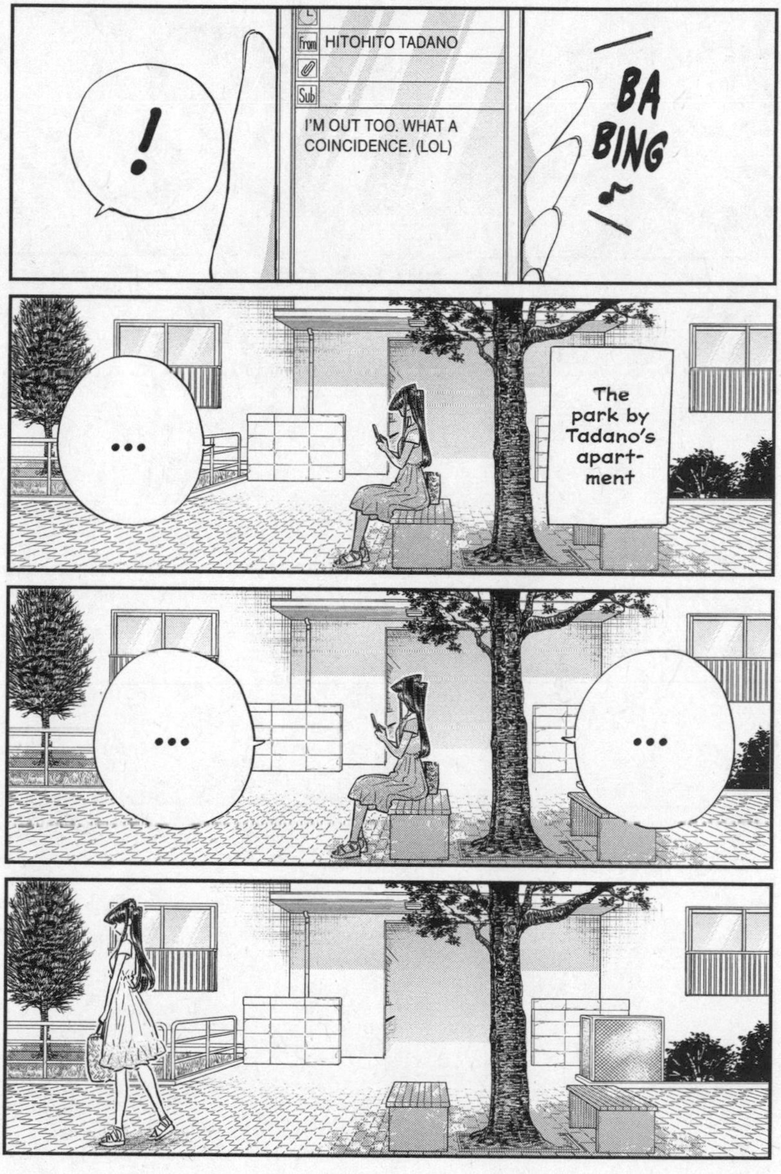
BA BING ♪
From HITOHITO TADANO
Sub
I'M OUT TOO. WHAT A COINCIDENCE. (LOL)
!
The park by Tadano's apartment
...
...
...

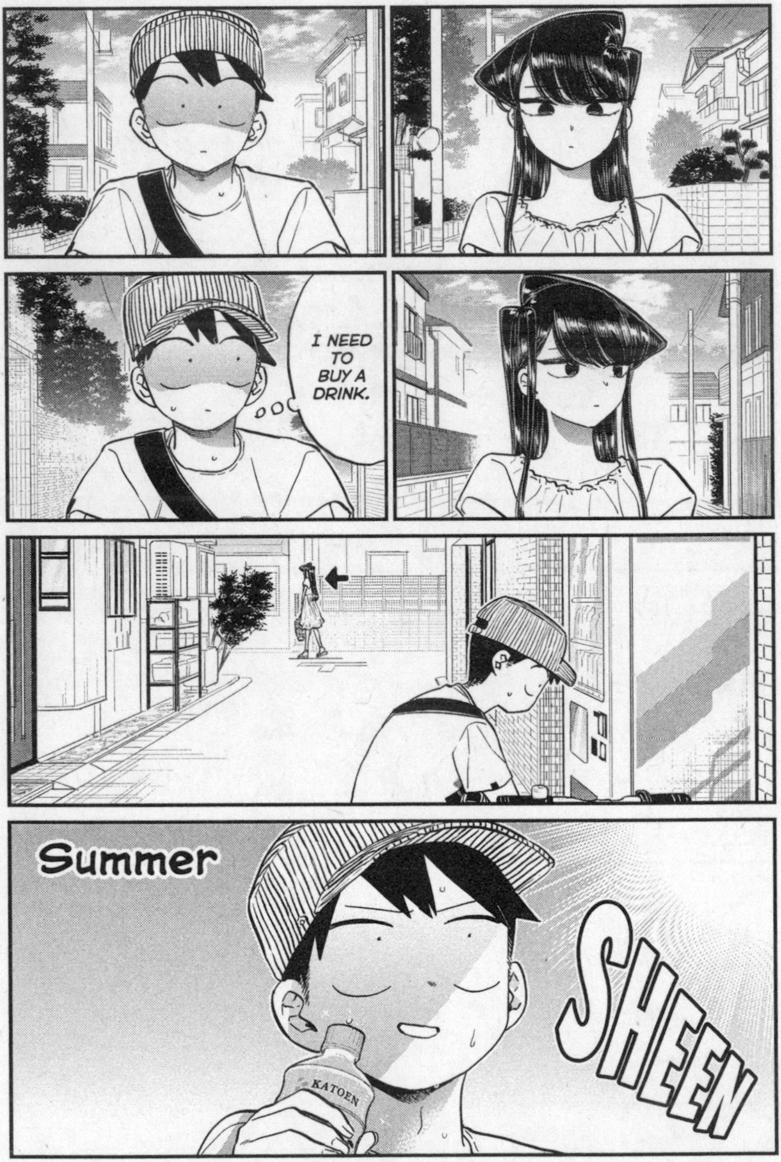
I NEED TO BUY A DRINK.
Summer
SHEEN
KATOEN

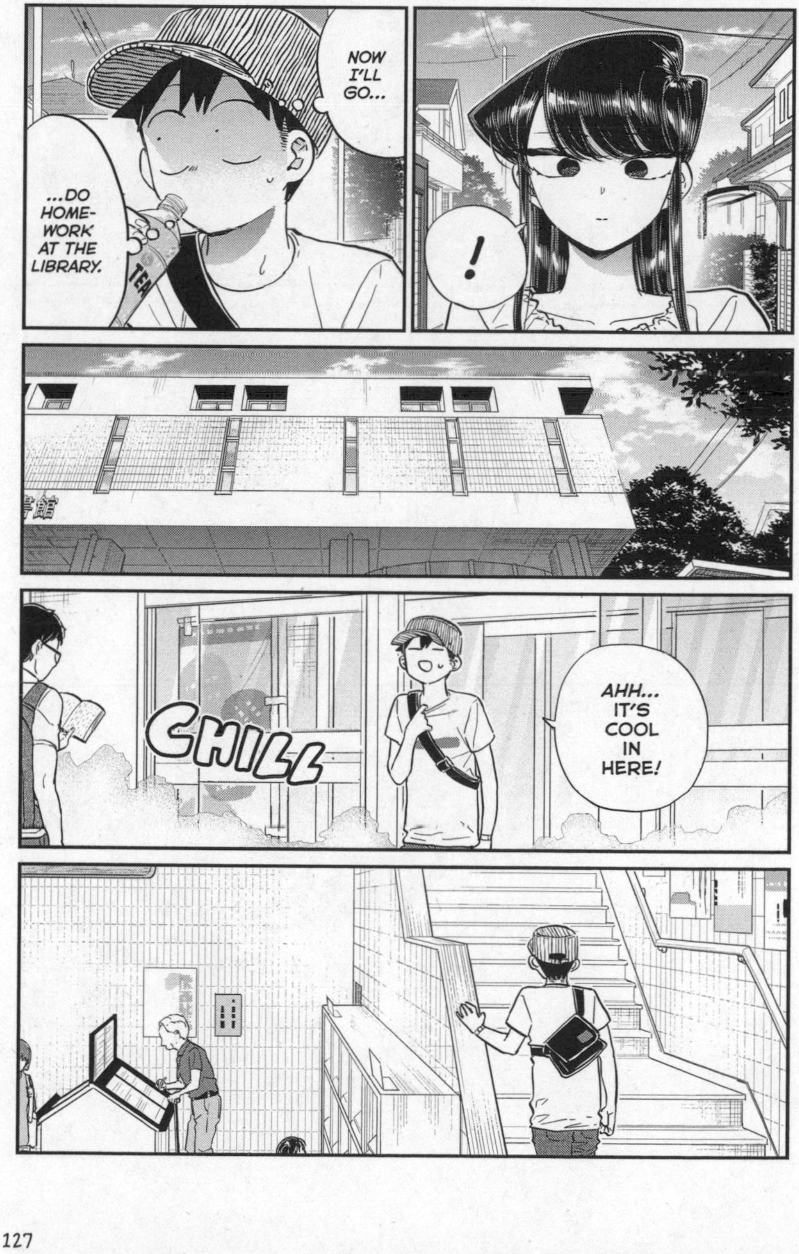
!
NOW I'LL GO...
...DO HOME-WORK AT THE LIBRARY.
AHH... IT'S COOL IN HERE!
CHILL

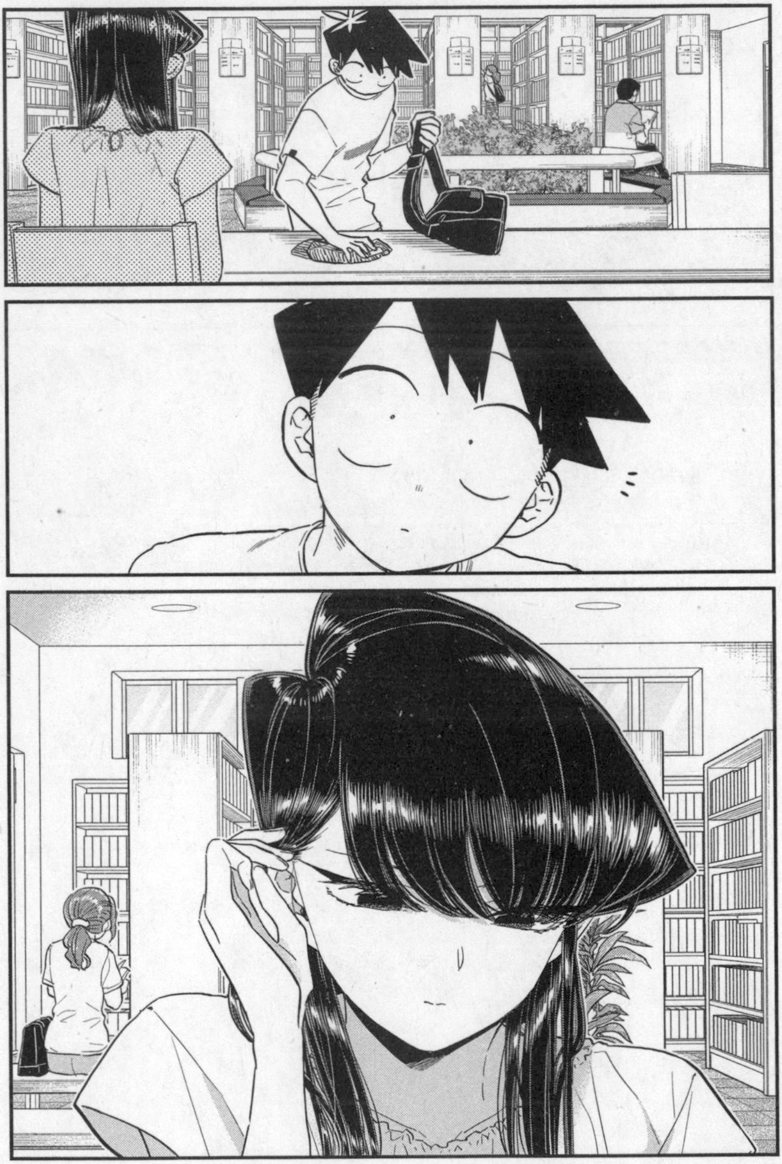

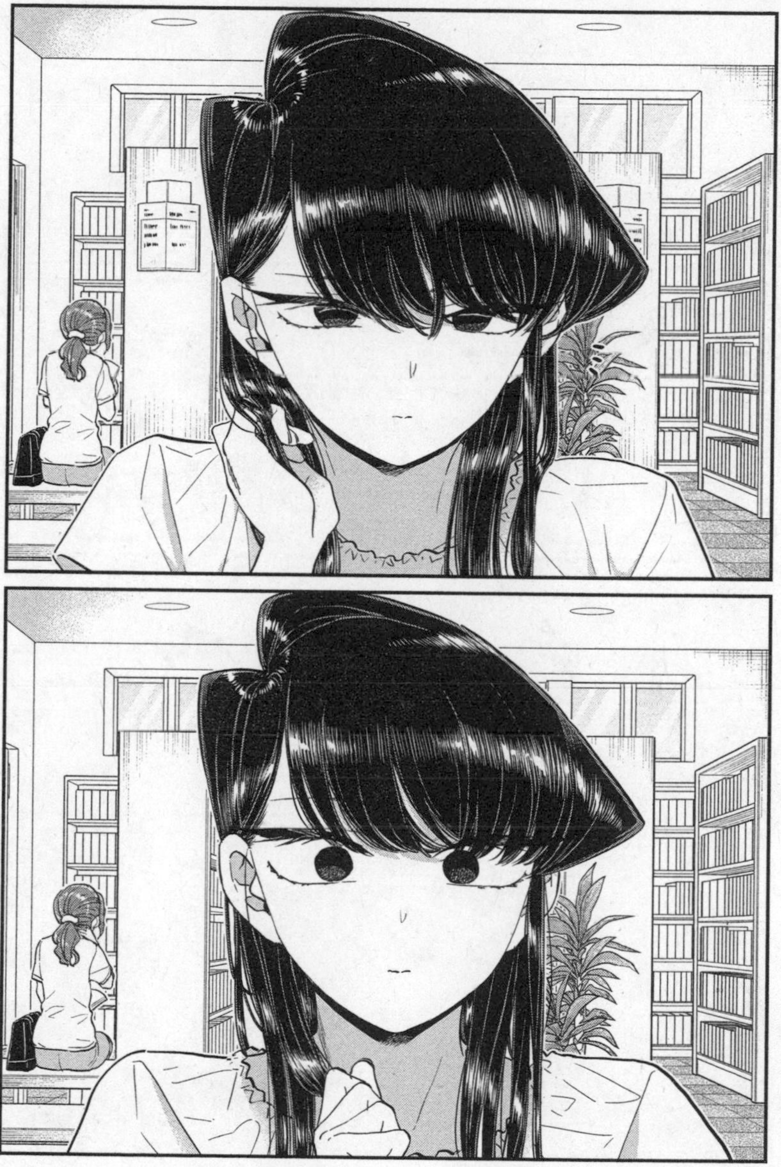

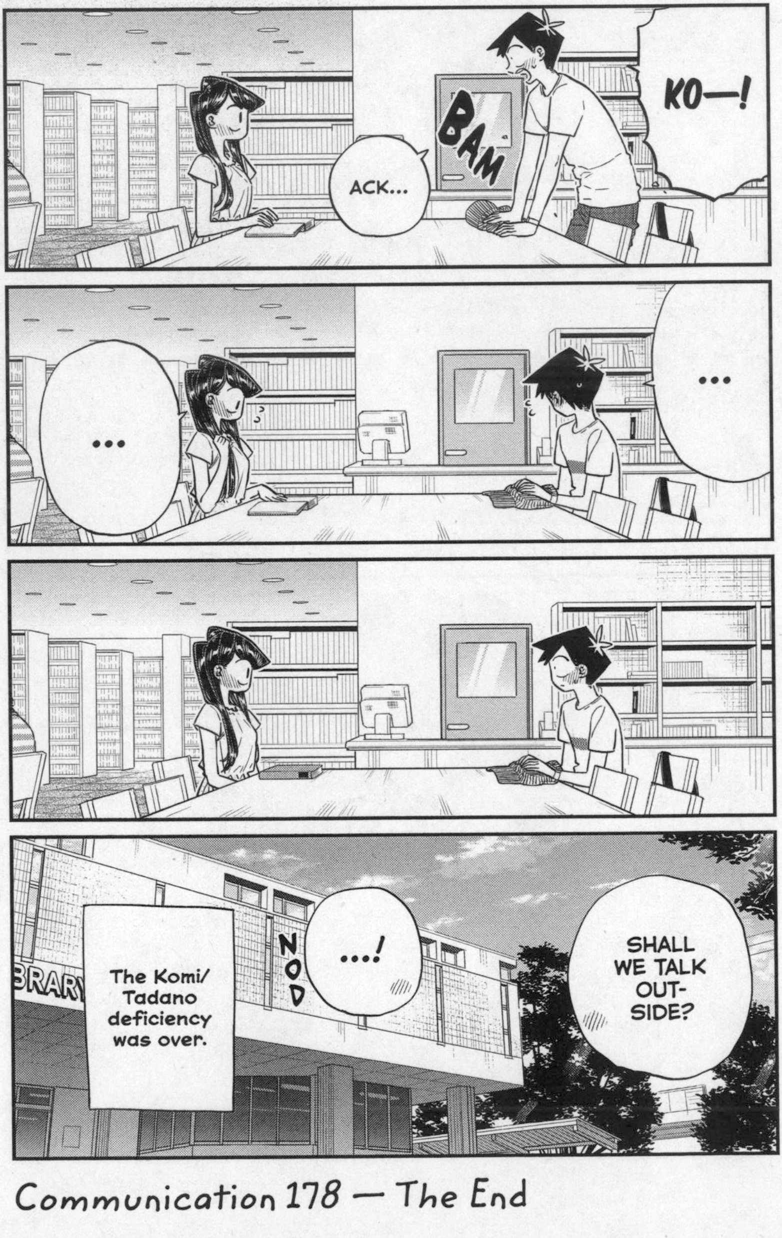
KO—!
BAM
ACK...
...
...
SHALL WE TALK OUT-SIDE?
NOD
...!
The Komi/ Tadano deficiency was over.
BRARY

Communication 178 — The End

Komi Can't Communicate

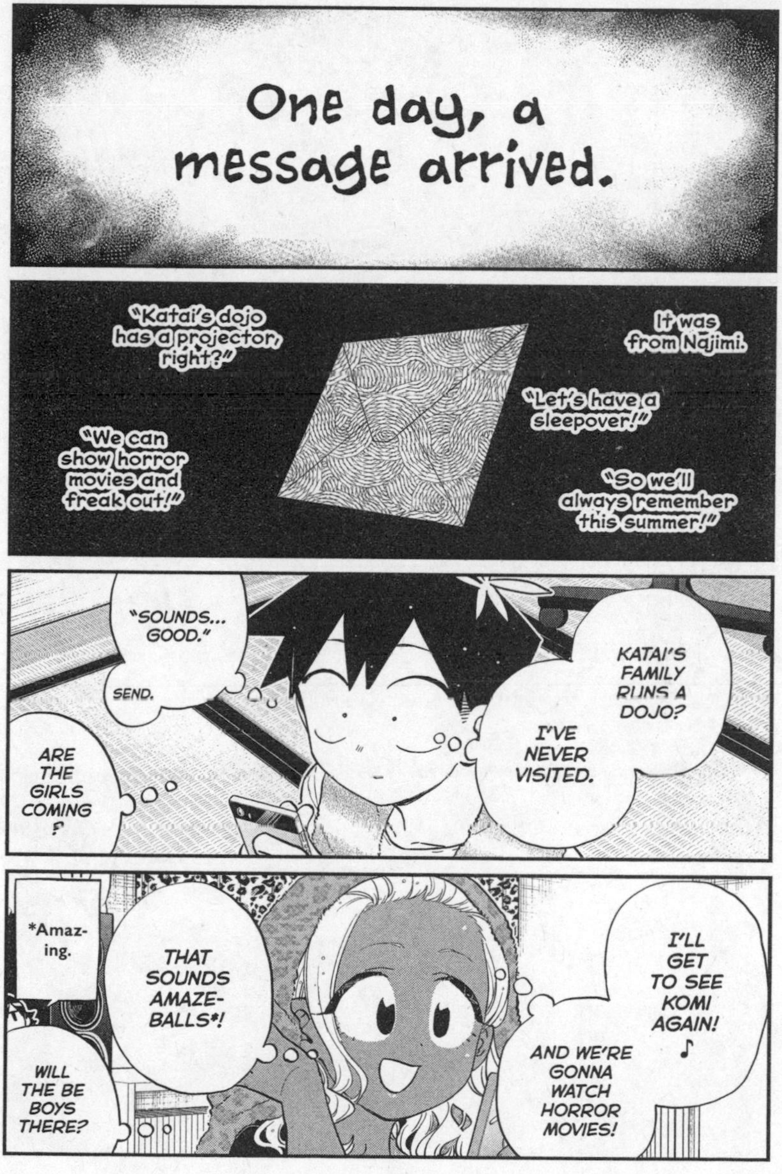
One day, a message arrived.
It was from Najimi.
"Katai's dojo has a projector, right?"
"Let's have a sleepover!"
"We can show horror movies and freak out!"
"So we'll always remember this summer!"
KATAI'S FAMILY RUNS A DOJO? I'VE NEVER VISITED.
"SOUNDS... GOOD."
SEND.
ARE THE GIRLS COMING?
I'LL GET TO SEE KOMI AGAIN! ♪
AND WE'RE GONNA WATCH HORROR MOVIES!
THAT SOUNDS AMAZE-BALLS*!
*Amaz-ing.
WILL THE BE BOYS THERE?

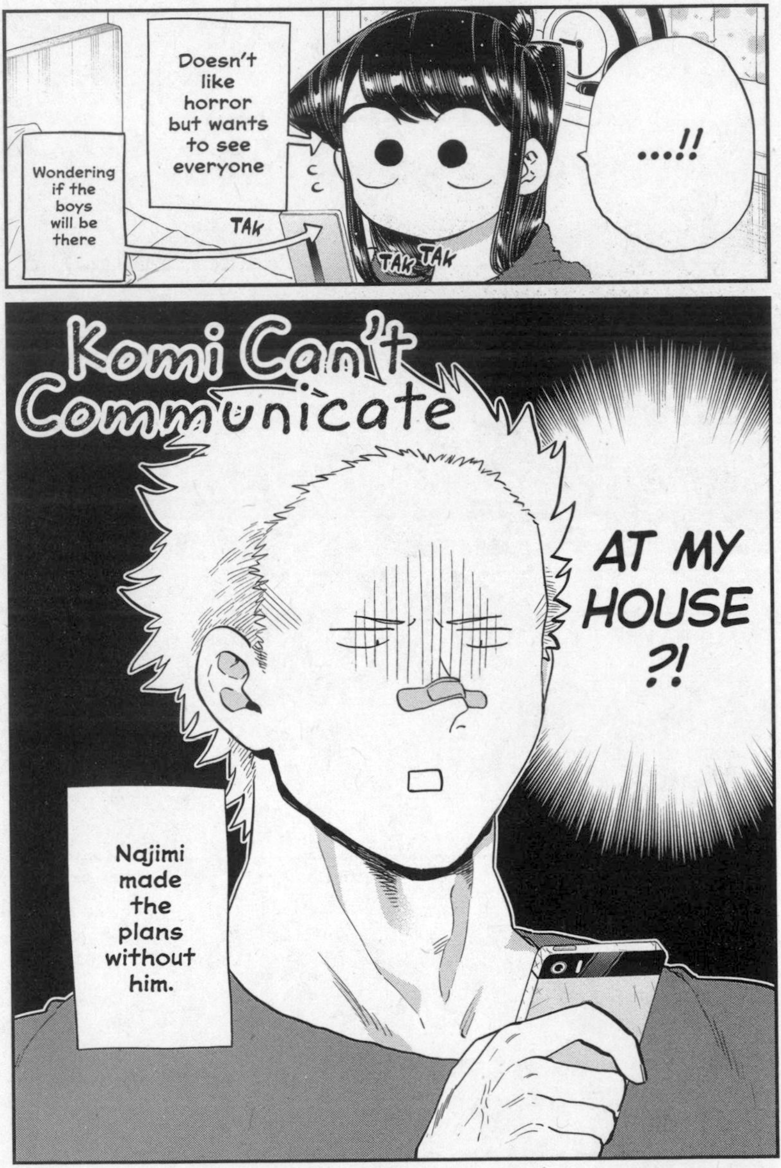
...!!
Doesn't like horror but wants to see everyone
TAK TAK
TAK
Wondering if the boys will be there
Komi Can't Communicate
AT MY HOUSE ?!
Najimi made the plans without him.

Communication 179: The Fearsome Katai Clan

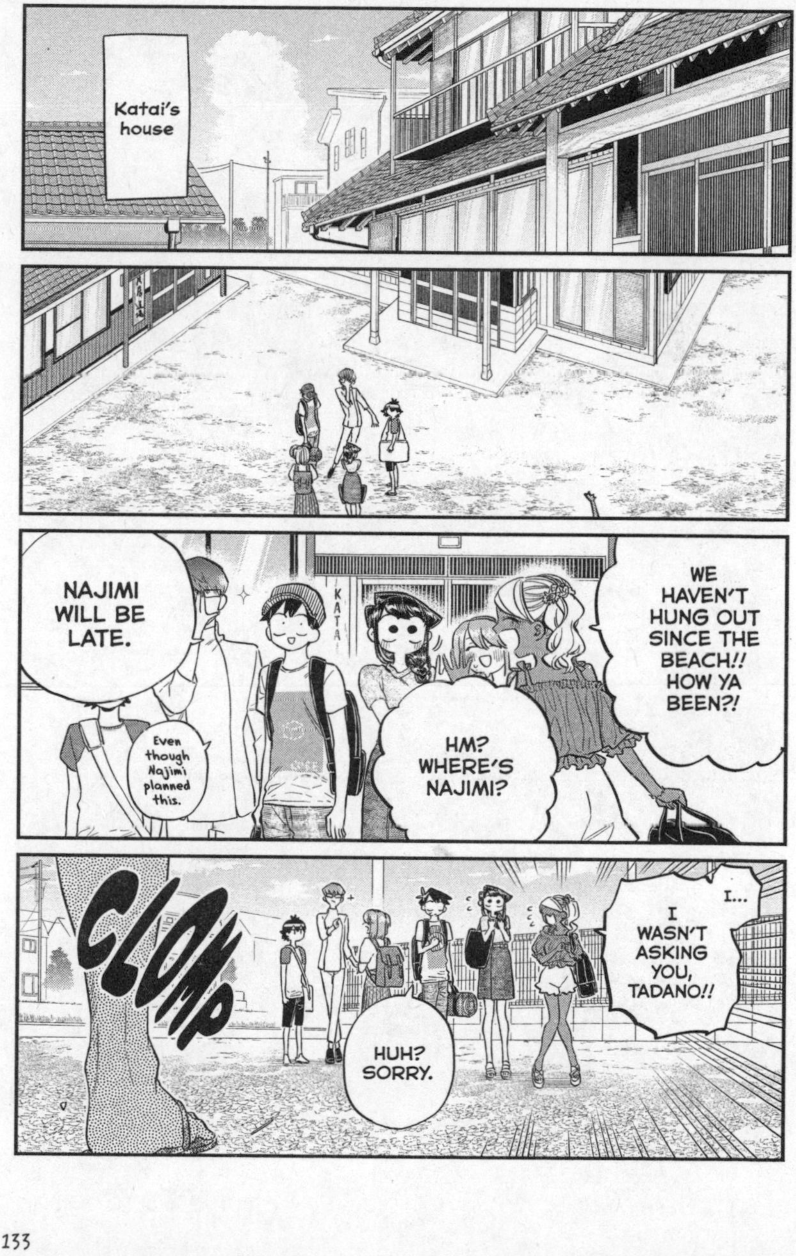
Katai's house
WE HAVEN'T HUNG OUT SINCE THE BEACH!! HOW YA BEEN?!
HM? WHERE'S NAJIMI?
NAJIMI WILL BE LATE.
Even though Najimi planned this.
I... I WASN'T ASKING YOU, TADANO!!
HUH? SORRY.
CLOMP

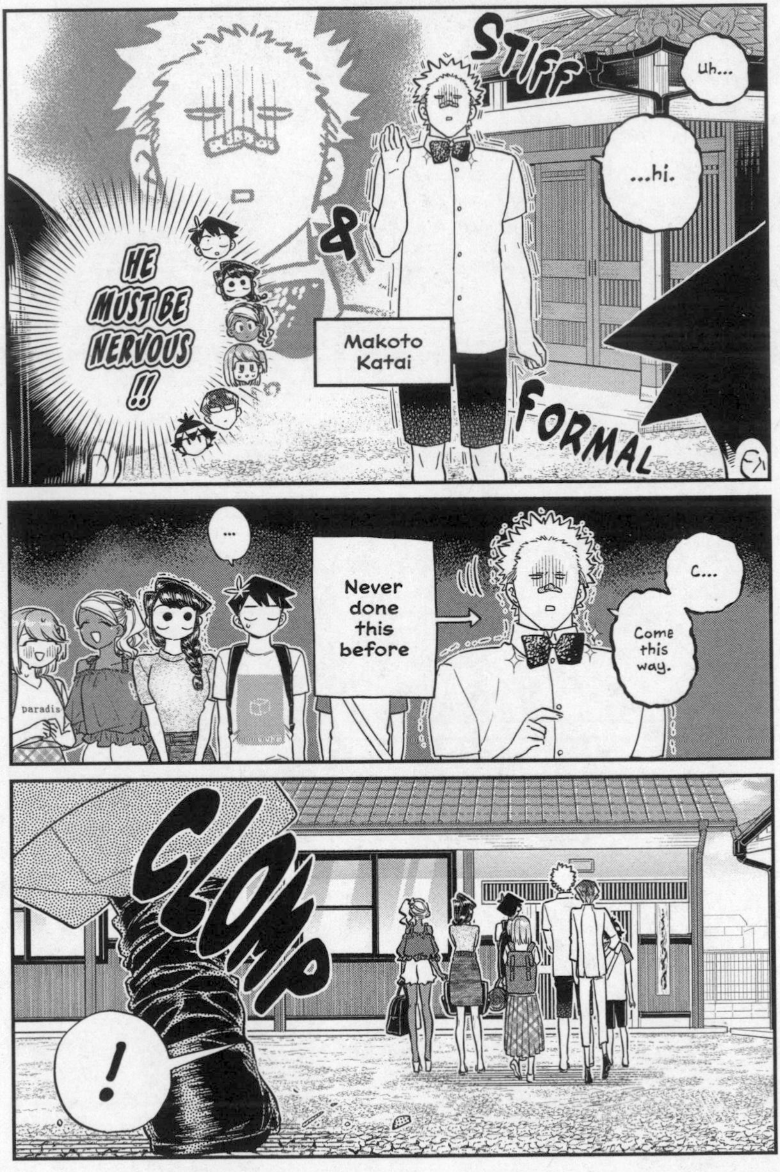
Uh...
...hi.
STIFF
&
FORMAL
Makoto Katai
HE MUST BE NERVOUS!!
C...
Come this way.
Never done this before
...
paradis
CLOMP
!

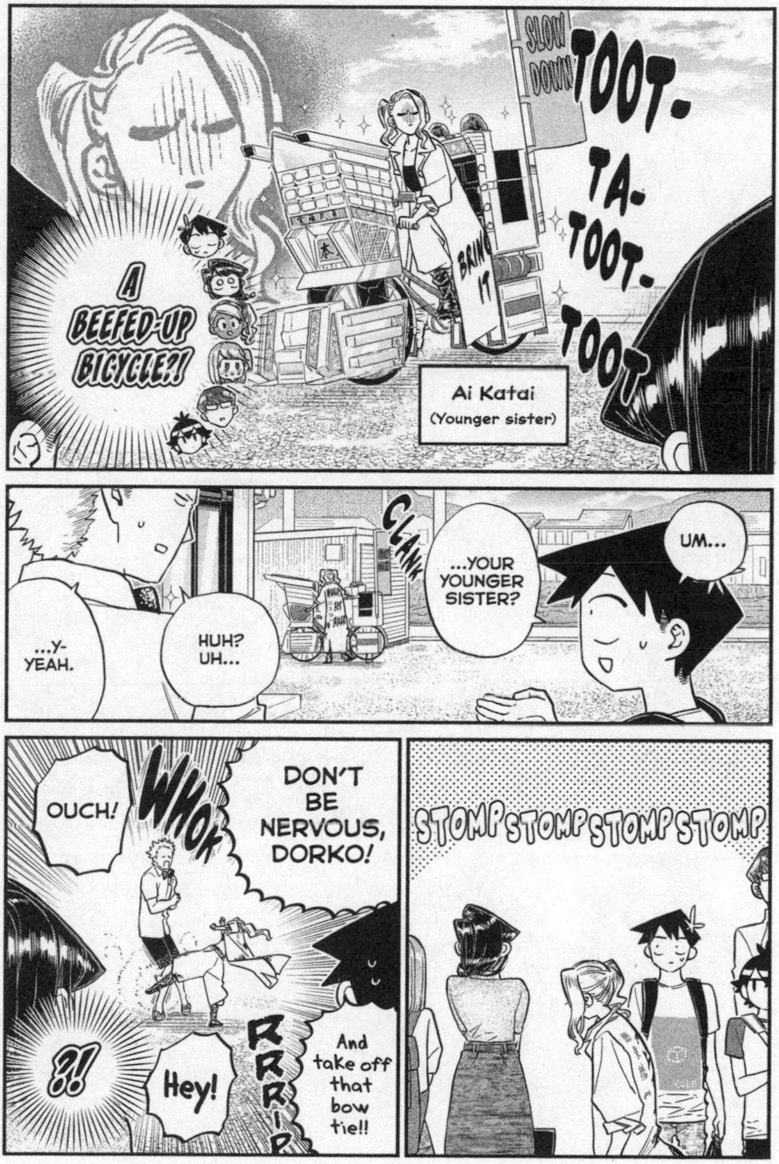
SLOW DOWN
TOOT-TA-TOOT-TOOT
BRING IT
A BEEFED-UP BICYCLE?!
Ai Katai (Younger sister)
UM...
...YOUR YOUNGER SISTER?
CLANK
HUH? UH...
...Y-YEAH.
STOMP STOMP STOMP STOMP
DON'T BE NERVOUS, DORKO!
WHOK
OUCH!
And take off that bow tie!!
RRRIP
Hey!
?!

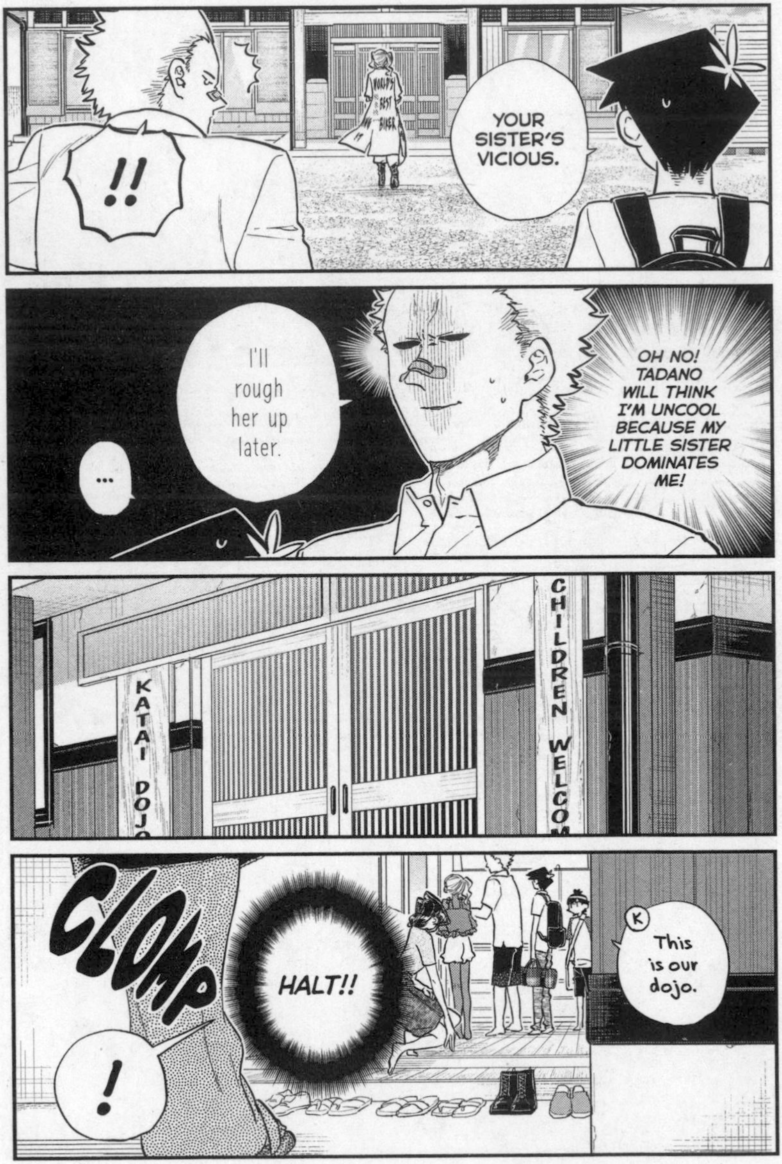
YOUR SISTER'S VICIOUS.
WORLD'S BEST BIKER
!!
OH NO! TADANO WILL THINK I'M UNCOOL BECAUSE MY LITTLE SISTER DOMINATES ME!
I'll rough her up later.
...
CHILDREN WELCOM
KATAI DOJO
K
This is our dojo.
HALT!!
CLOMP
!

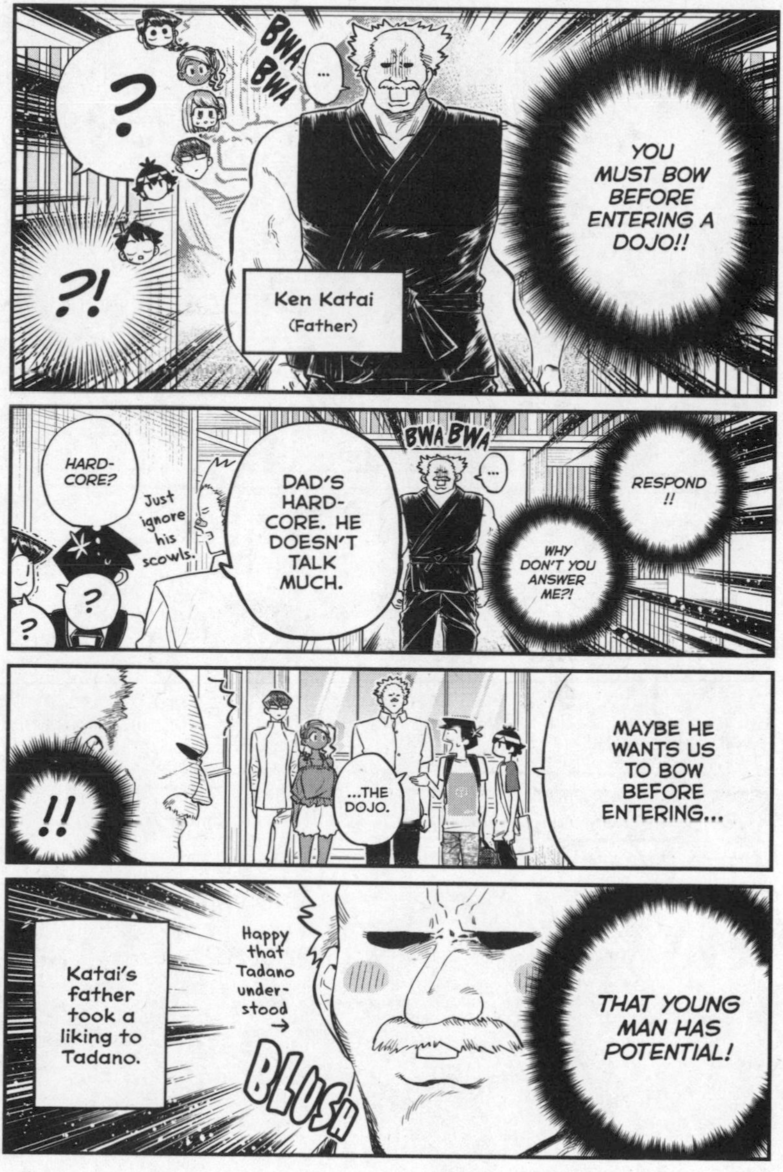
YOU MUST BOW BEFORE ENTERING A DOJO!!
...
BWA BWA
Ken Katai (Father)
?
?!
RESPOND !!
WHY DON'T YOU ANSWER ME?!
...
BWA BWA
DAD'S HARD-CORE. HE DOESN'T TALK MUCH.
Just ignore his scowls.
HARD-CORE?
?
?
MAYBE HE WANTS US TO BOW BEFORE ENTERING...
...THE DOJO.
!!
THAT YOUNG MAN HAS POTENTIAL!
BLUSH
Happy that Tadano under-stood →
Katai's father took a liking to Tadano.

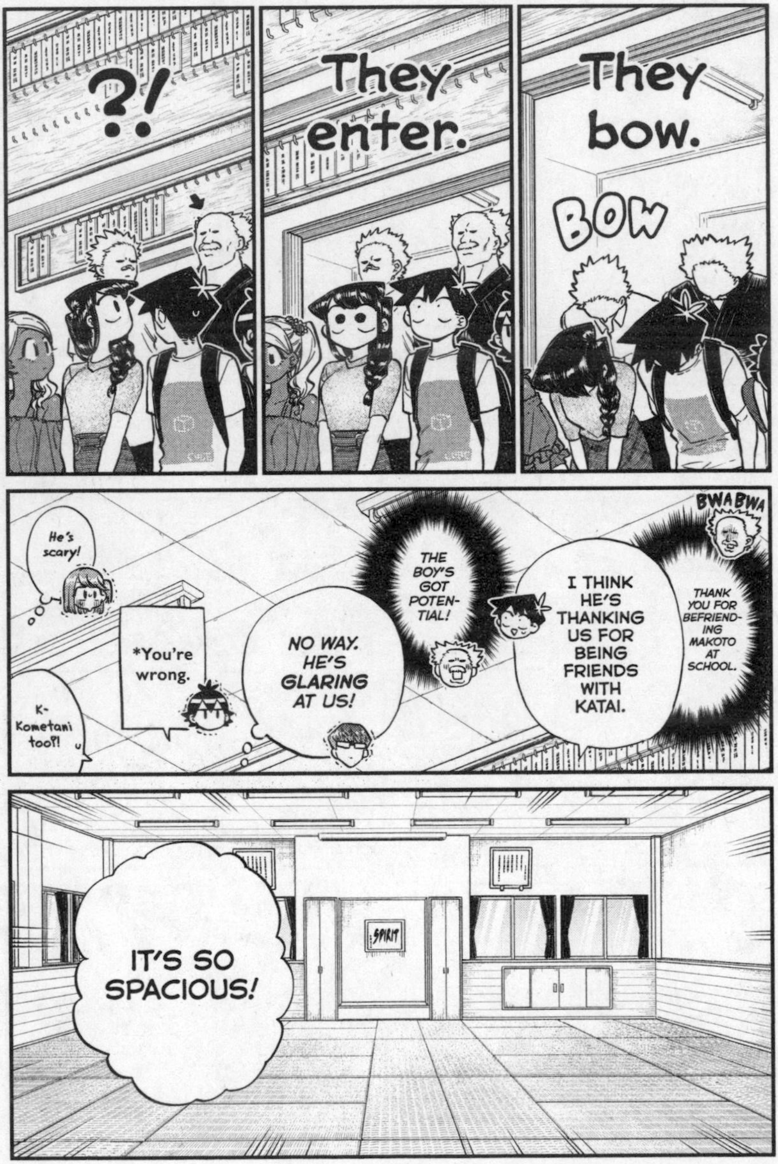
They bow.
BOW
They enter.
?!
BWABWA
THANK YOU FOR BEFRIENDING MAKOTO AT SCHOOL.
I THINK HE'S THANKING US FOR BEING FRIENDS WITH KATAI.
THE BOY'S GOT POTENTIAL!
NO WAY. HE'S GLARING AT US!
*You're wrong.
He's scary!
K-Kometani too?!
SPIRIT
IT'S SO SPACIOUS!

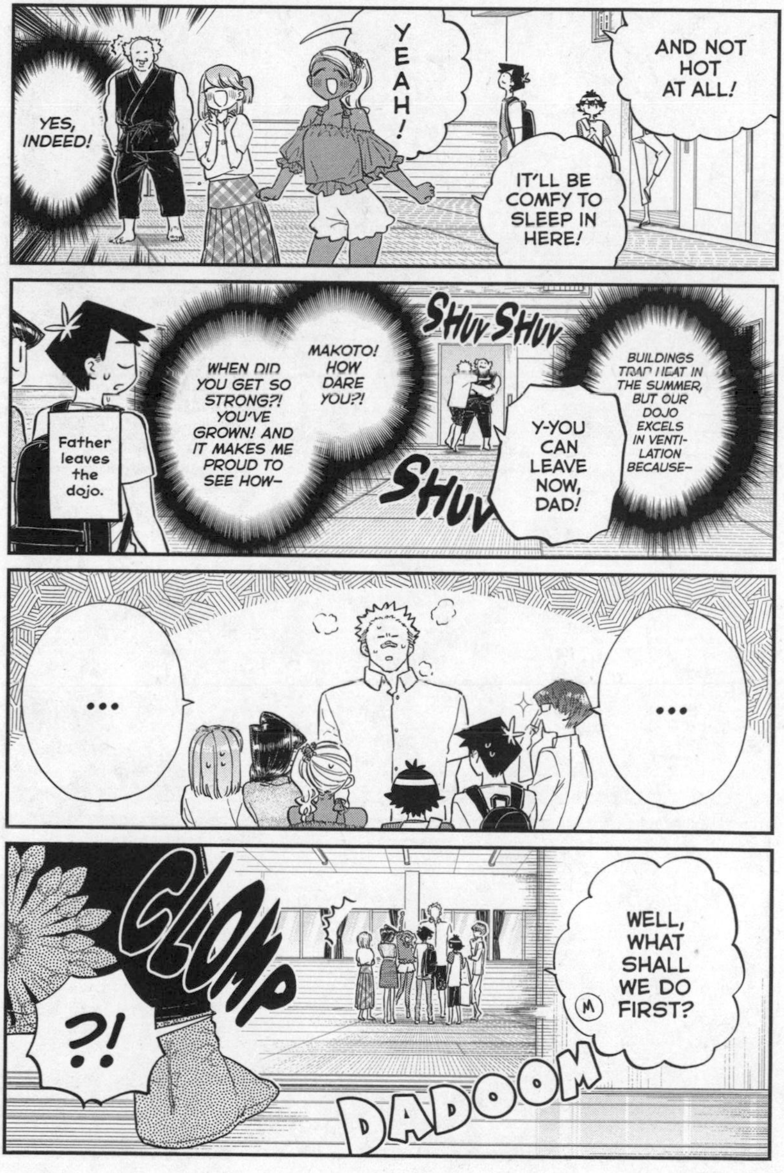
AND NOT HOT AT ALL!
IT'LL BE COMFY TO SLEEP IN HERE!
YEAH!
YES, INDEED!
BUILDINGS TRAP HEAT IN THE SUMMER, BUT OUR DOJO EXCELS IN VENTILATION BECAUSE–
SHUV SHUV
Y-YOU CAN LEAVE NOW, DAD!
SHUV
MAKOTO! HOW DARE YOU?!
WHEN DID YOU GET SO STRONG?! YOU'VE GROWN! AND IT MAKES ME PROUD TO SEE HOW–
Father leaves the dojo.
...
...
WELL, WHAT SHALL WE DO FIRST?
M
DADOOM
GLOMP
?!

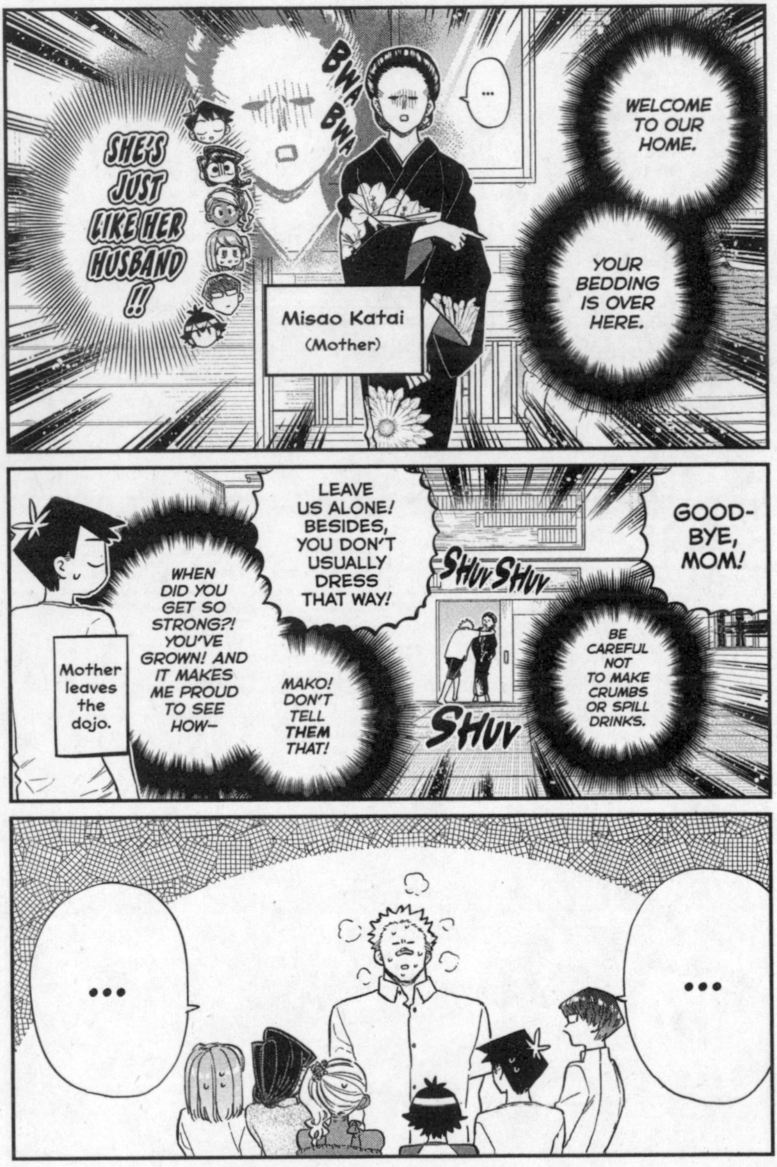
WELCOME TO OUR HOME.
YOUR BEDDING IS OVER HERE.
...
BWA BWA
Misao Katai (Mother)
SHE'S JUST LIKE HER HUSBAND!!
GOOD-BYE, MOM!
BE CAREFUL NOT TO MAKE CRUMBS OR SPILL DRINKS.
SHUV SHUV
SHUV
LEAVE US ALONE! BESIDES, YOU DON'T USUALLY DRESS THAT WAY!
MAKO! DON'T TELL THEM THAT!
WHEN DID YOU GET SO STRONG?! YOU'VE GROWN! AND IT MAKES ME PROUD TO SEE HOW–
Mother leaves the dojo.
...
...

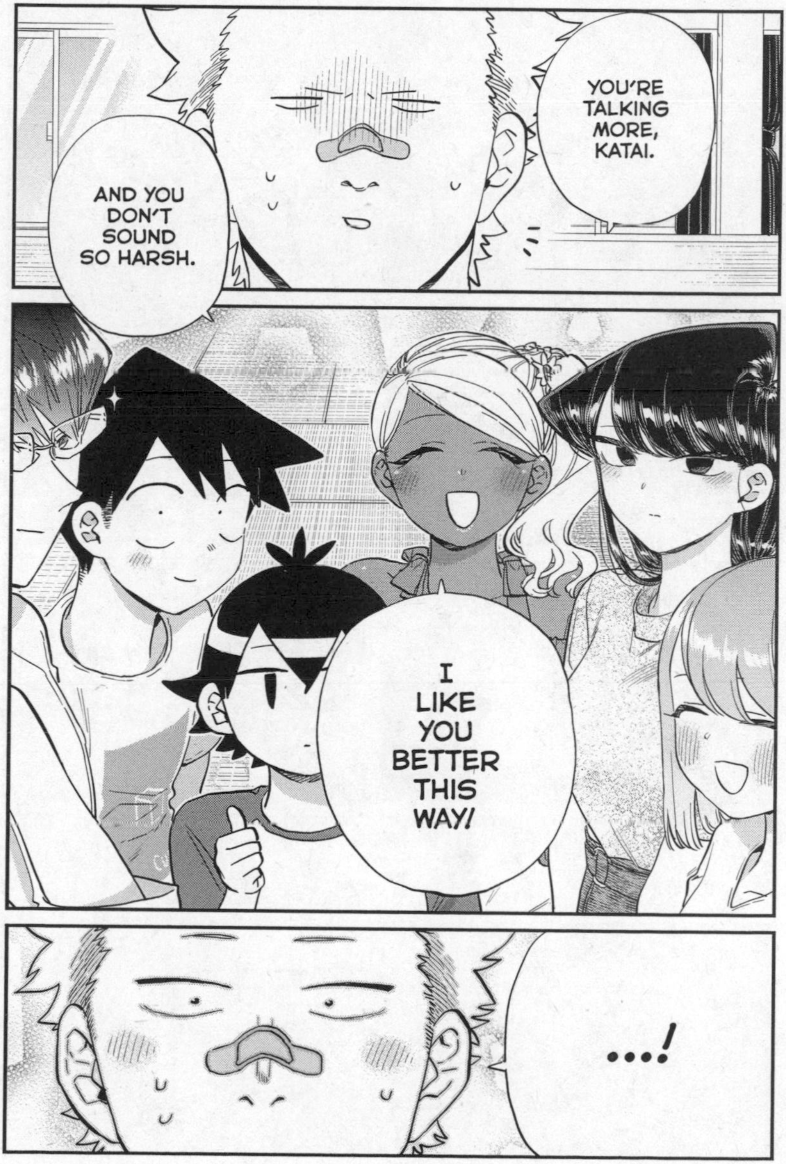
YOU'RE TALKING MORE, KATAI.
AND YOU DON'T SOUND SO HARSH.
I LIKE YOU BETTER THIS WAY!
...!

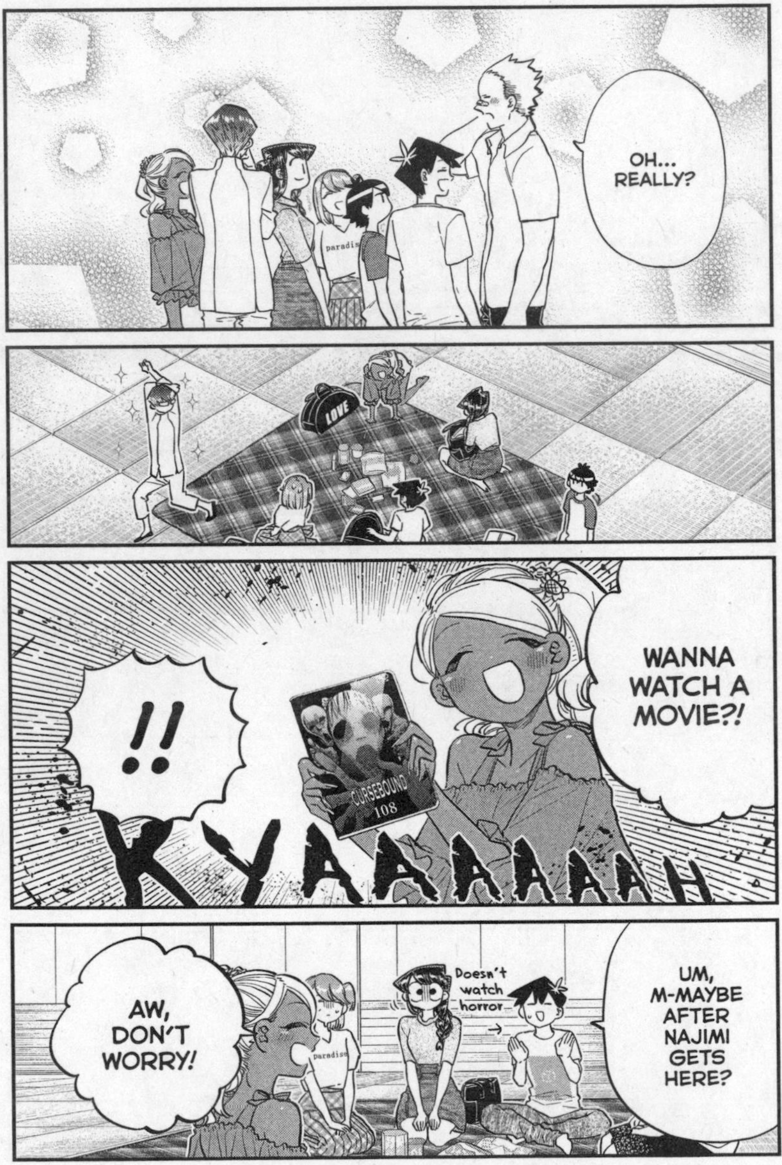
OH... REALLY?
WANNA WATCH A MOVIE?!
CURSEBOUND 108
!!
KYAAAAAAH
UM, M-MAYBE AFTER NAJIMI GETS HERE?
Doesn't watch horror
AW, DON'T WORRY!

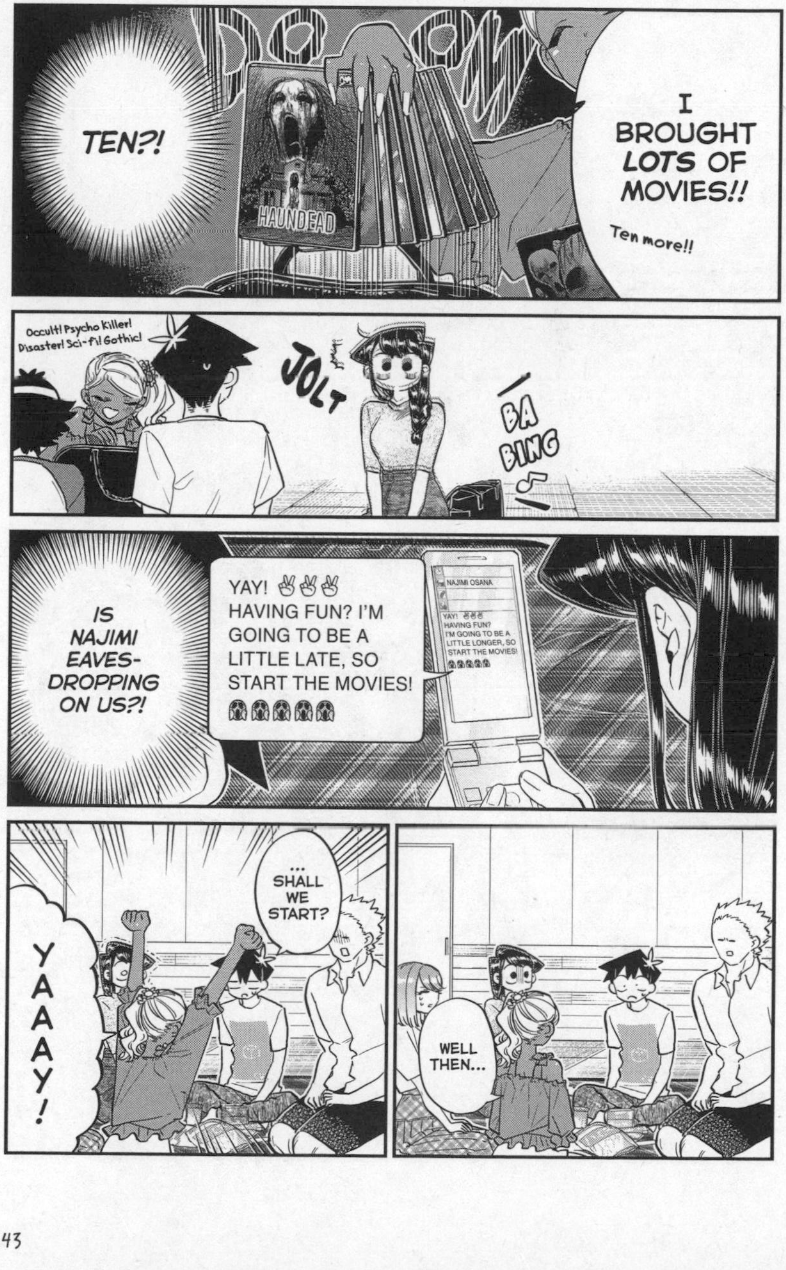
I BROUGHT LOTS OF MOVIES!!
Ten more!!
HAUNDEAD
TEN?!
BA BING
JOLT
Occult! Psycho Killer! Disaster! Sci-fi! Gothic!
NAJIMI OSANA
YAY! ✌✌✌ HAVING FUN? I'M GOING TO BE A LITTLE LATE, SO START THE MOVIES! 😱😱😱😱😱
IS NAJIMI EAVES-DROPPING ON US?!
WELL THEN...
...SHALL WE START?
YAAAAY!

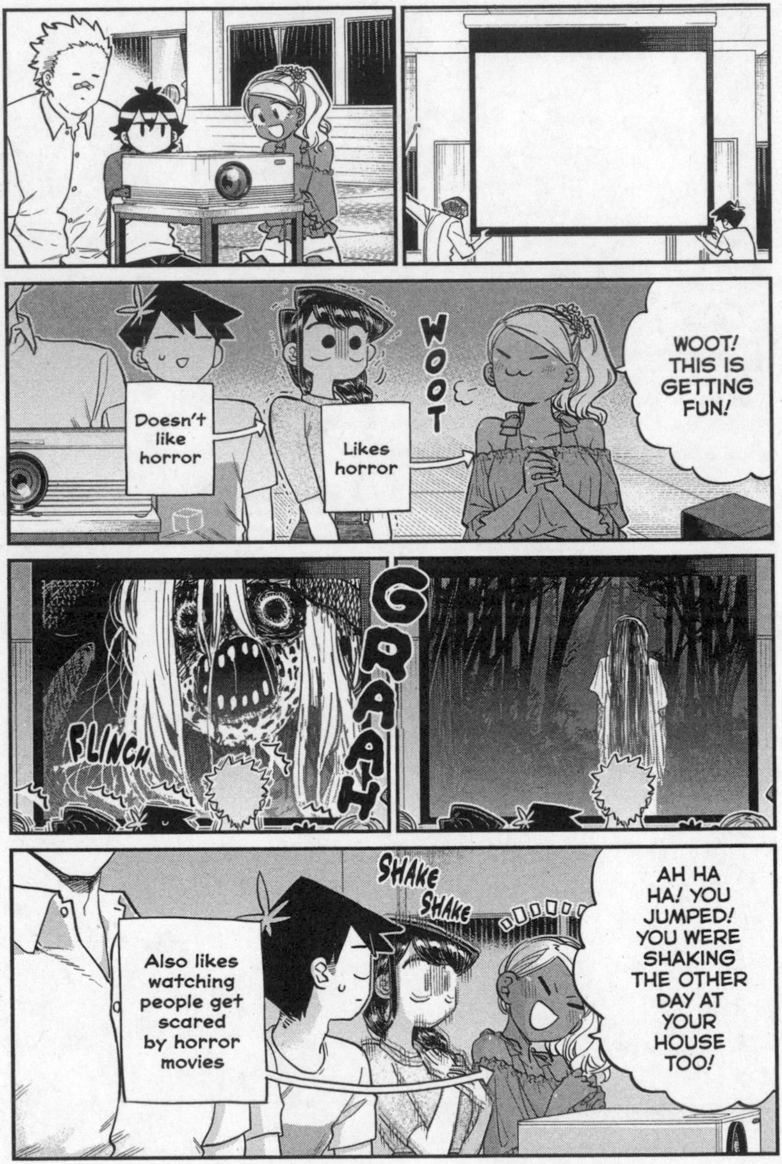
WOOT! THIS IS GETTING FUN!
WOOT WOOT
Likes horror
Doesn't like horror
GRAAAH
FLINCH
AH HA HA! YOU JUMPED! YOU WERE SHAKING THE OTHER DAY AT YOUR HOUSE TOO!
SHAKE SHAKE
Also likes watching people get scared by horror movies

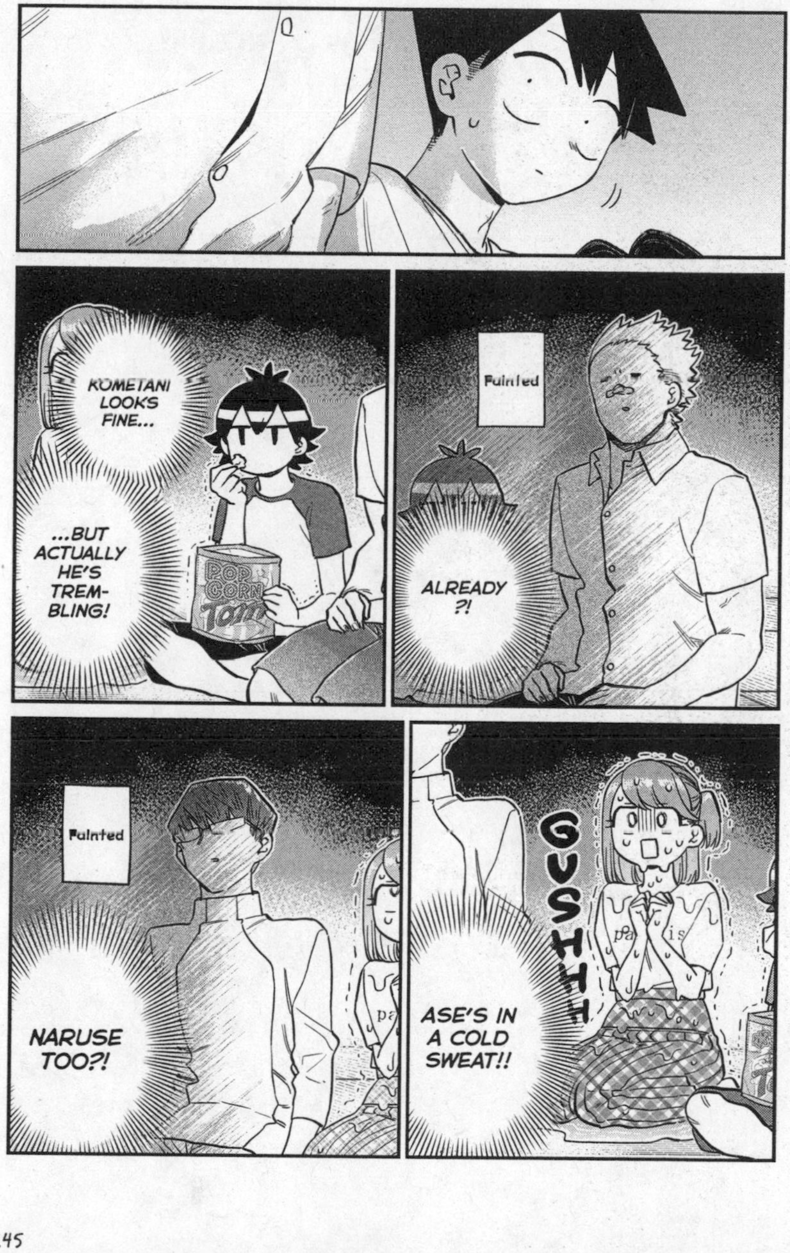
Fainted
ALREADY?!
KOMETANI LOOKS FINE...
...BUT ACTUALLY HE'S TREM-BLING!
POP CORN
GUSHHH
ASE'S IN A COLD SWEAT!!
Fainted
NARUSE TOO?!

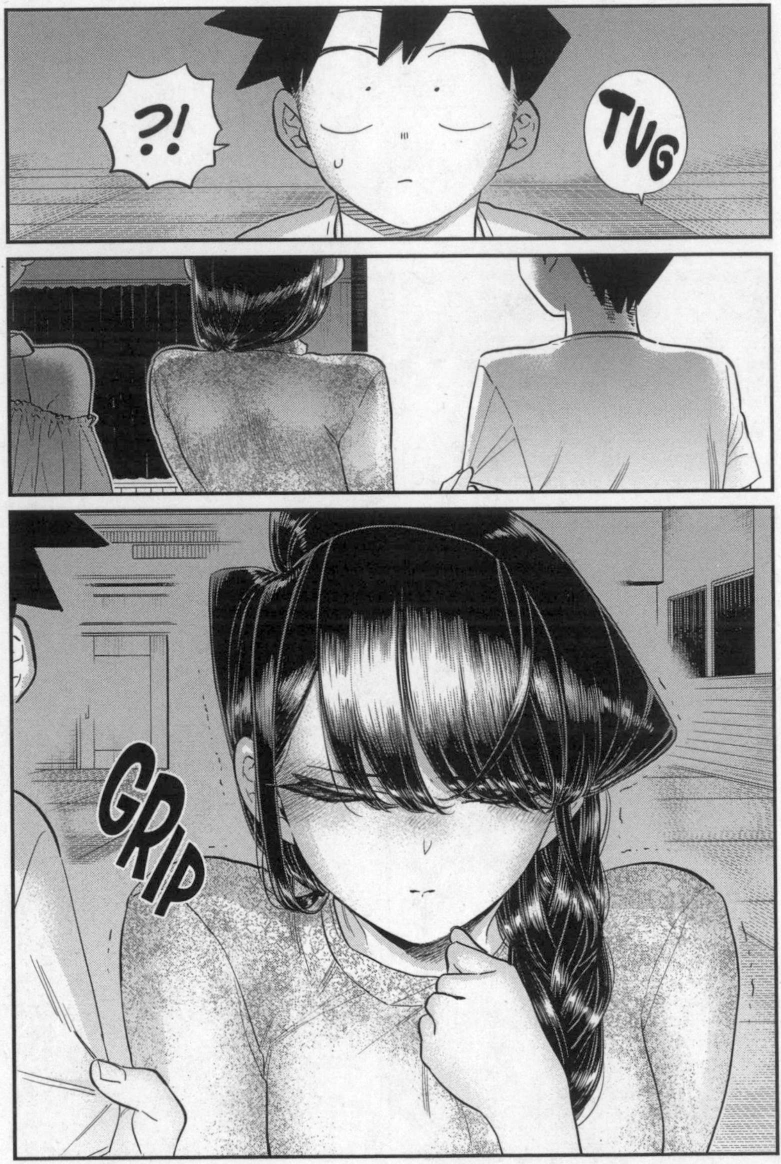
TUG
?!
GRIP

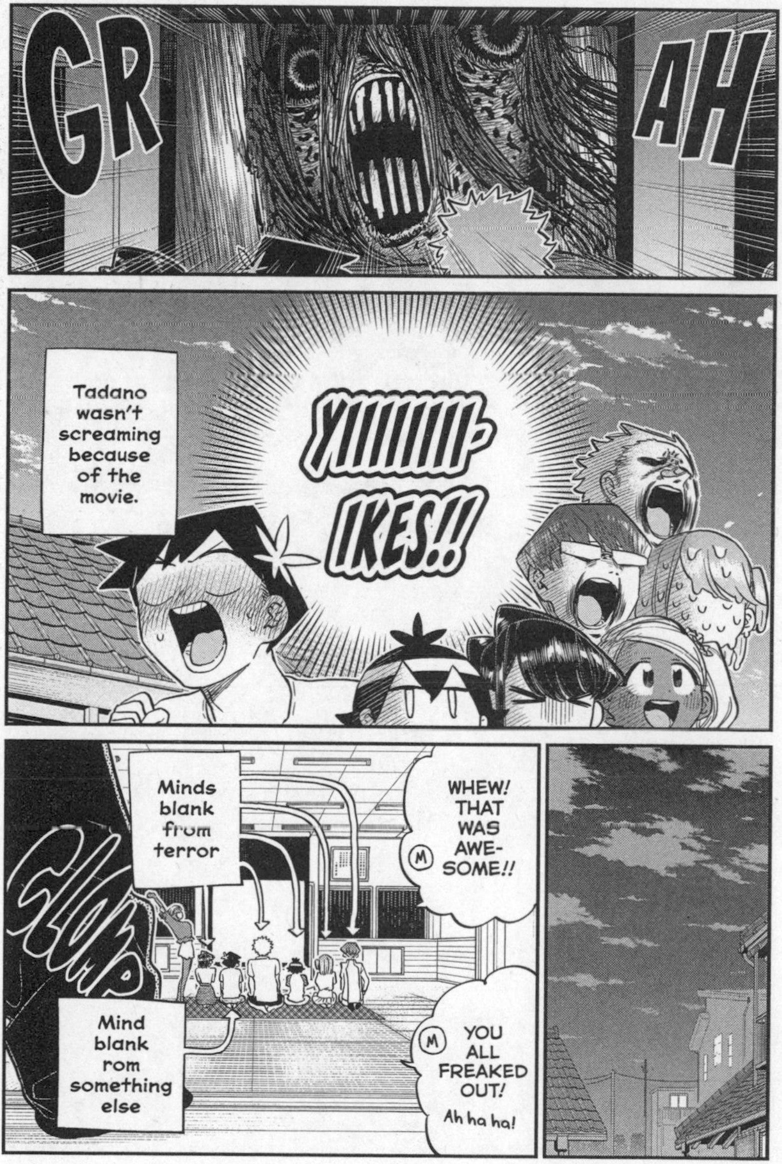
GR
AH
YIIIIIII-
IKES!!
Tadano wasn't screaming because of the movie.
WHEW! THAT WAS AWE-SOME!!
Minds blank from terror
GLOMP
YOU ALL FREAKED OUT!
Ah ha ha!
Mind blank rom something else

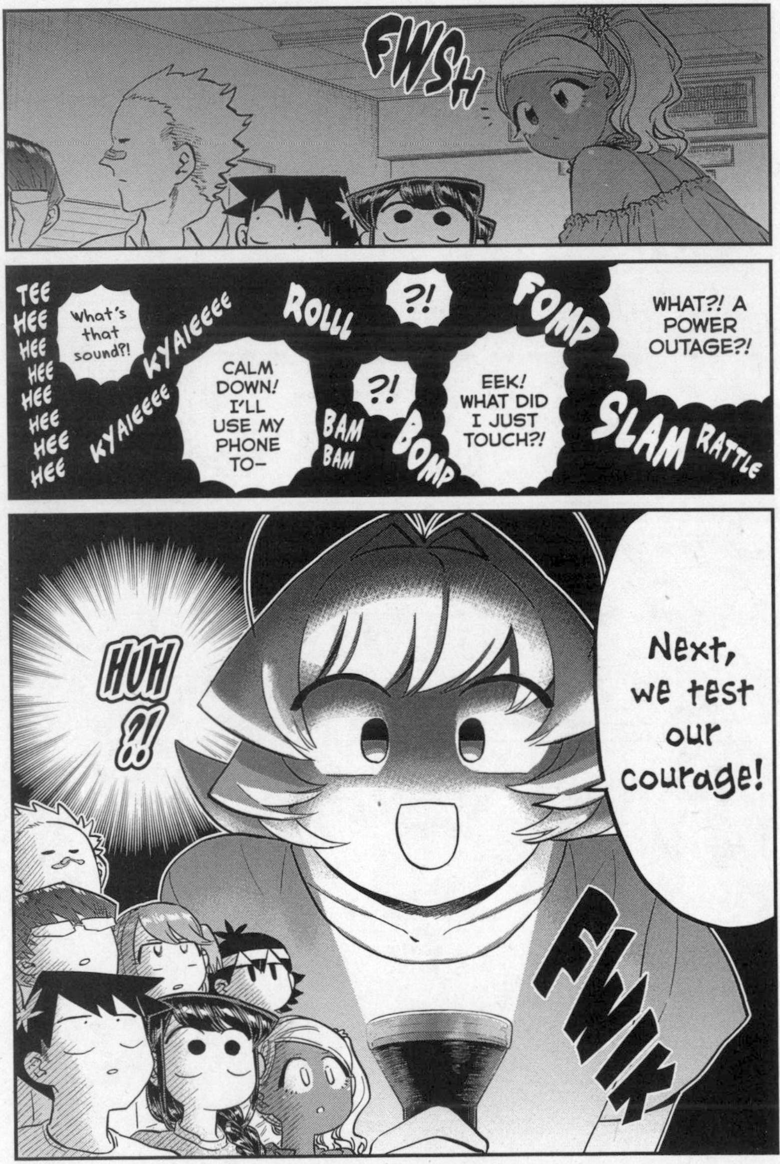
FWSH
WHAT?! A POWER OUTAGE?!
SLAM
RATTLE
FOMP
EEK! WHAT DID I JUST TOUCH?!
?!
BOMP
?!
ROLLL
BAM BAM
CALM DOWN! I'LL USE MY PHONE TO—
KYAIEEEE
KYAIEEEE
What's that sound?!
TEE HEE HEE HEE HEE HEE HEE HEE
Next, we test our courage!
FWIK
HUH?!

Communication 179 — The End

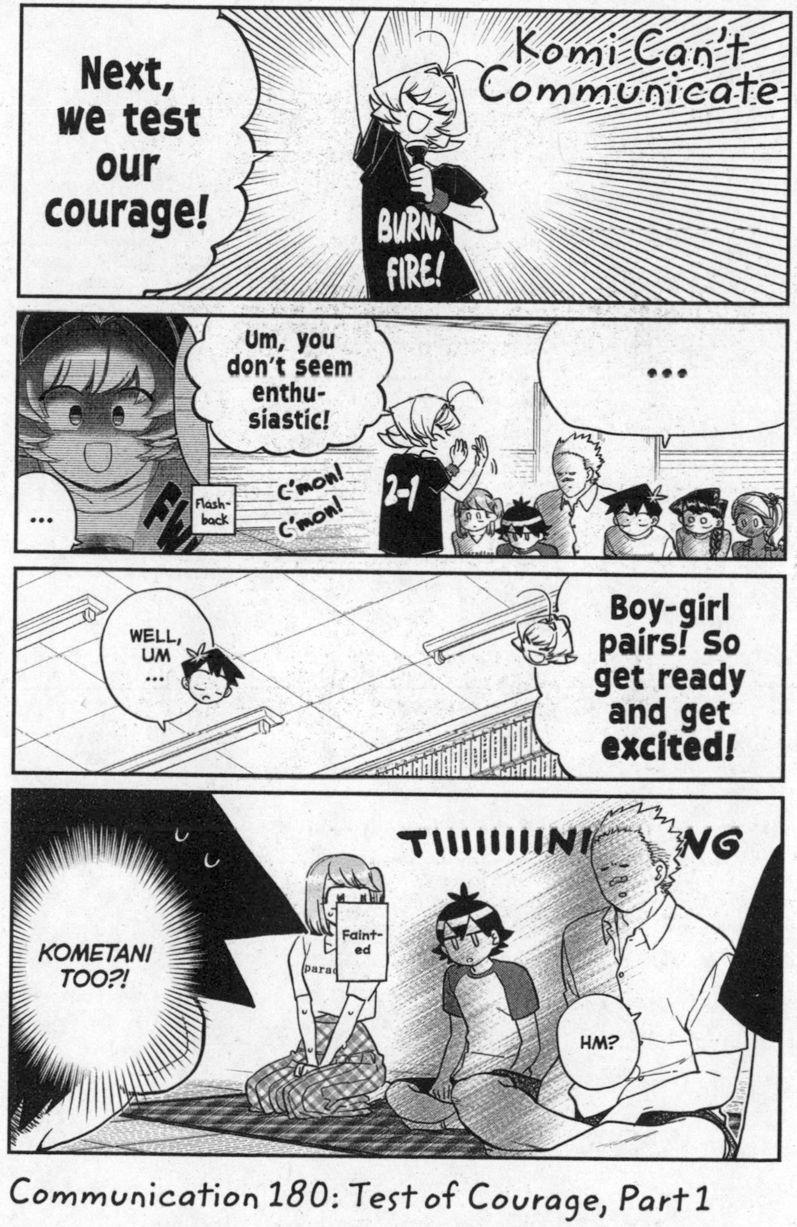
Komi Can't Communicate
Next, we test our courage!
BURN, FIRE!
...
Um, you don't seem enthu-siastic!
2-1
C'mon! C'mon!
Flash-back
...
Boy-girl pairs! So get ready and get excited!
WELL, UM ...
HM?
Faint-ed
KOMETANI TOO?!

Communication 180: Test of Courage, Part 1

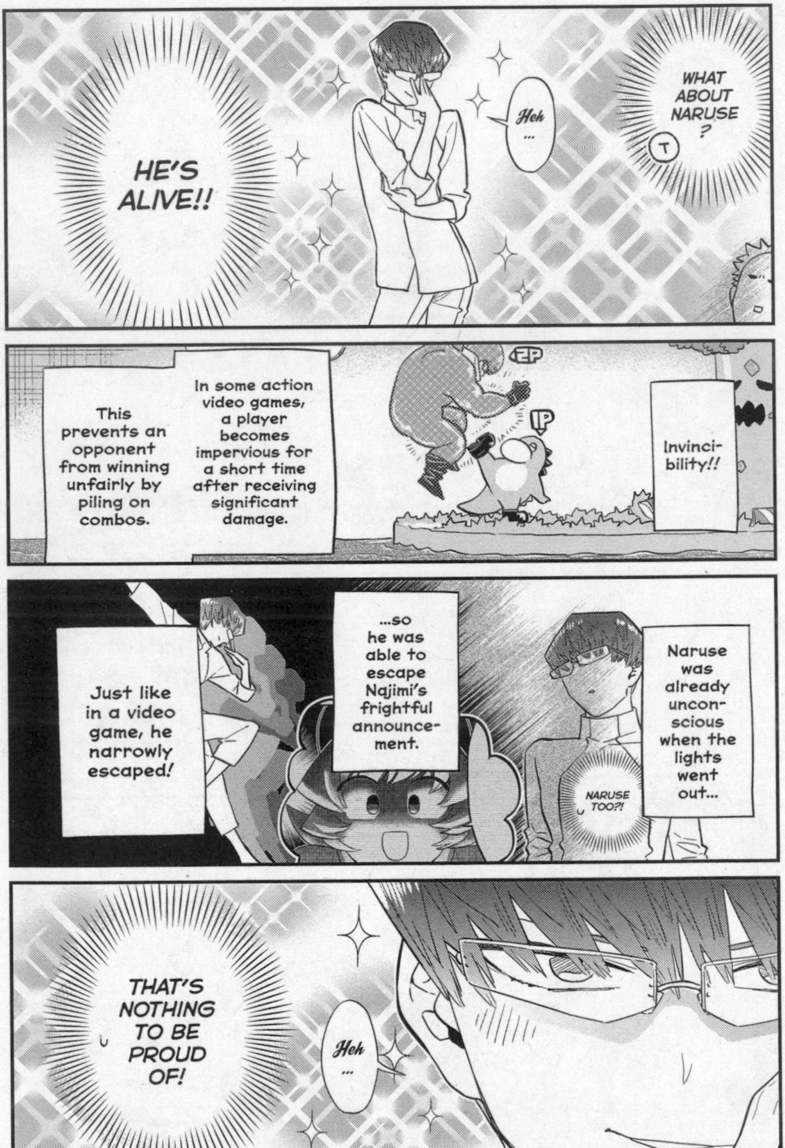
WHAT ABOUT NARUSE?
T
Heh...
HE'S ALIVE!!
Invincibility!!
2P
1P
In some action video games, a player becomes impervious for a short time after receiving significant damage.
This prevents an opponent from winning unfairly by piling on combos.
Naruse was already unconscious when the lights went out...
NARUSE TOO?!
...so he was able to escape Najimi's frightful announcement.
Just like in a video game, he narrowly escaped!
Heh...
THAT'S NOTHING TO BE PROUD OF!

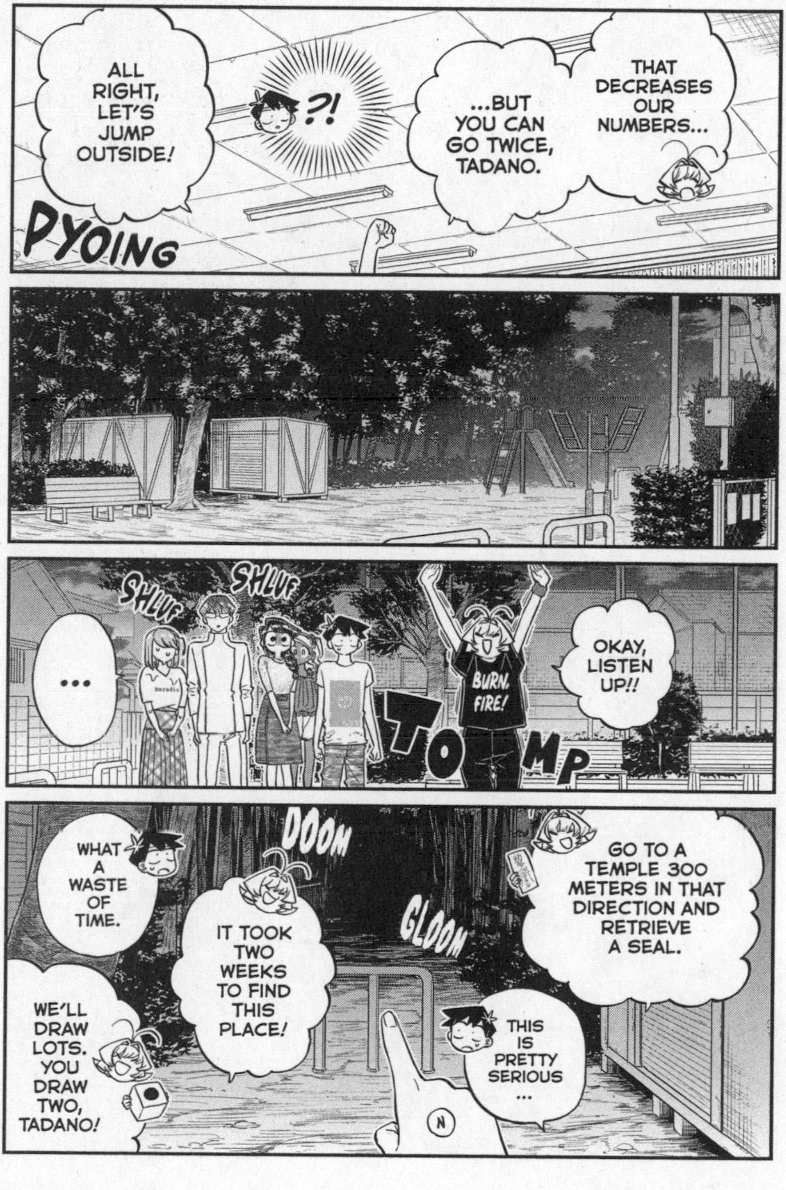
THAT DECREASES OUR NUMBERS...
...BUT YOU CAN GO TWICE, TADANO.
?!
ALL RIGHT, LET'S JUMP OUTSIDE!
PYOING
OKAY, LISTEN UP!!
BURN, FIRE!
TOMP
SHLUF
SHLUF
...
GO TO A TEMPLE 300 METERS IN THAT DIRECTION AND RETRIEVE A SEAL.
GLOOM
DOOM
THIS IS PRETTY SERIOUS ...
IT TOOK TWO WEEKS TO FIND THIS PLACE!
WHAT A WASTE OF TIME.
WE'LL DRAW LOTS. YOU DRAW TWO, TADANO!
N

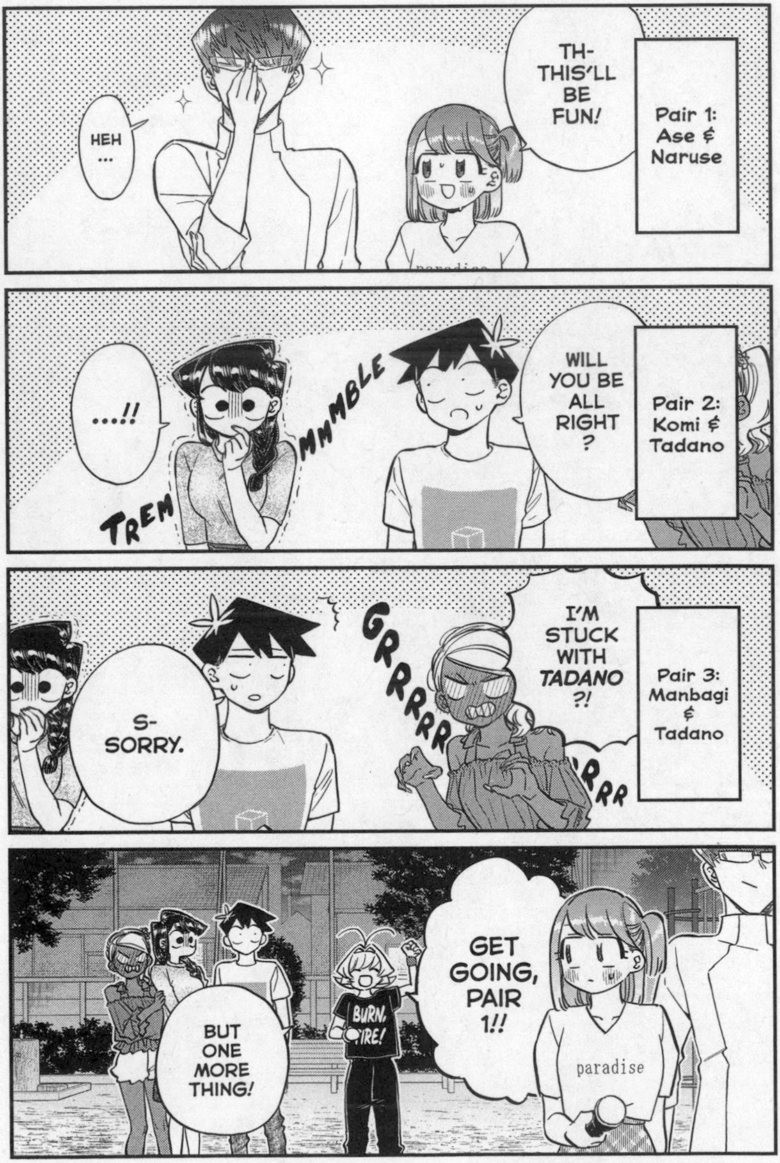
Pair 1: Ase & Naruse
TH-THIS'LL BE FUN!
HEH ...
Pair 2: Komi & Tadano
WILL YOU BE ALL RIGHT?
....!!
TREM MMMBLE
Pair 3: Manbagi & Tadano
I'M STUCK WITH *TADANO*?!
GRRRRR RRRR
S-SORRY.
GET GOING, PAIR 1!!
paradise
BUT ONE MORE THING!

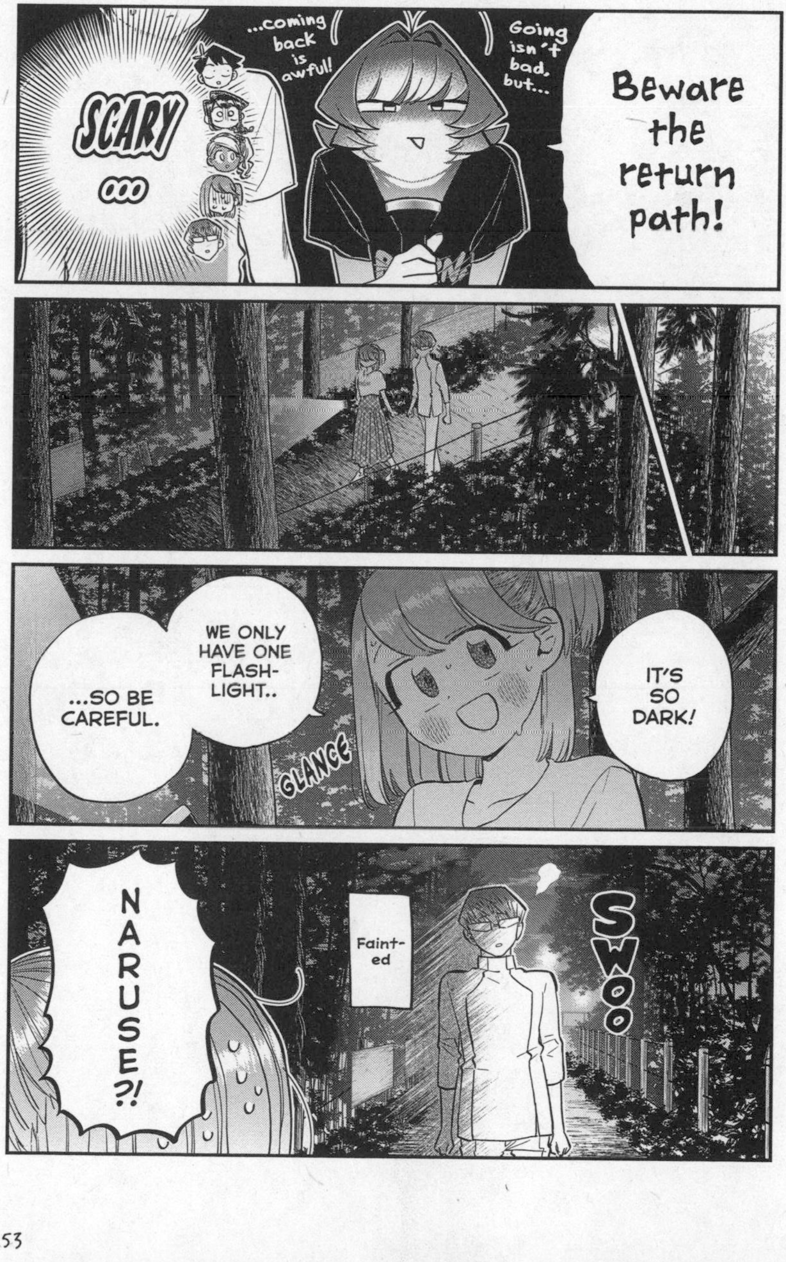
Beware the return path!
Going isn't bad, but...
...coming back is awful!
SCARY
ooo
IT'S SO DARK!
GLANCE
WE ONLY HAVE ONE FLASH-LIGHT..
...SO BE CAREFUL.
SWOO
Faint-ed
NARUSE?!

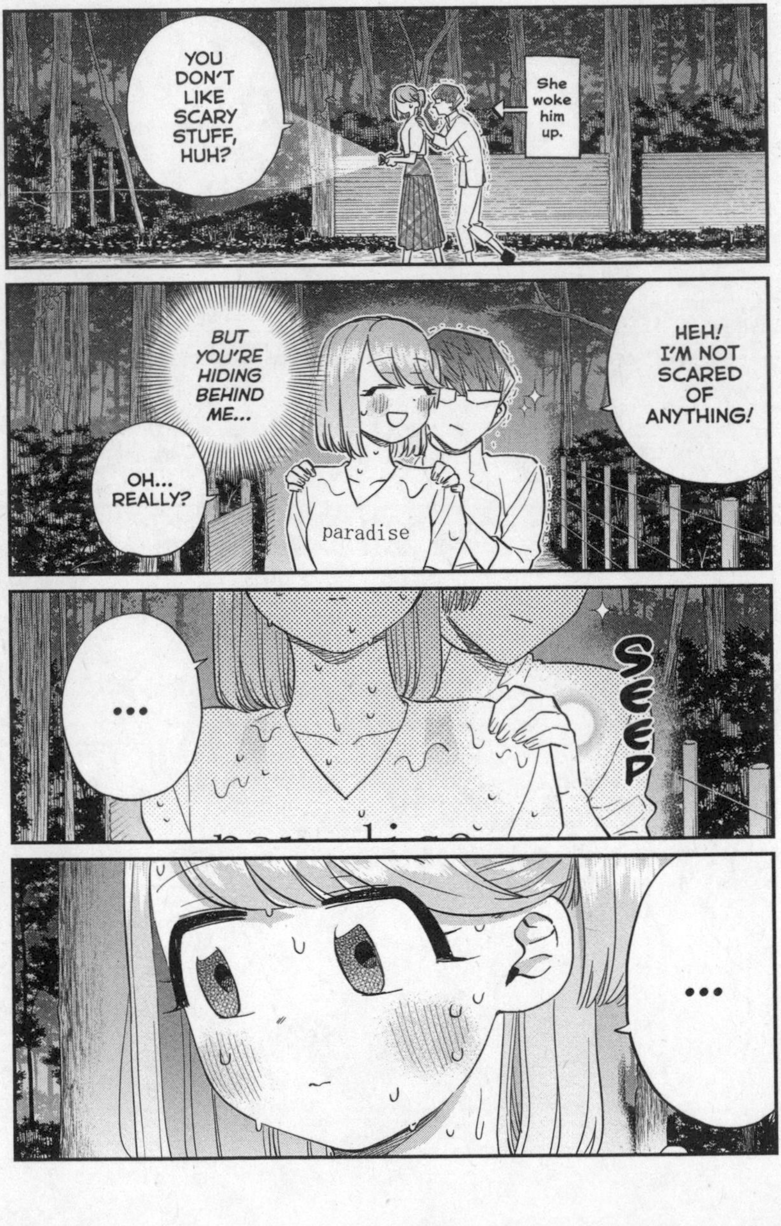
YOU DON'T LIKE SCARY STUFF, HUH?
She woke him up.
HEH! I'M NOT SCARED OF ANYTHING!
BUT YOU'RE HIDING BEHIND ME...
OH... REALLY?
paradise
SEEP
...
...

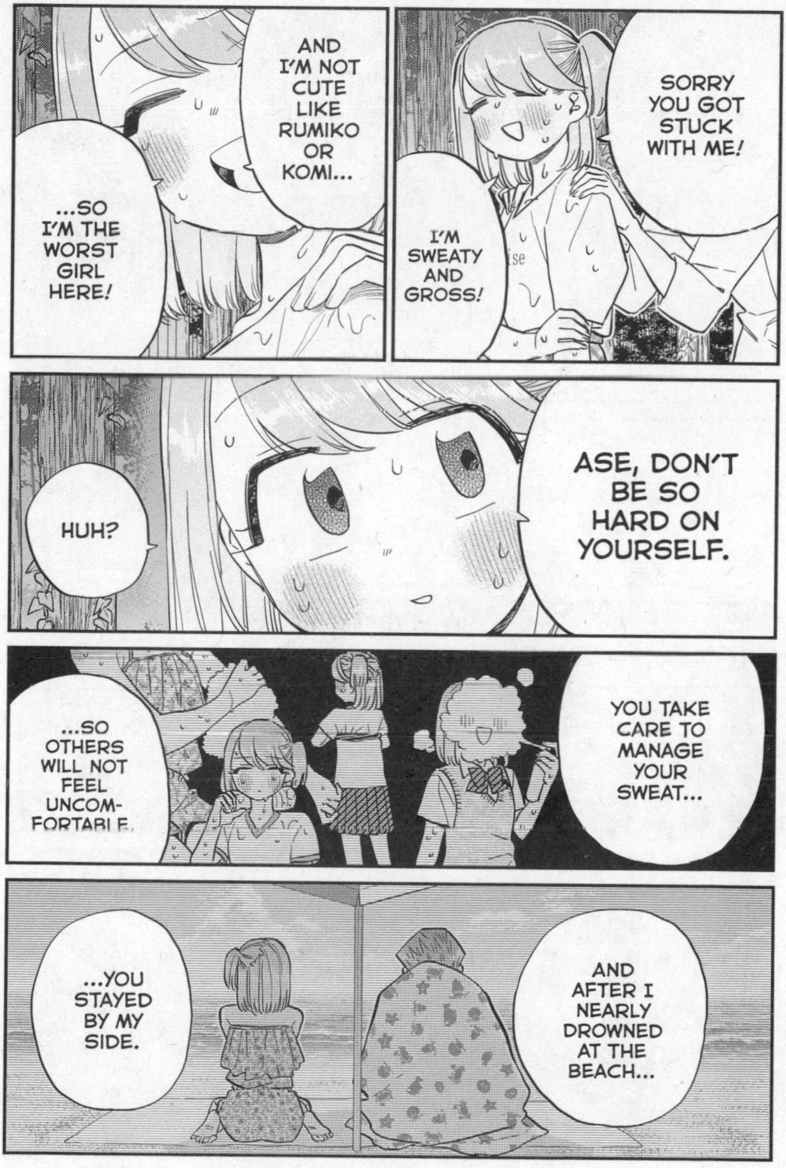
SORRY YOU GOT STUCK WITH ME!
I'M SWEATY AND GROSS!
AND I'M NOT CUTE LIKE RUMIKO OR KOMI...
...SO I'M THE WORST GIRL HERE!
ASE, DON'T BE SO HARD ON YOURSELF.
HUH?
YOU TAKE CARE TO MANAGE YOUR SWEAT...
...SO OTHERS WILL NOT FEEL UNCOM-FORTABLE.
AND AFTER I NEARLY DROWNED AT THE BEACH...
...YOU STAYED BY MY SIDE.

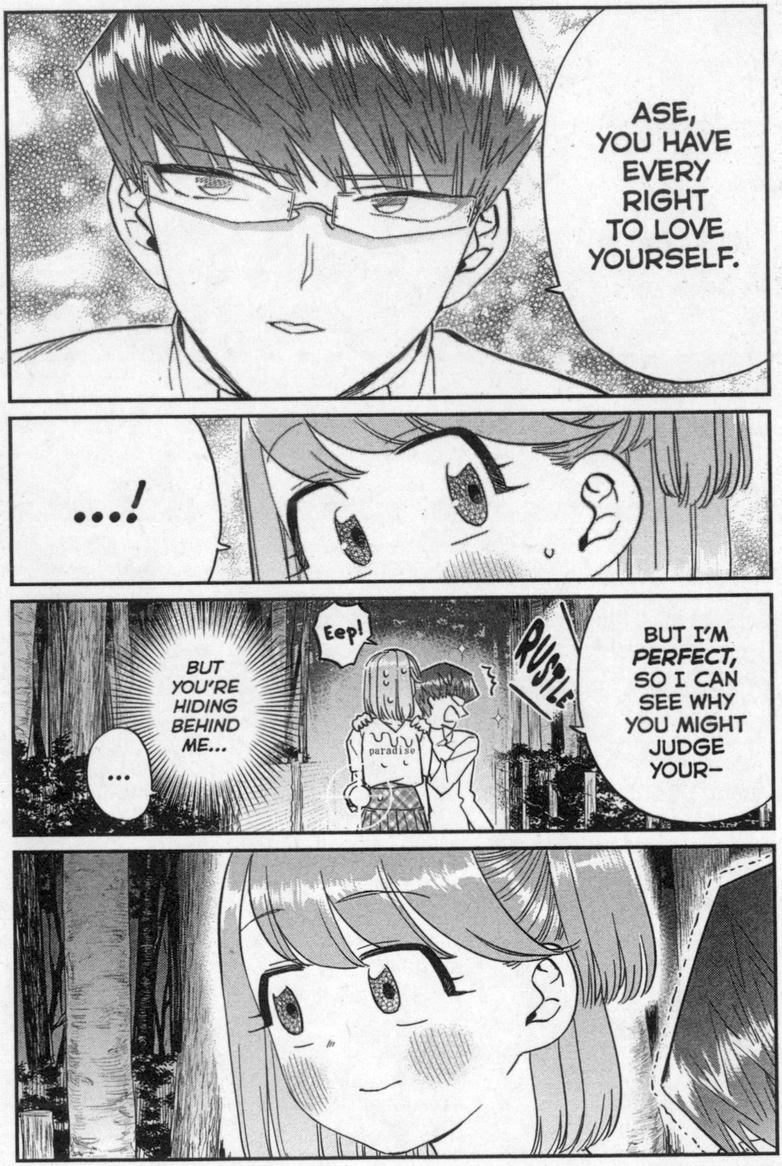
ASE, YOU HAVE EVERY RIGHT TO LOVE YOURSELF.
....!
BUT I'M PERFECT, SO I CAN SEE WHY YOU MIGHT JUDGE YOUR–
RUSTLE
Eep!
paradise
BUT YOU'RE HIDING BEHIND ME...
...

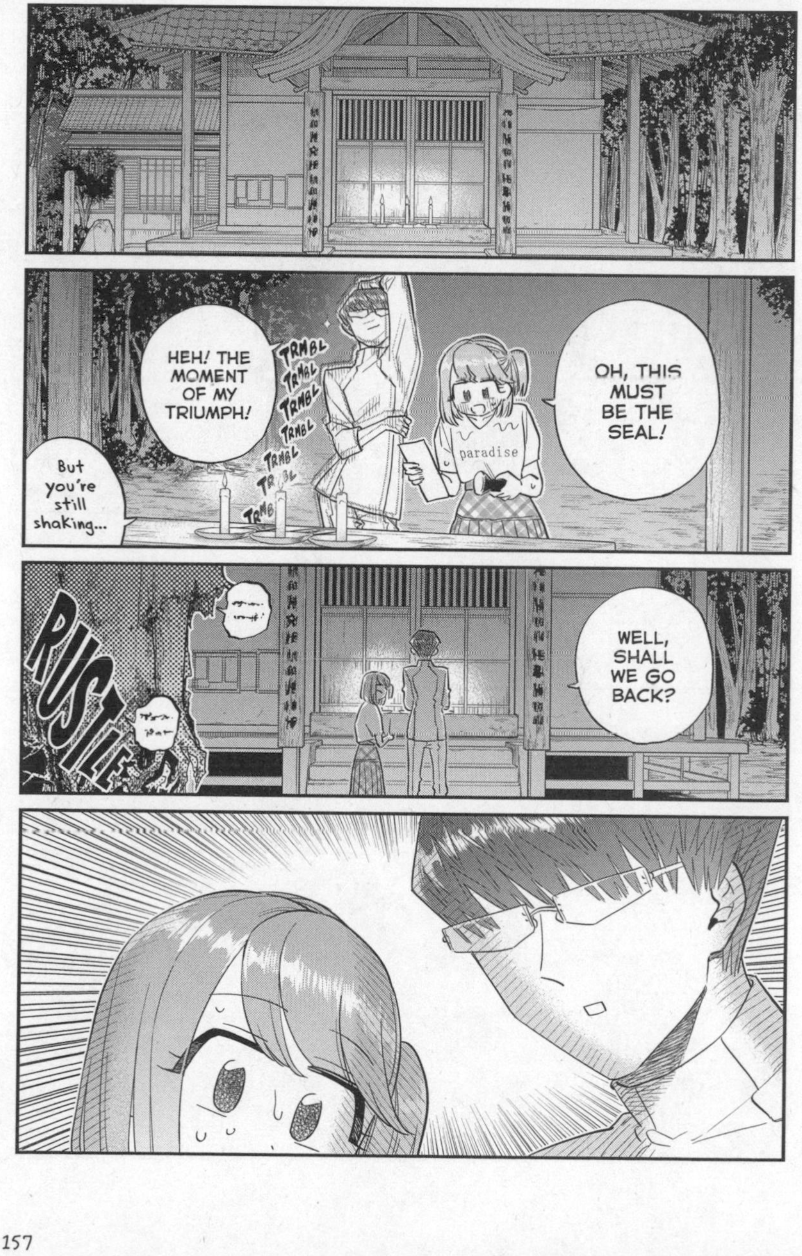
OH, THIS MUST BE THE SEAL!
paradise
HEH! THE MOMENT OF MY TRIUMPH!
TRMBL TRMBL TRMBL TRMBL TRMBL TRMBL TRMBL
But you're still shaking...
WELL, SHALL WE GO BACK?
RUSTLE

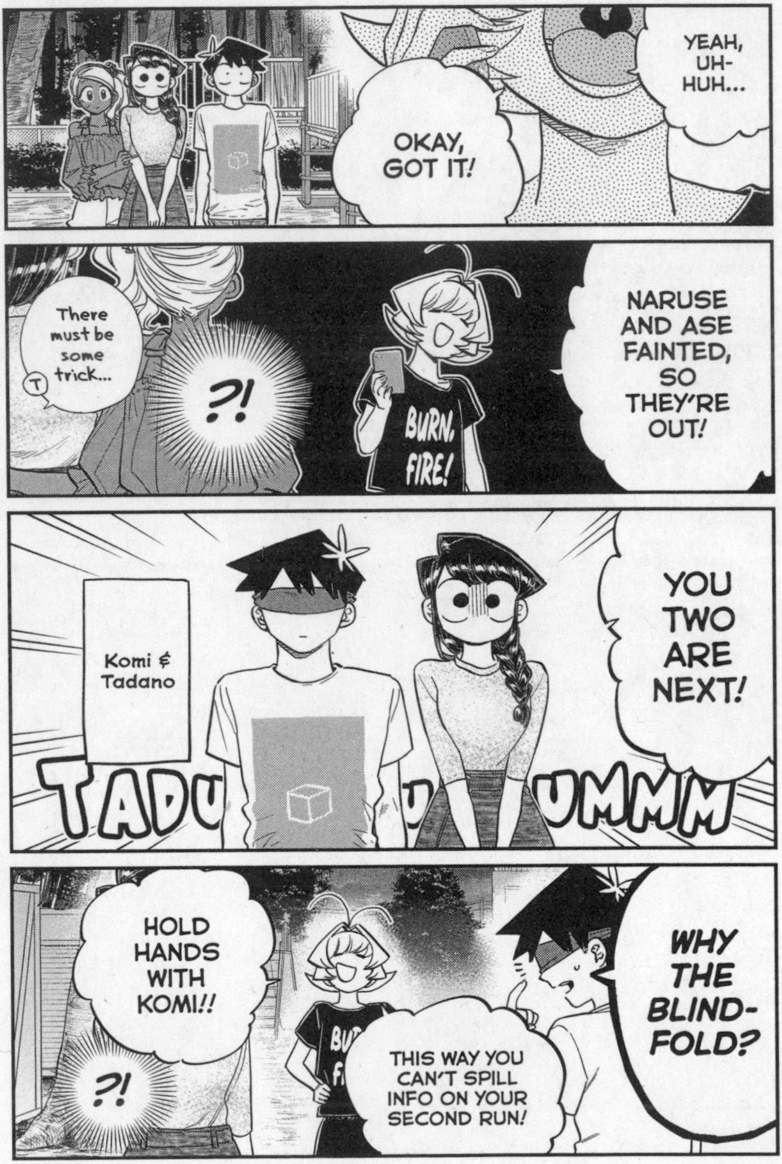
YEAH, UH-HUH...
OKAY, GOT IT!
NARUSE AND ASE FAINTED, SO THEY'RE OUT!
?!
There must be some trick...
YOU TWO ARE NEXT!
Komi & Tadano
TADU U UMMMM
WHY THE BLIND-FOLD?
THIS WAY YOU CAN'T SPILL INFO ON YOUR SECOND RUN!
HOLD HANDS WITH KOMI!!
?!

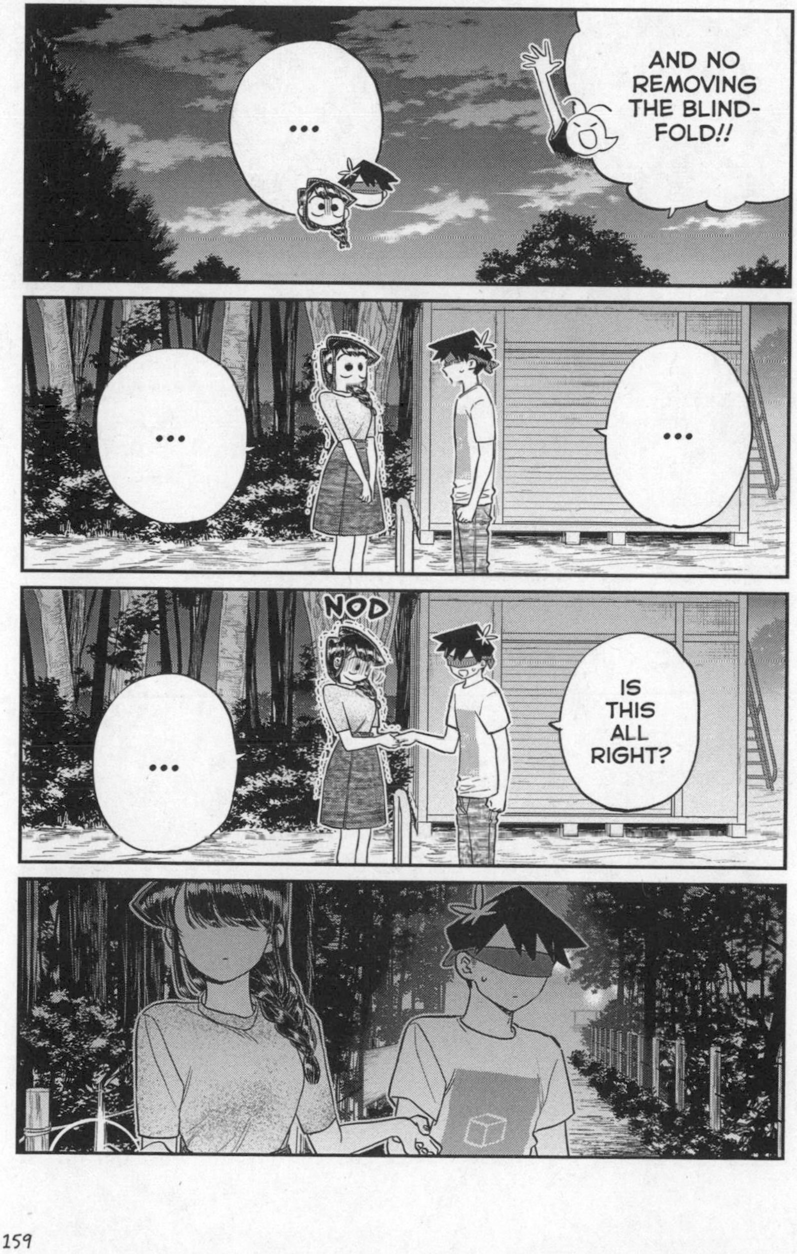
AND NO REMOVING THE BLIND-FOLD!!
...
...
...
IS THIS ALL RIGHT?
NOD
...

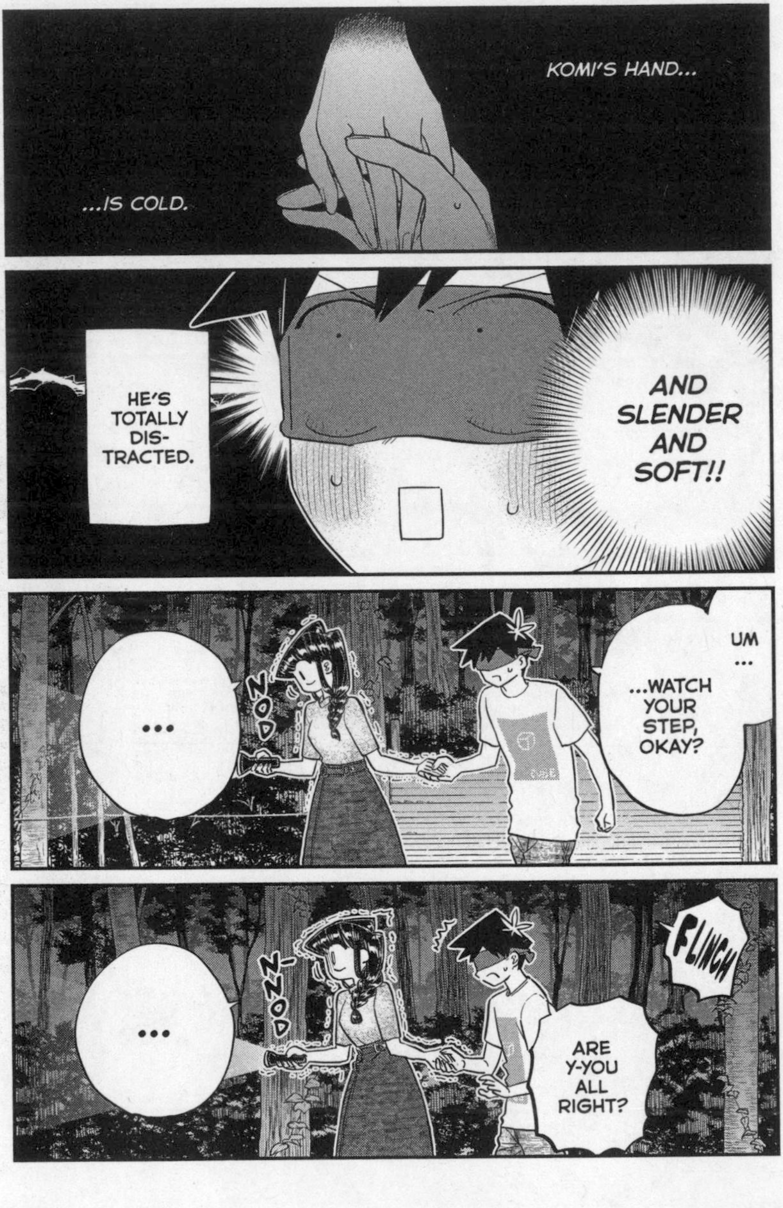
KOMI'S HAND...
...IS COLD.
AND SLENDER AND SOFT!!
HE'S TOTALLY DIS- TRACTED.
UM ...
...WATCH YOUR STEP, OKAY?
NOD
...
FLINCH
ARE Y-YOU ALL RIGHT?
N-NOD
...

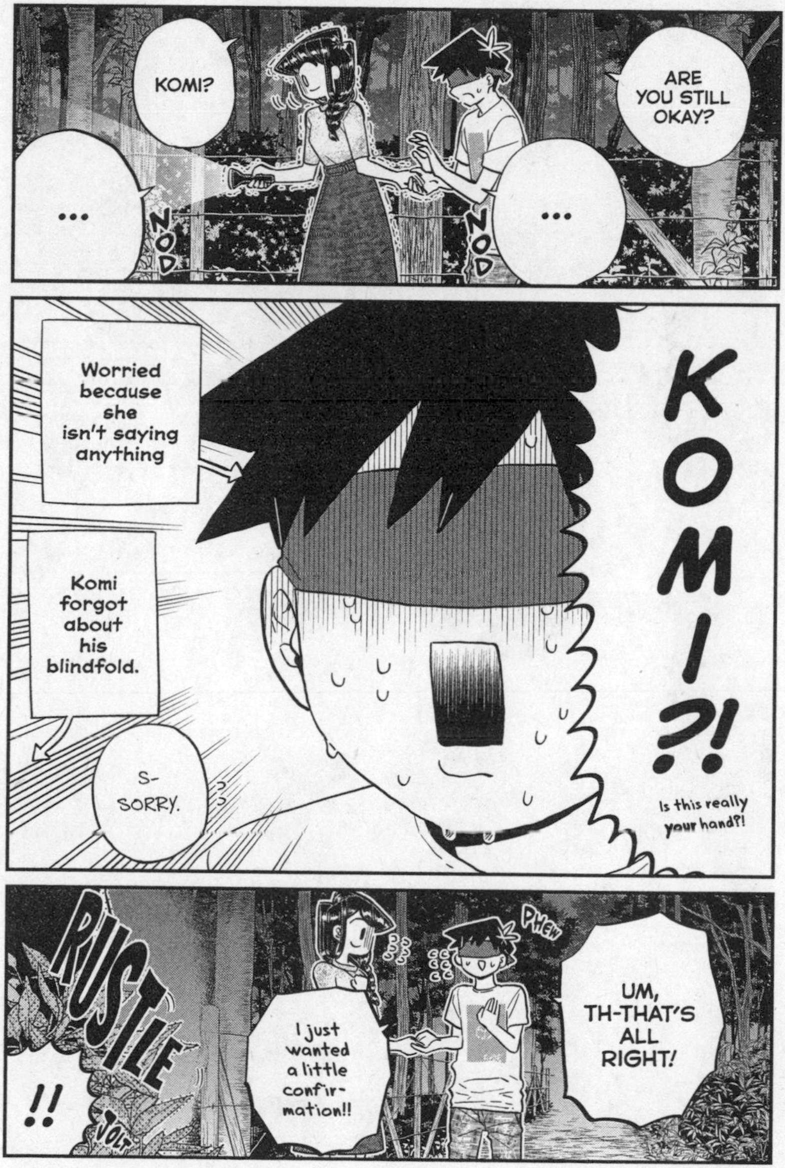
ARE YOU STILL OKAY?
...
NOD
KOMI?
...
NOD
KOMI?!
Is this really your hand?!
Worried because she isn't saying anything
Komi forgot about his blindfold.
S-SORRY.
UM, TH-THAT'S ALL RIGHT!
PHEW
I just wanted a little confir-mation!!
RUSTLE
!!
JOLT

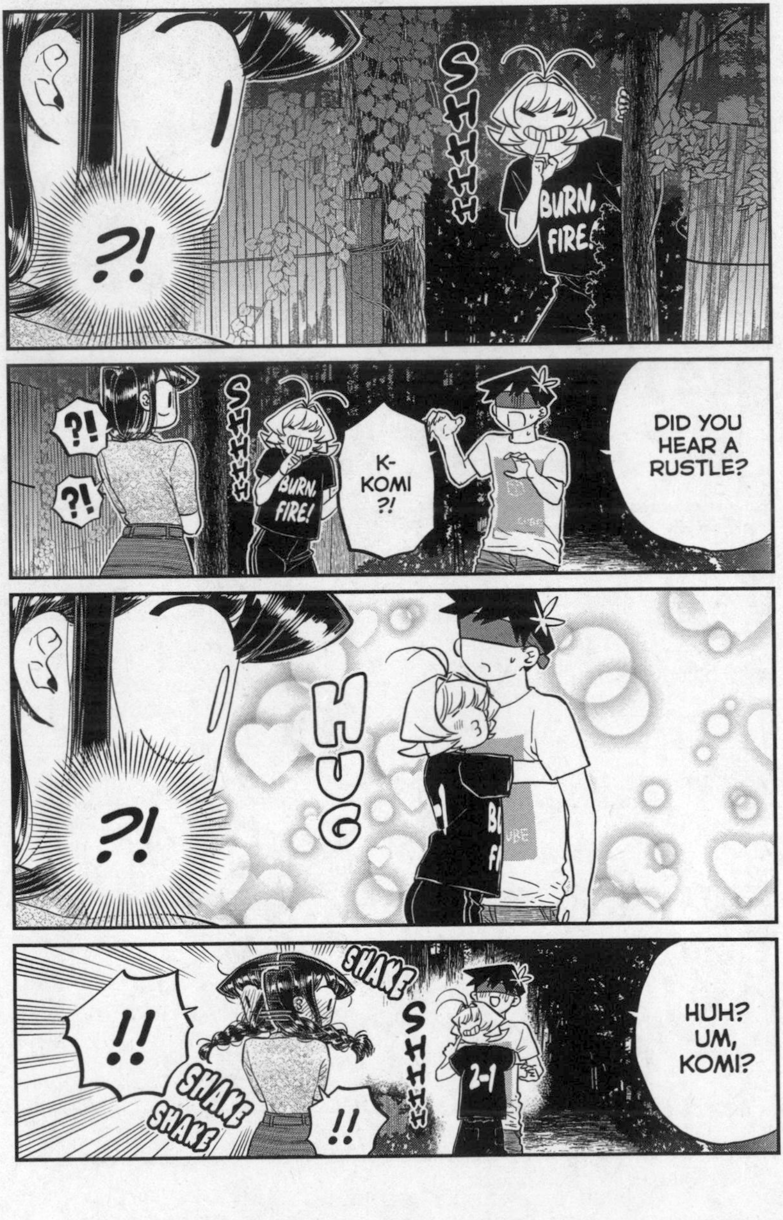
SHHHHH
?!
DID YOU HEAR A RUSTLE?
K-KOMI ?!
SHHHHH
?!
?!
HUG
?!
HUH? UM, KOMI?
SHAKE
SHHHHH
!!
SHAKE
SHAKE
!!

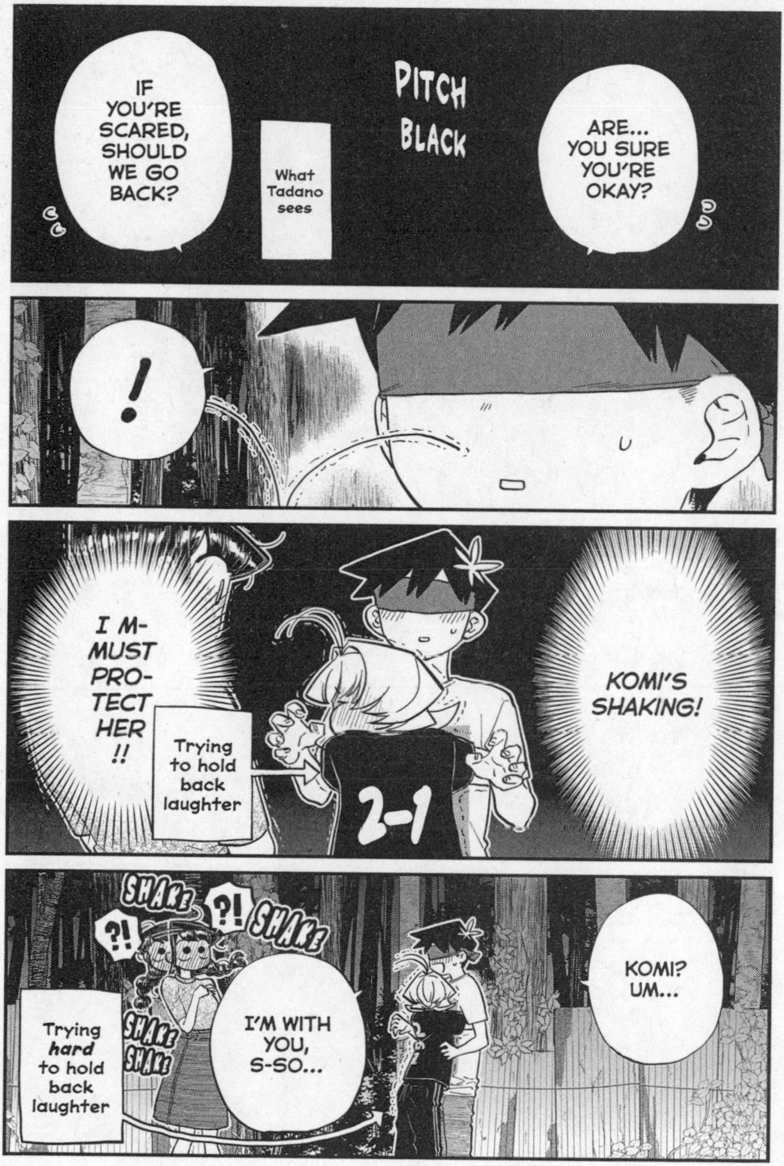
ARE... YOU SURE YOU'RE OKAY?
PITCH BLACK
What Tadano sees
IF YOU'RE SCARED, SHOULD WE GO BACK?
!
KOMI'S SHAKING!
2-1
Trying to hold back laughter
I M-MUST PRO-TECT HER!!
KOMI? UM...
SHAKE
?!
I'M WITH YOU, S-SO...
SHAKE
?!
SHAKE SHAKE
Trying *hard* to hold back laughter

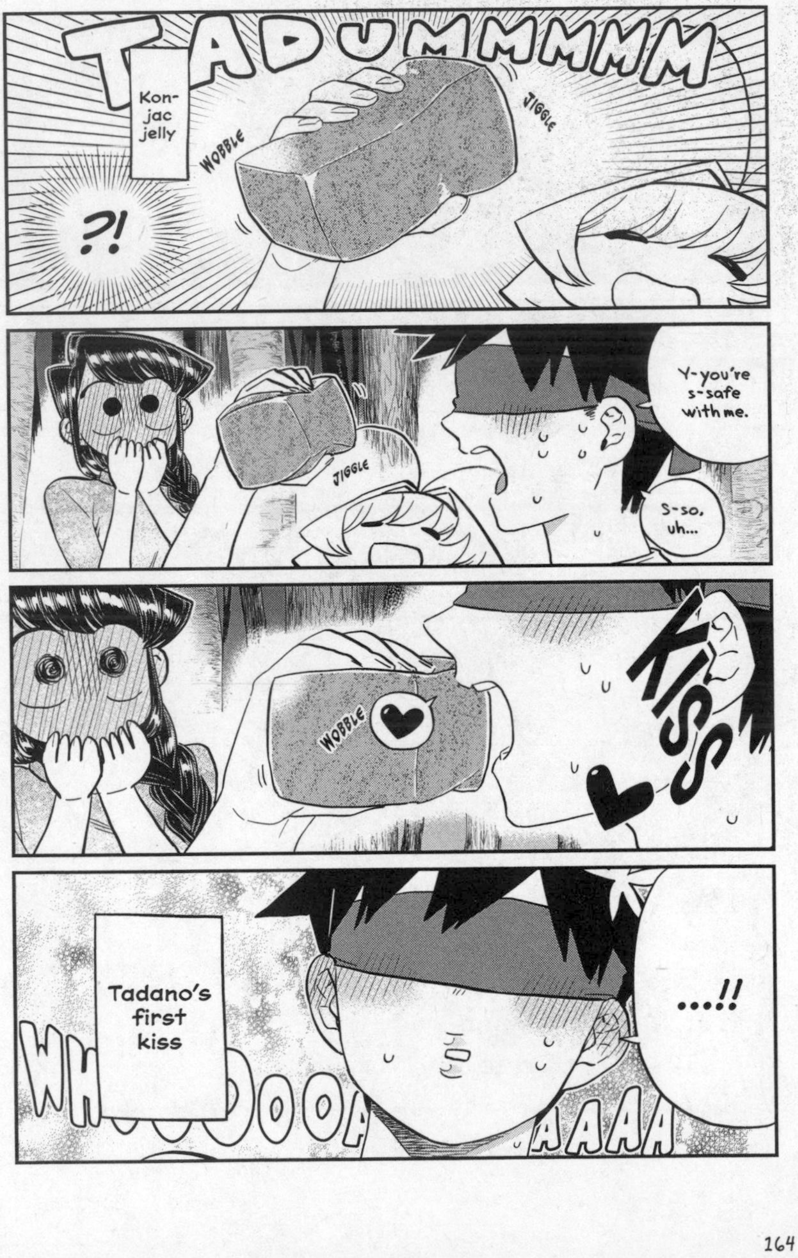
TADUMMMMMM
JIGGLE
Kon-jac jelly
WOBBLE
?!
Y-you're s-safe with me.
S-so, uh...
JIGGLE
KISS
WOBBLE
...!!
Tadano's first kiss

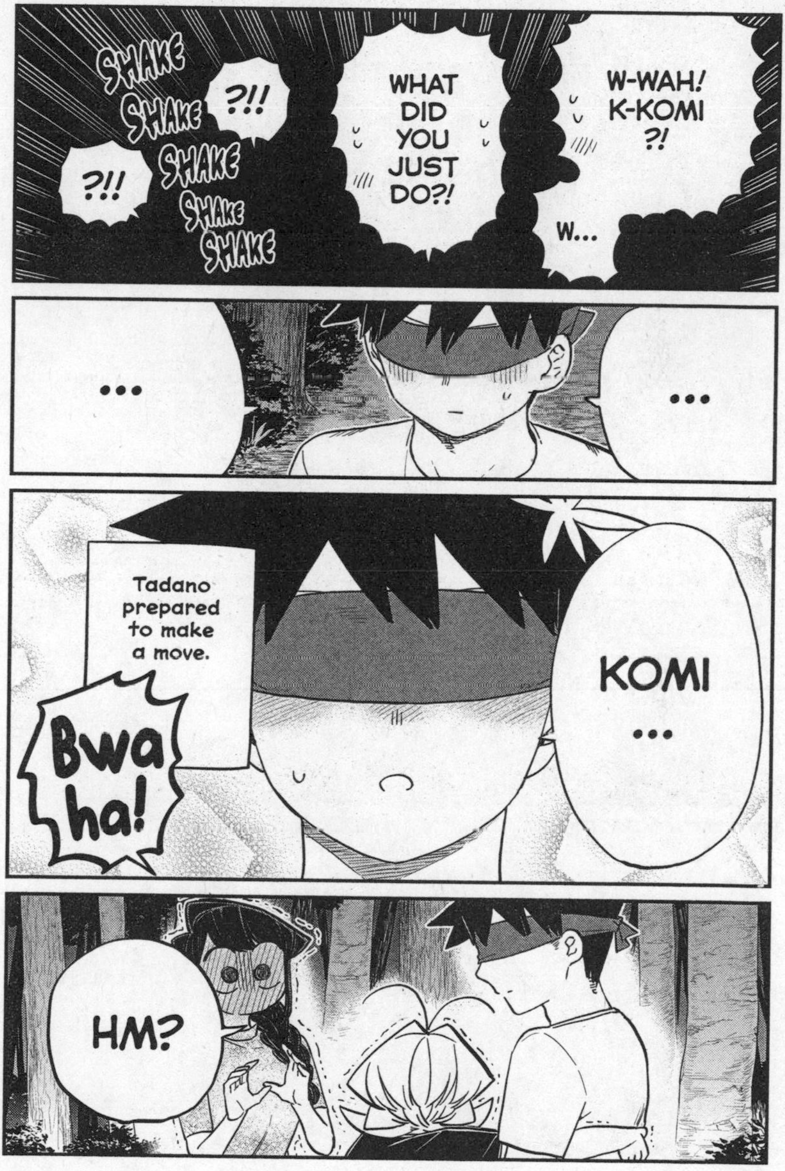
W-WAH! K-KOMI ?!
W...
WHAT DID YOU JUST DO?!
?!!
SHAKE SHAKE SHAKE SHAKE SHAKE
?!!
...
...
KOMI ...
Tadano prepared to make a move.
Bwa ha!
HM?

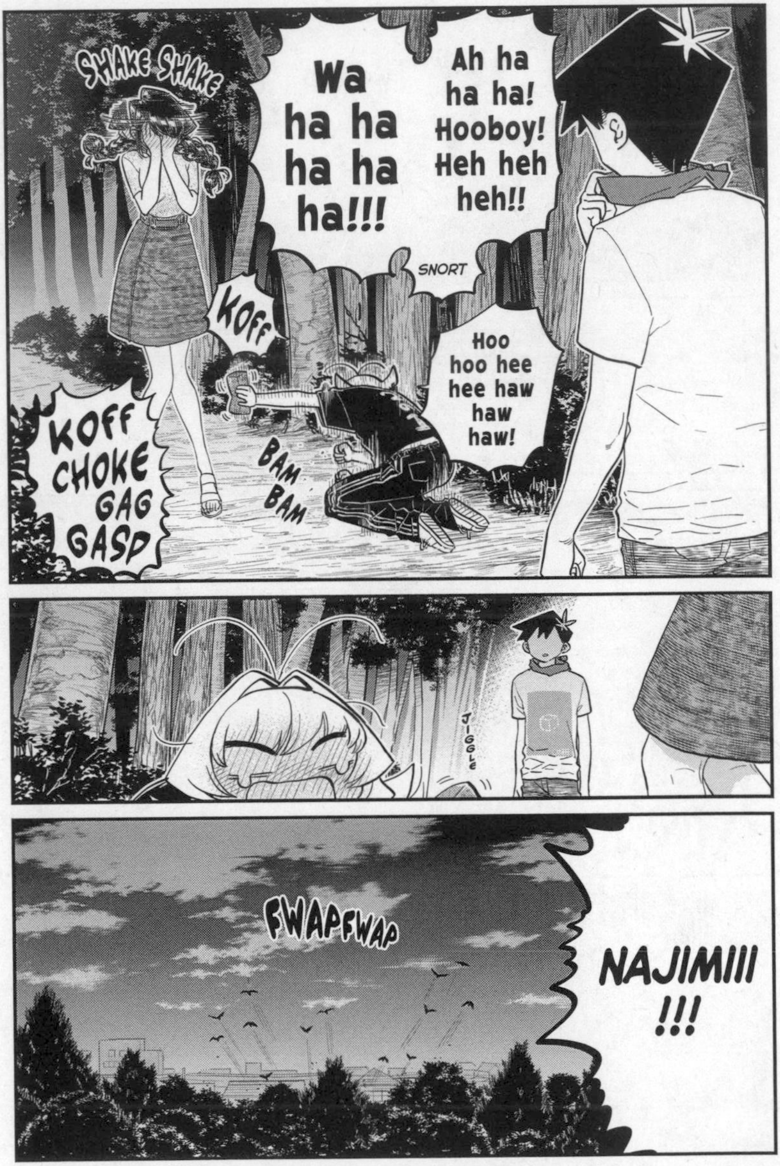
Ah ha ha ha! Hooboy! Heh heh heh!!
Wa ha ha ha ha ha!!!
SNORT
Hoo hoo hee hee haw haw haw!
SHAKE SHAKE
KOFF
BAM BAM
KOFF CHOKE GAG GASP
JIGGLE
NAJIMIII !!!
FWAPFWAP

Communication 180 — The End

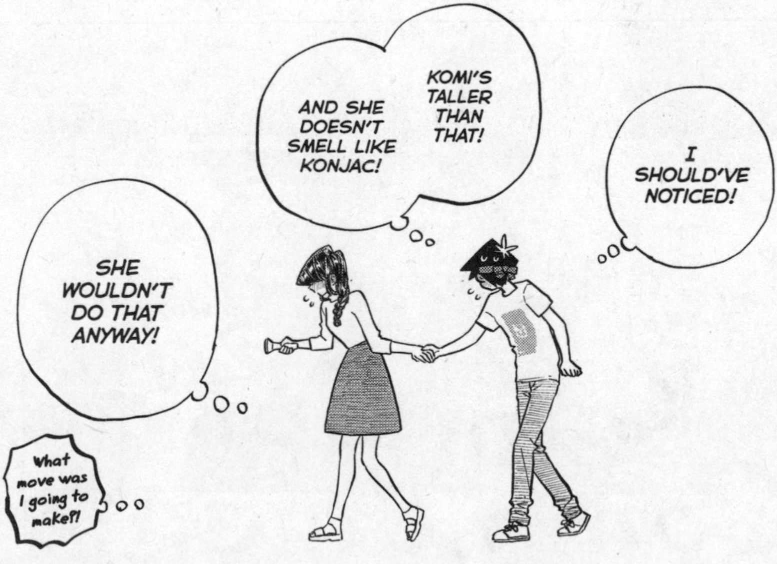
I SHOULD'VE NOTICED!
KOMI'S TALLER THAN THAT!
AND SHE DOESN'T SMELL LIKE KONJAC!
SHE WOULDN'T DO THAT ANYWAY!
What move was I going to make?!

Komi Can't
Communicate

Komi Can't Communicate

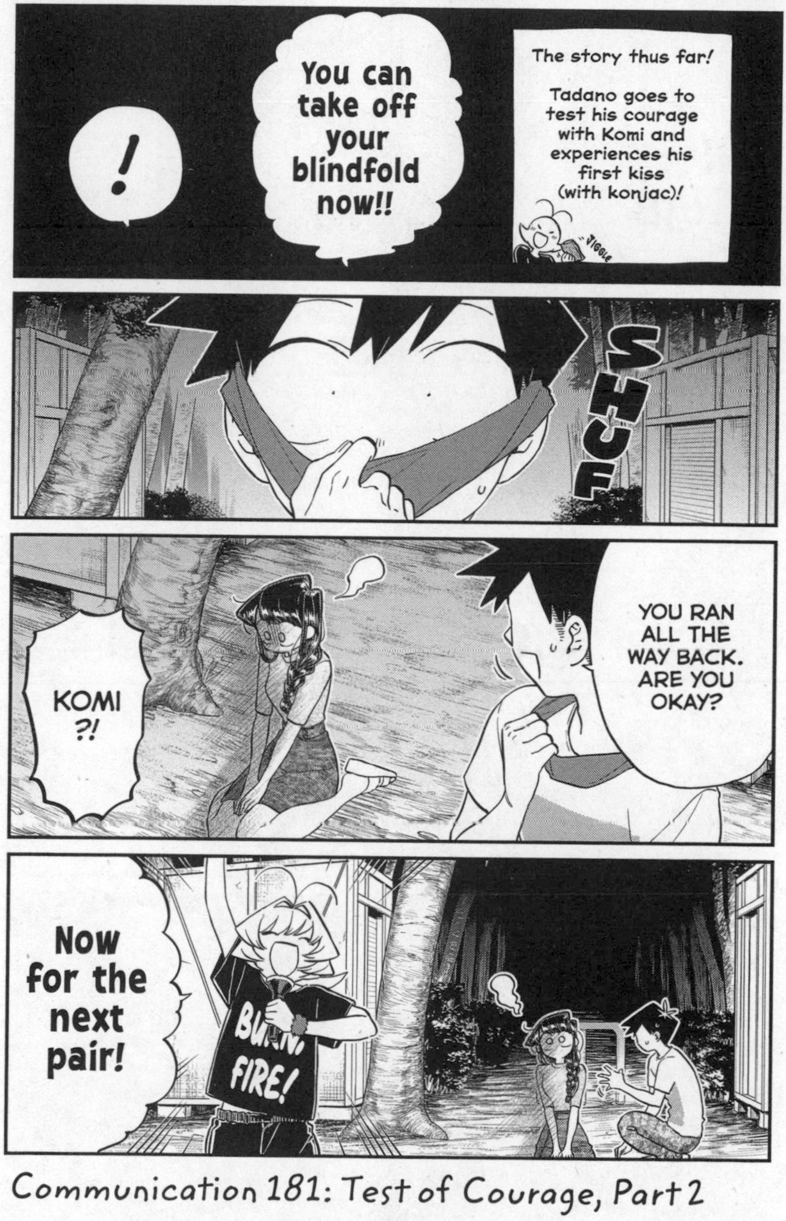
The story thus far!
Tadano goes to test his courage with Komi and experiences his first kiss (with konjac)!
JIGGLE
You can take off your blindfold now!!
!
SHUF
YOU RAN ALL THE WAY BACK. ARE YOU OKAY?
KOMI ?!
Now for the next pair!
BURN! FIRE!

Communication 181: Test of Courage, Part 2

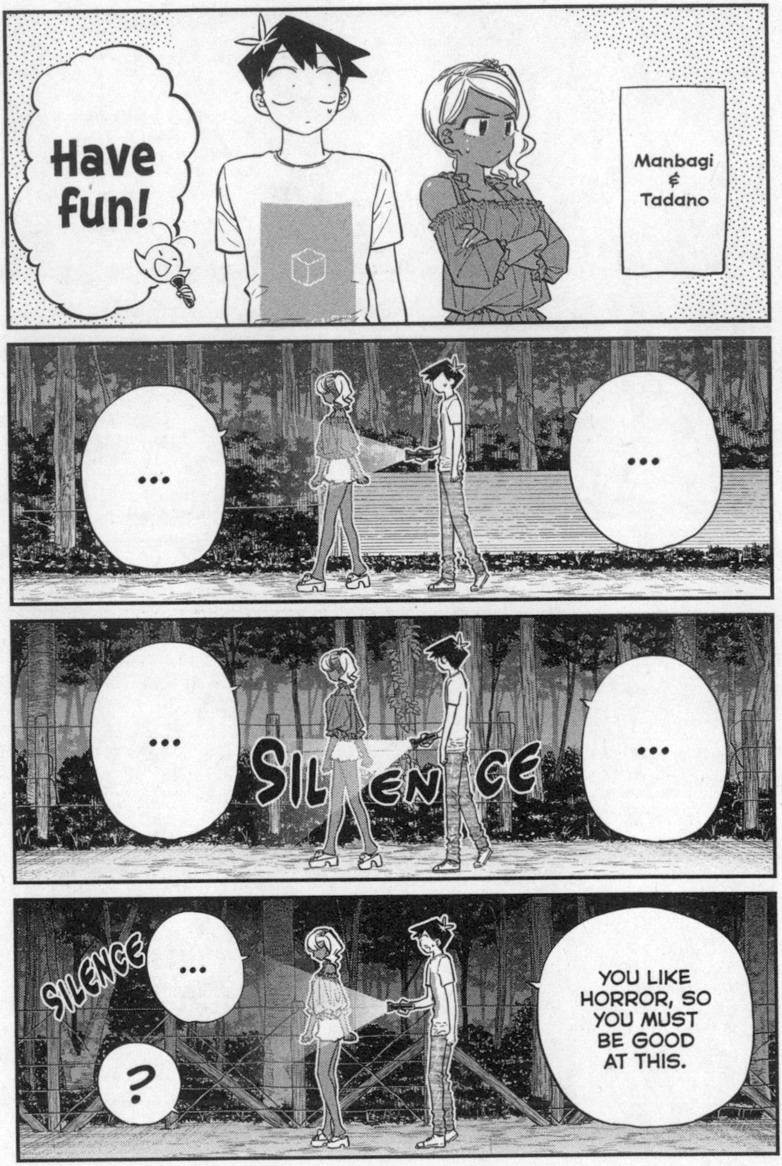
Manbagi & Tadano
Have fun!
...
...
...
SILENCE
...
YOU LIKE HORROR, SO YOU MUST BE GOOD AT THIS.
...
SILENCE
?

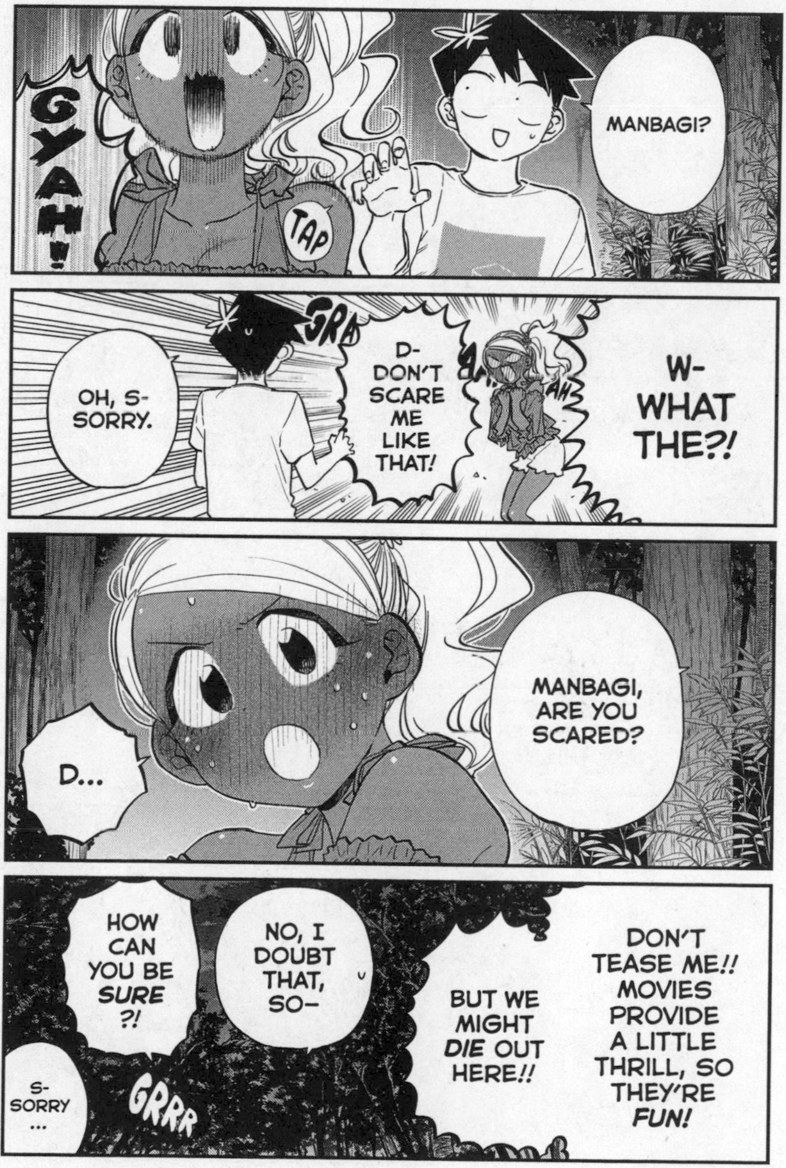
MANBAGI?
GYAH!!
TAP
W-WHAT THE?!
D-DON'T SCARE ME LIKE THAT!
OH, S-SORRY.
MANBAGI, ARE YOU SCARED?
D...
DON'T TEASE ME!! MOVIES PROVIDE A LITTLE THRILL, SO THEY'RE FUN!
BUT WE MIGHT DIE OUT HERE!!
NO, I DOUBT THAT, SO–
HOW CAN YOU BE SURE?!
GRRR
S-SORRY...

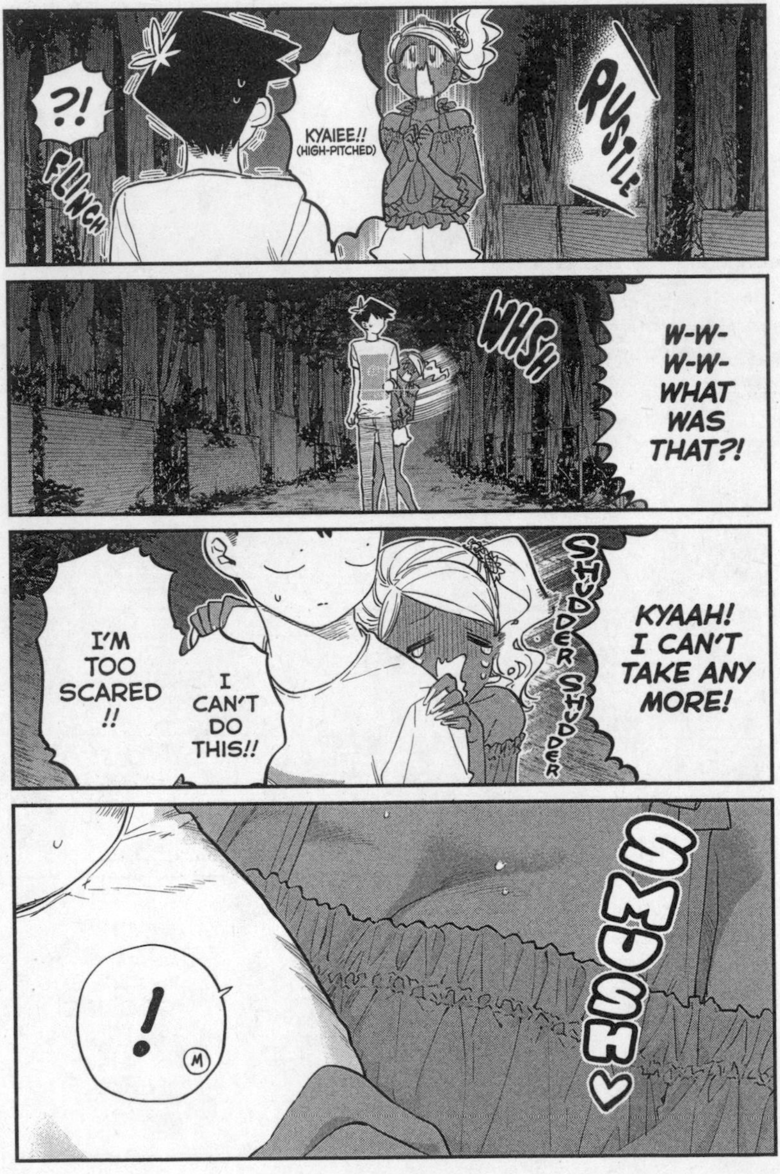
RUSTLE
KYAIEE!!
(HIGH-PITCHED)
?!
FLINCH
WHSH
W-W-
W-W-
WHAT
WAS
THAT?!
KYAAH!
I CAN'T
TAKE ANY
MORE!
SHUDDER SHUDDER
I
CAN'T
DO
THIS!!
I'M
TOO
SCARED
!!
SMUSH♥
!

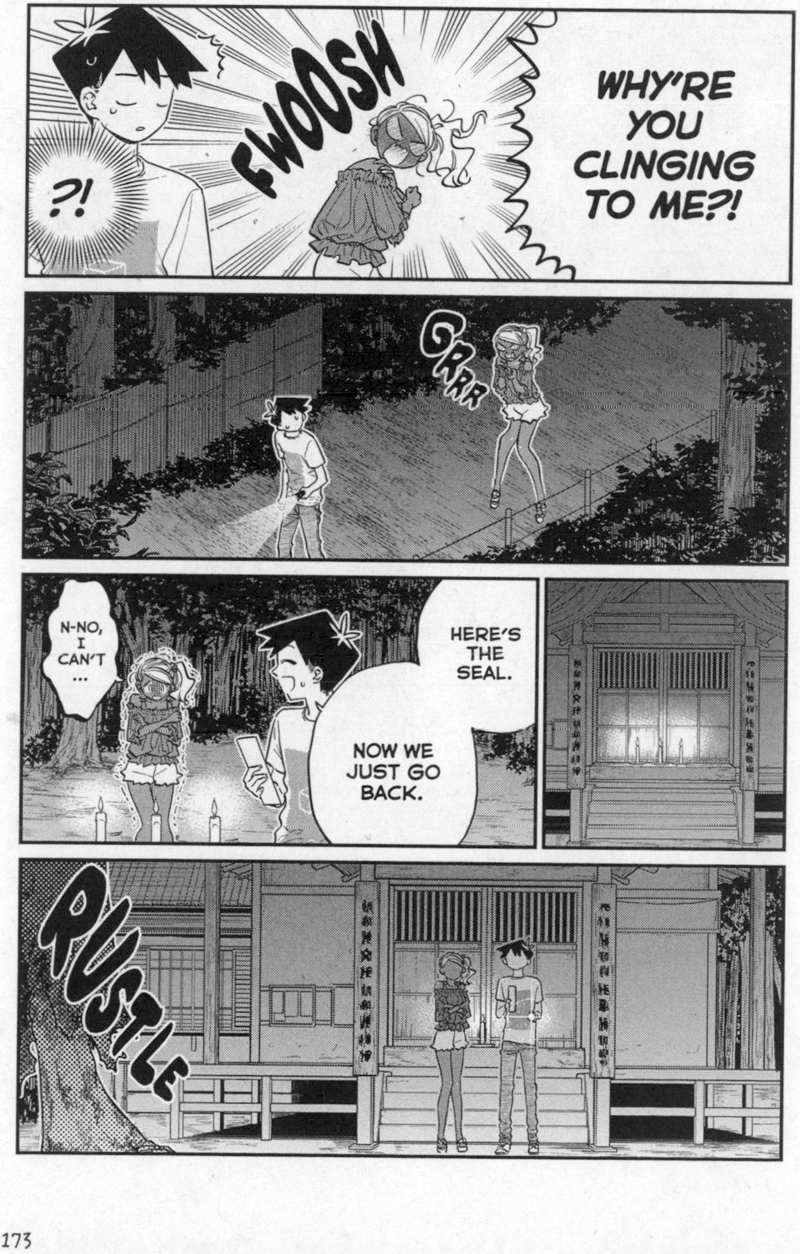
WHY'RE YOU CLINGING TO ME?!
FWOOSH
?!
GRRR
HERE'S THE SEAL.
NOW WE JUST GO BACK.
N-NO, I CAN'T ...
RUSTLE

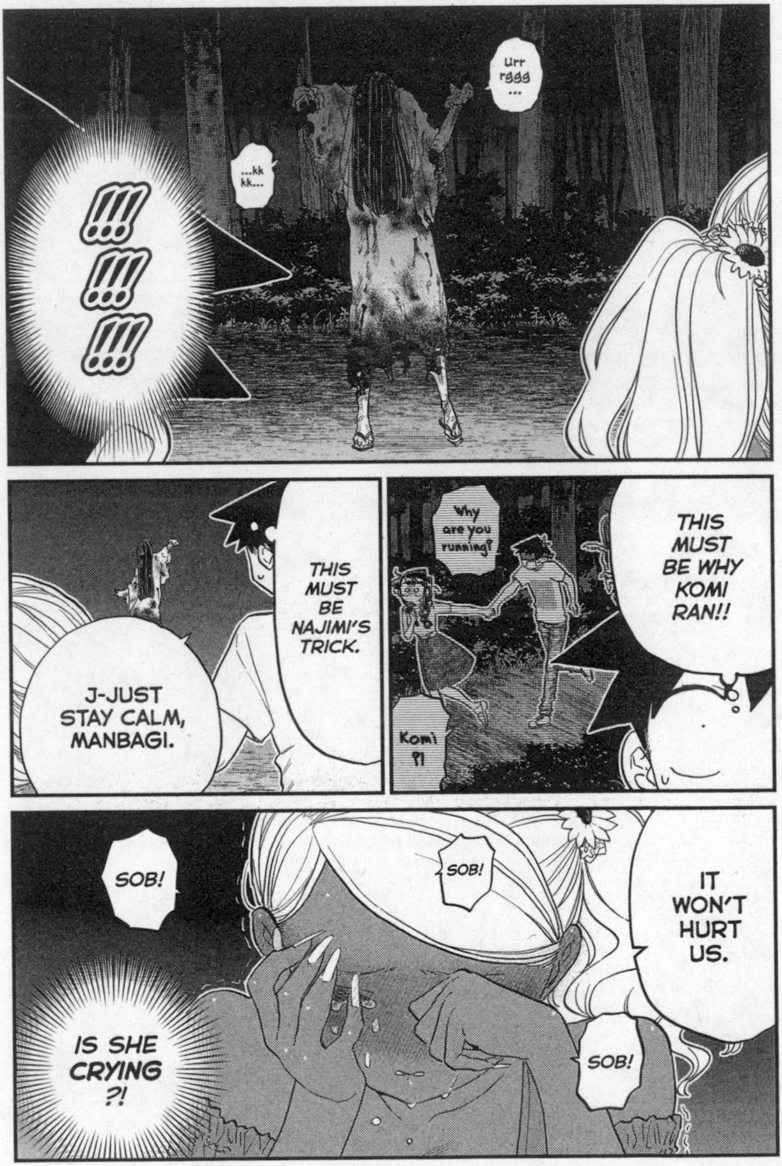
Urr rggg ...
...kk kk...
!!!... !!!... !!!...
THIS MUST BE WHY KOMI RAN!!
Why are you running?
Komi ?!
THIS MUST BE NAJIMI'S TRICK.
J-JUST STAY CALM, MANBAGI.
IT WON'T HURT US.
SOB!
SOB!
SOB!
IS SHE CRYING ?!

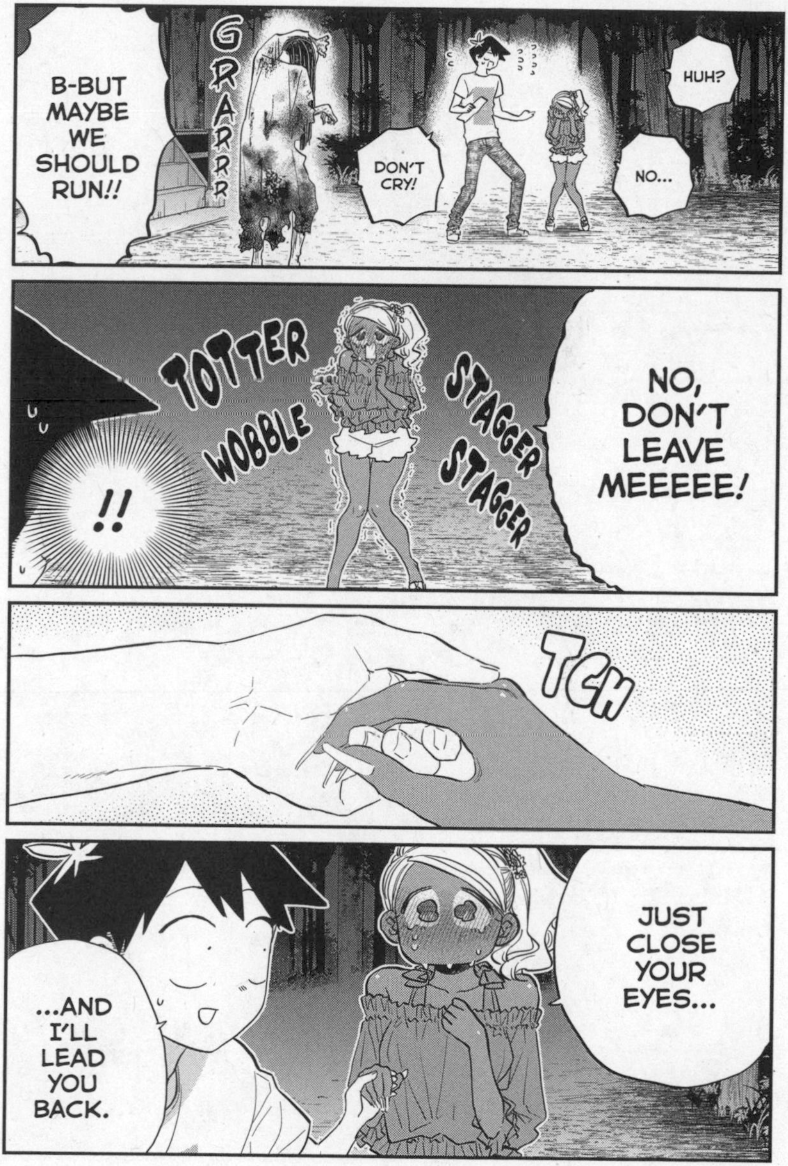
HUH?
NO...
DON'T CRY!
GRARRRR
B-BUT MAYBE WE SHOULD RUN!!
NO, DON'T LEAVE MEEEEE!
STAGGER STAGGER
TOTTER WOBBLE
!!
TCH
JUST CLOSE YOUR EYES...
...AND I'LL LEAD YOU BACK.

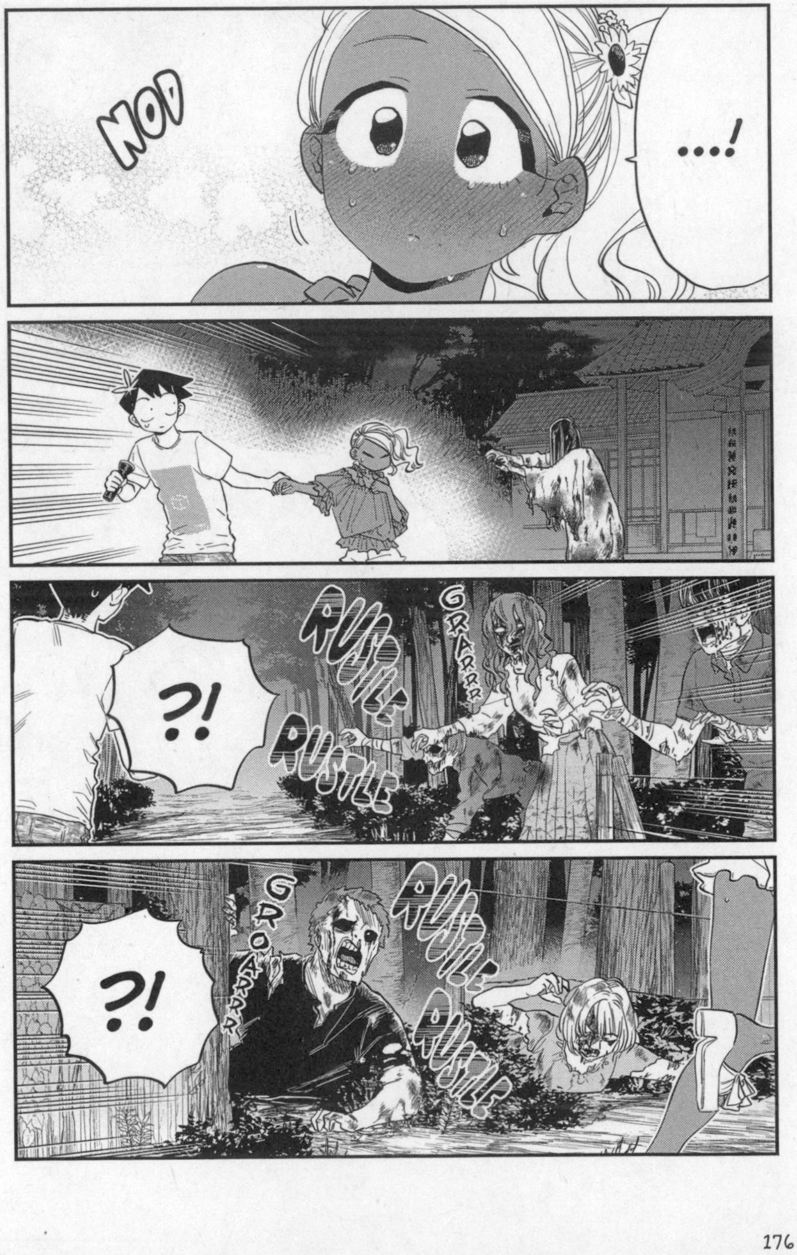
...!
NOD
?!
GRARRR
RUSTLE RUSTLE
RUSTLE RUSTLE
GROARRRR
?!

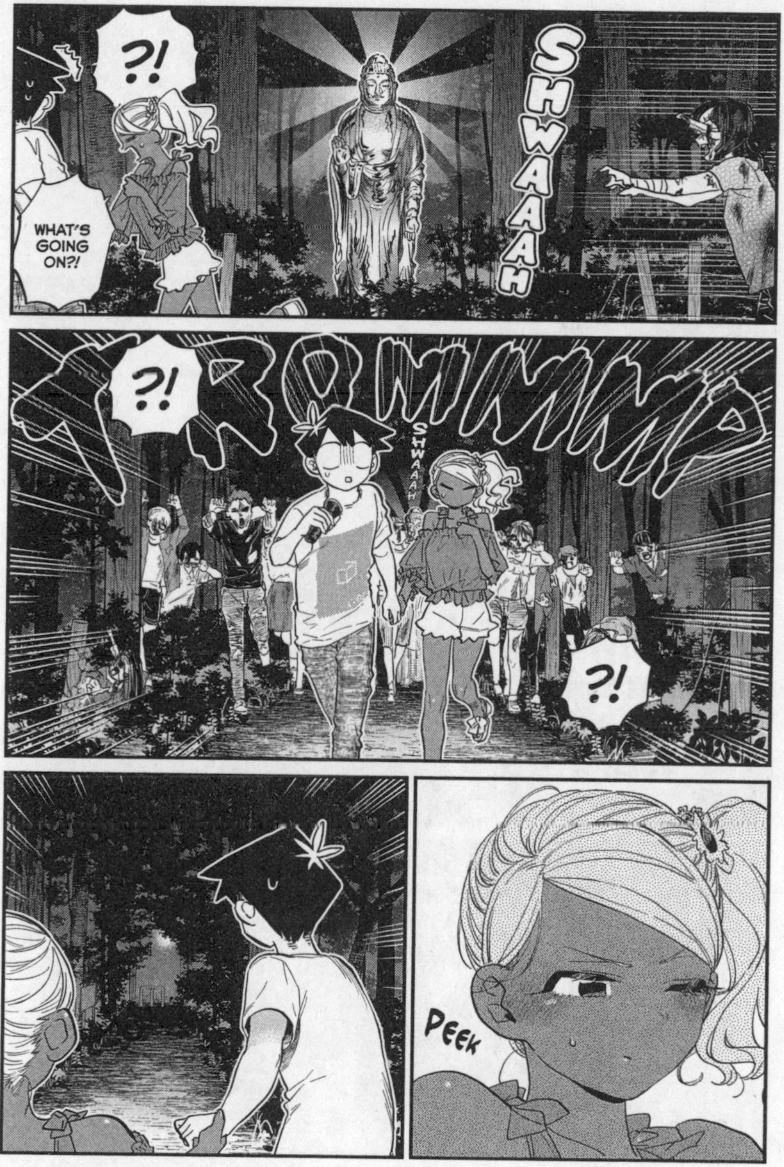
SHWAAAAH
?!
WHAT'S GOING ON?!
TROMMMP
?!
SHWAAAH
?!
PEEK

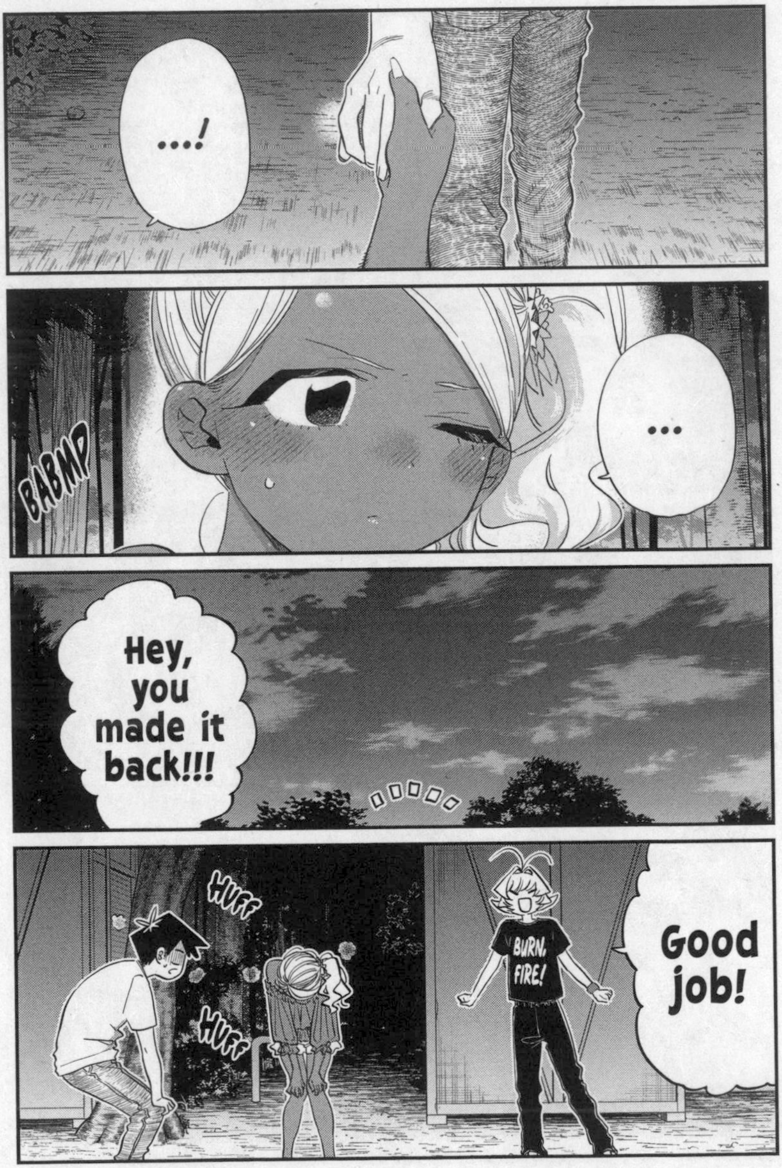
...!
...
BABMP
Hey, you made it back!!!
Good job!
BURN, FIRE!
HUFF
HUFF

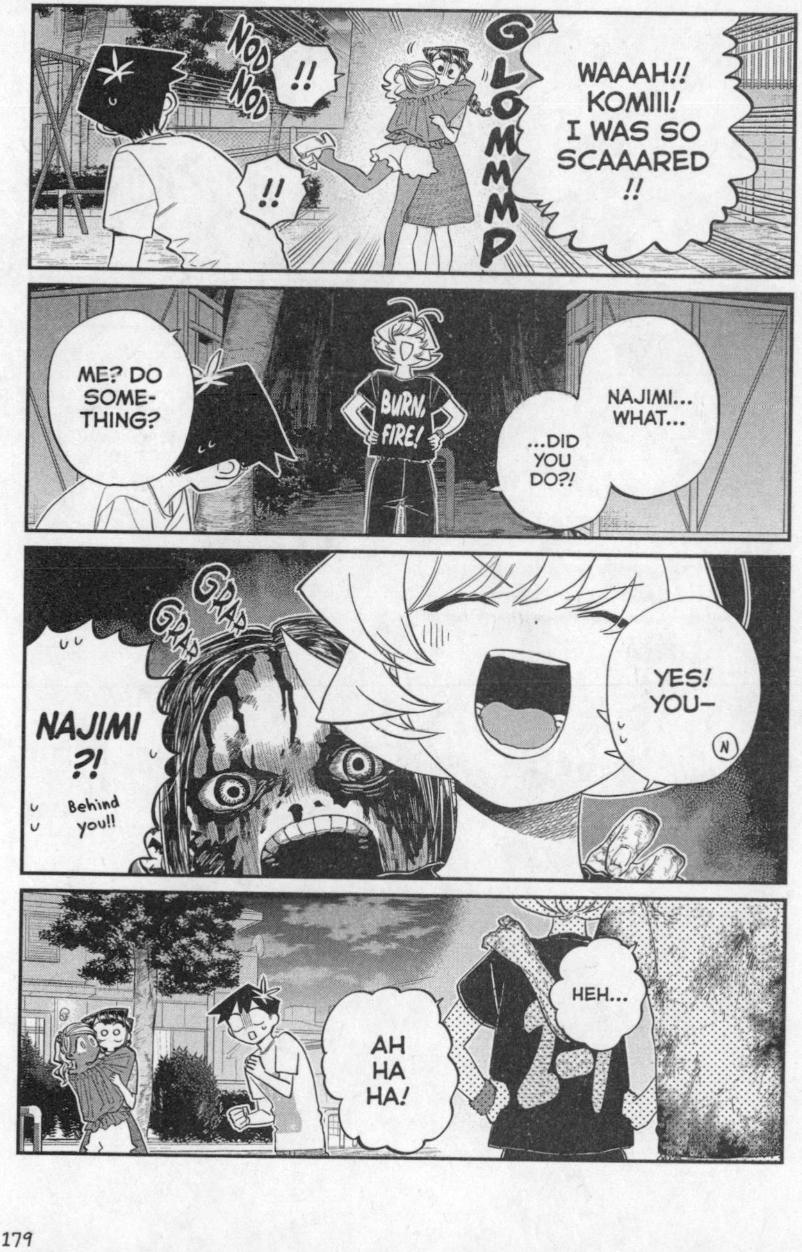
WAAAH!! KOMIII! I WAS SO SCAAARED !!
GLOMMMP
!!
NOD NOD
!!
NAJIMI... WHAT... ...DID YOU DO?!
BURN, FIRE!
ME? DO SOME-THING?
YES! YOU—
GRAP GRAP
NAJIMI ?!
Behind you!!
HEH...
AH HA HA!

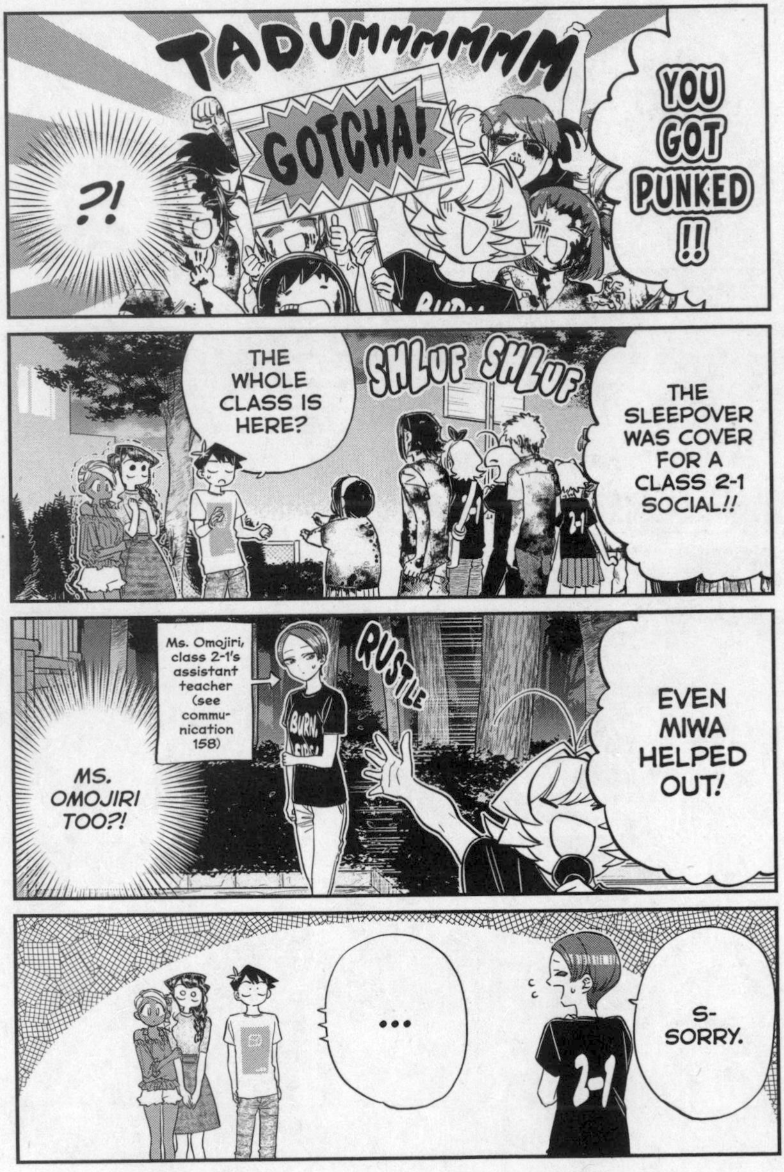
TADUMMMMMM
YOU GOT PUNKED!!
GOTCHA!
?!
THE SLEEPOVER WAS COVER FOR A CLASS 2-1 SOCIAL!!
SHLUF SHLUF
THE WHOLE CLASS IS HERE?
EVEN MIWA HELPED OUT!
RUSTLE
Ms. Omojiri, class 2-1's assistant teacher (see communication 158)
MS. OMOJIRI TOO?!
S-SORRY.
...

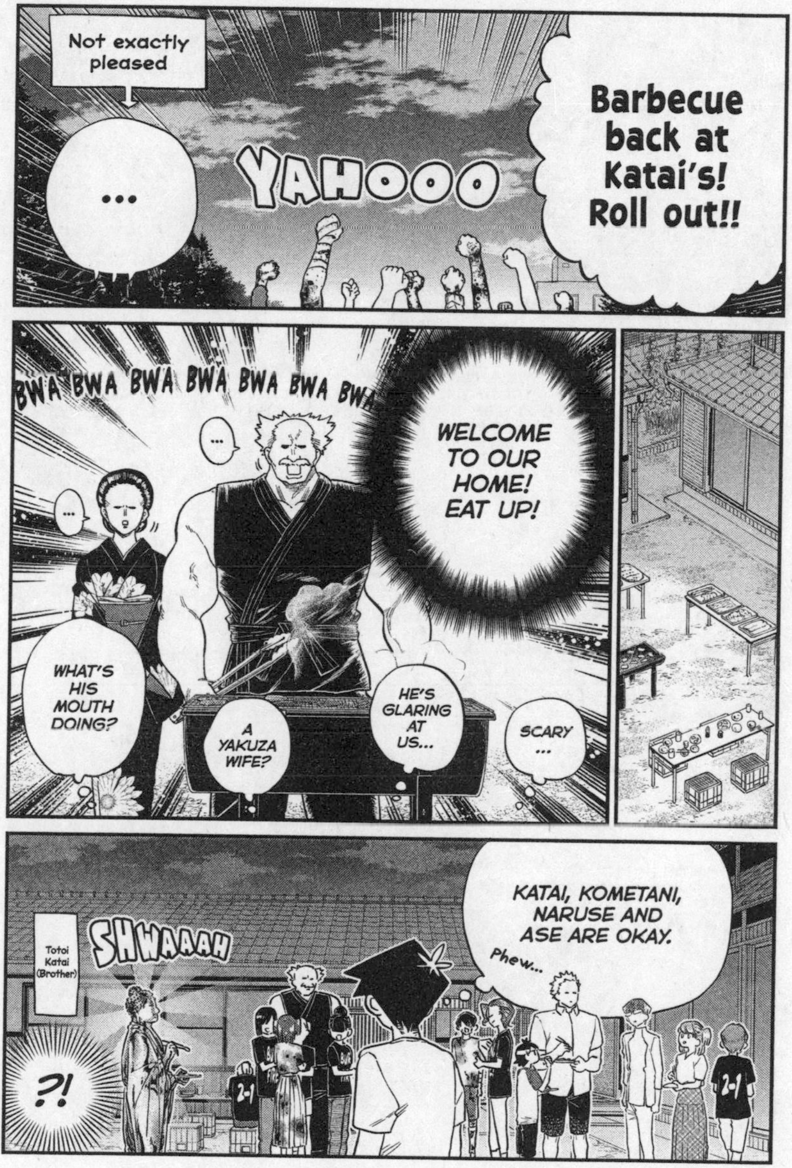
Barbecue back at Katai's! Roll out!!
YAHOOO
Not exactly pleased
...
WELCOME TO OUR HOME! EAT UP!
BWA BWA BWA BWA BWA BWA BWA
...
...
SCARY ...
HE'S GLARING AT US...
A YAKUZA WIFE?
WHAT'S HIS MOUTH DOING?
KATAI, KOMETANI, NARUSE AND ASE ARE OKAY.
Phew...
SHWAAAH
Totoi Katai (Brother)
?!

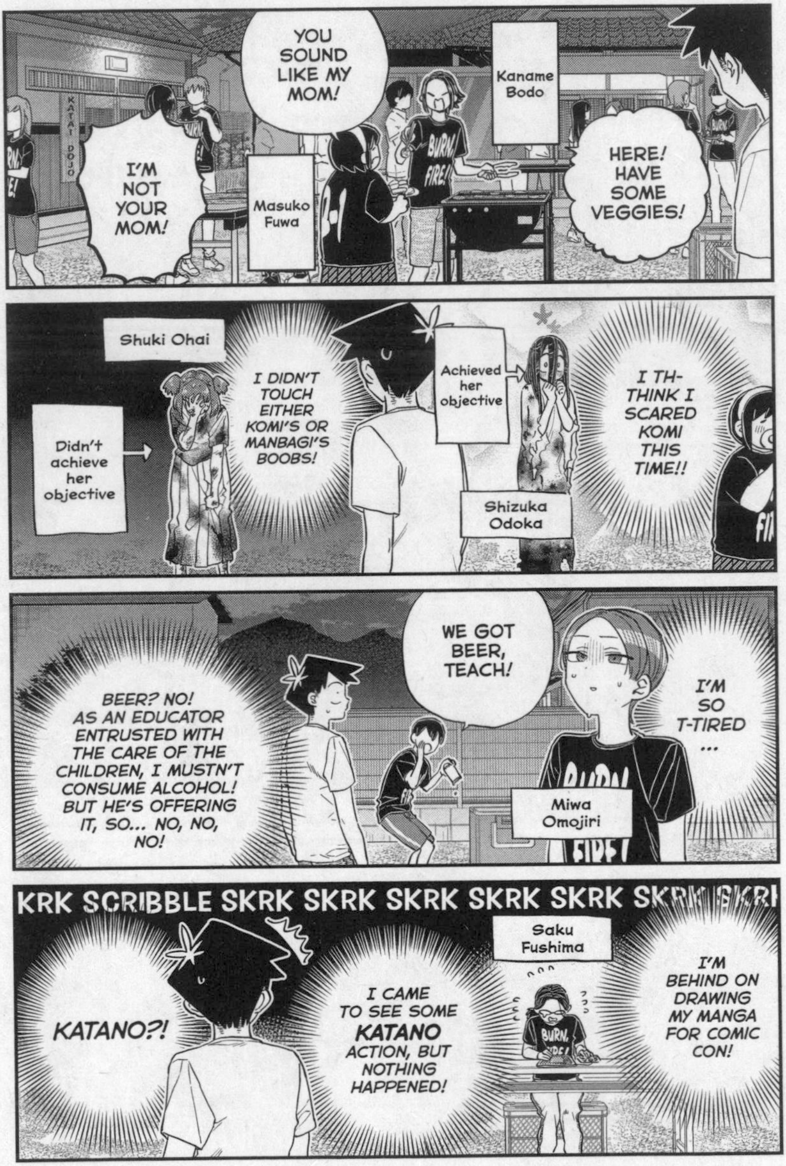
HERE! HAVE SOME VEGGIES!
Kaname Bodo
YOU SOUND LIKE MY MOM!
Masuko Fuwa
KATAI DOJO
I'M NOT YOUR MOM!
I TH-THINK I SCARED KOMI THIS TIME!!
Achieved her objective
Shizuka Odoka
I DIDN'T TOUCH EITHER KOMI'S OR MANBAGI'S BOOBS!
Shuki Ohai
Didn't achieve her objective
I'M SO T-TIRED ...
WE GOT BEER, TEACH!
Miwa Omojiri
BEER? NO! AS AN EDUCATOR ENTRUSTED WITH THE CARE OF THE CHILDREN, I MUSTN'T CONSUME ALCOHOL! BUT HE'S OFFERING IT, SO... NO, NO, NO!
KRK SCRIBBLE SKRK SKRK SKRK SKRK SKRK SKRK SKRI
I'M BEHIND ON DRAWING MY MANGA FOR COMIC CON!
Saku Fushima
I CAME TO SEE SOME KATANO ACTION, BUT NOTHING HAPPENED!
KATANO?!

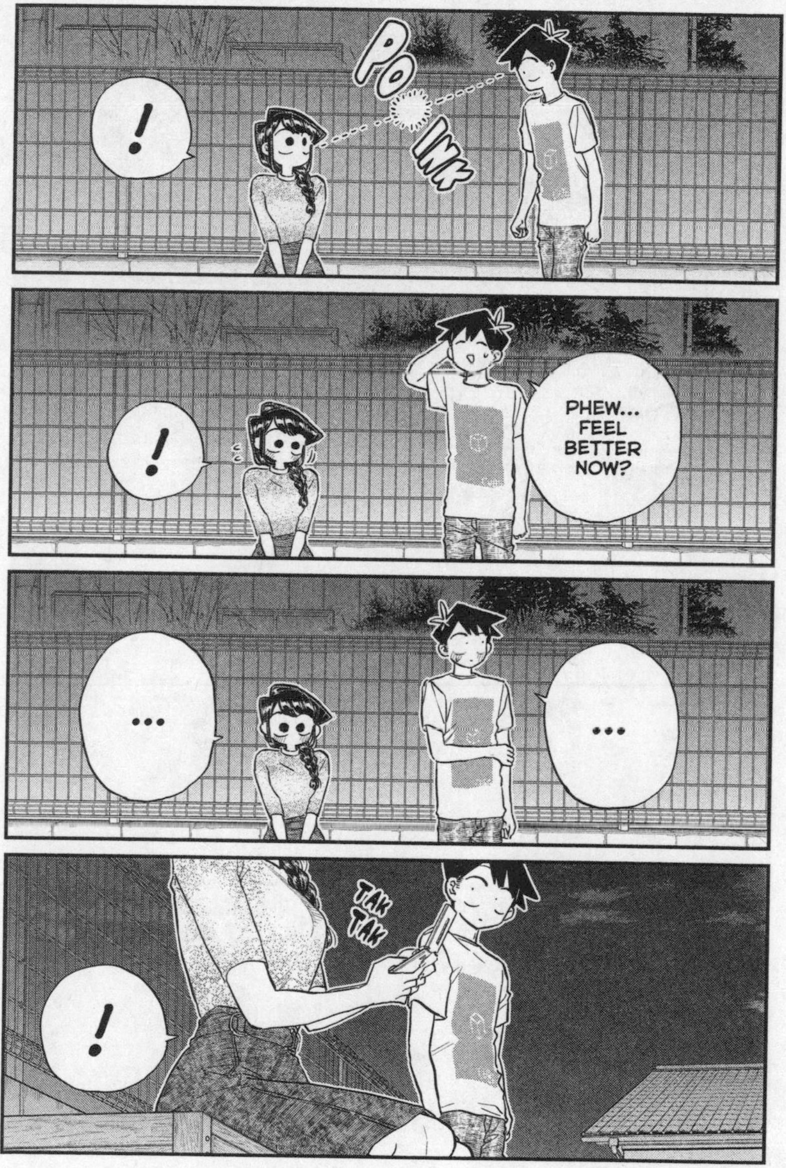
PO INK
!
PHEW... FEEL BETTER NOW?
!
...
...
TAK TAK
!

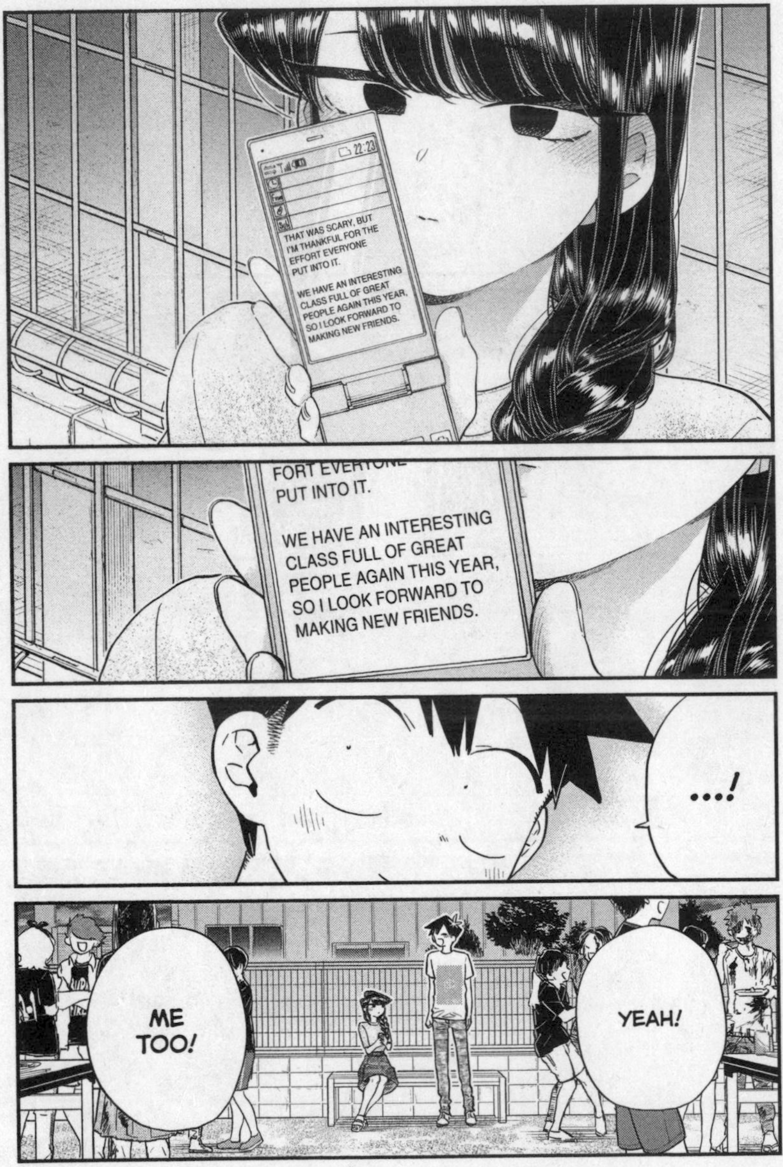
22:23
THAT WAS SCARY, BUT I'M THANKFUL FOR THE EFFORT EVERYONE PUT INTO IT.
WE HAVE AN INTERESTING CLASS FULL OF GREAT PEOPLE AGAIN THIS YEAR, SO I LOOK FORWARD TO MAKING NEW FRIENDS.
PUT INTO IT.
WE HAVE AN INTERESTING CLASS FULL OF GREAT PEOPLE AGAIN THIS YEAR, SO I LOOK FORWARD TO MAKING NEW FRIENDS.
...!
YEAH!
ME TOO!

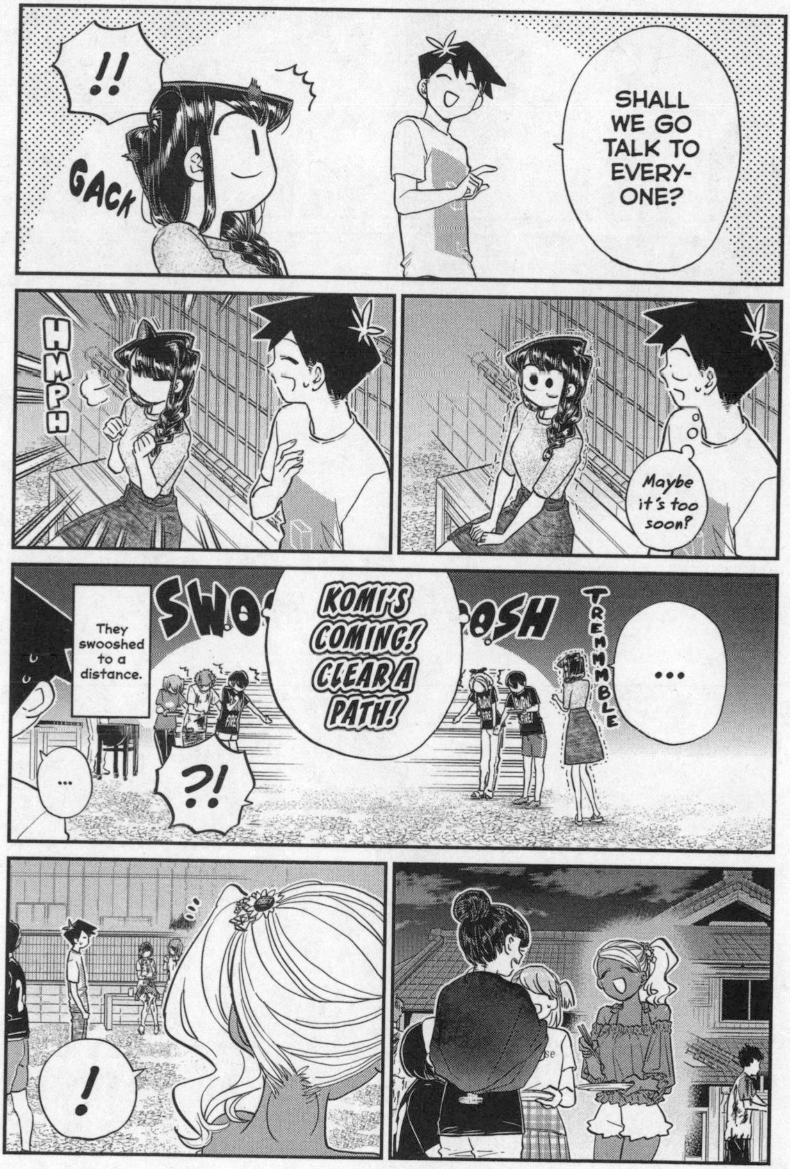
SHALL WE GO TALK TO EVERY-ONE?
!!
GACK
Maybe it's too soon?
HMPH
...
TREMMMBLE
OSH
KOMI'S COMING! CLEAR A PATH!
SWO
?!
They swooshed to a distance.
...
...
!

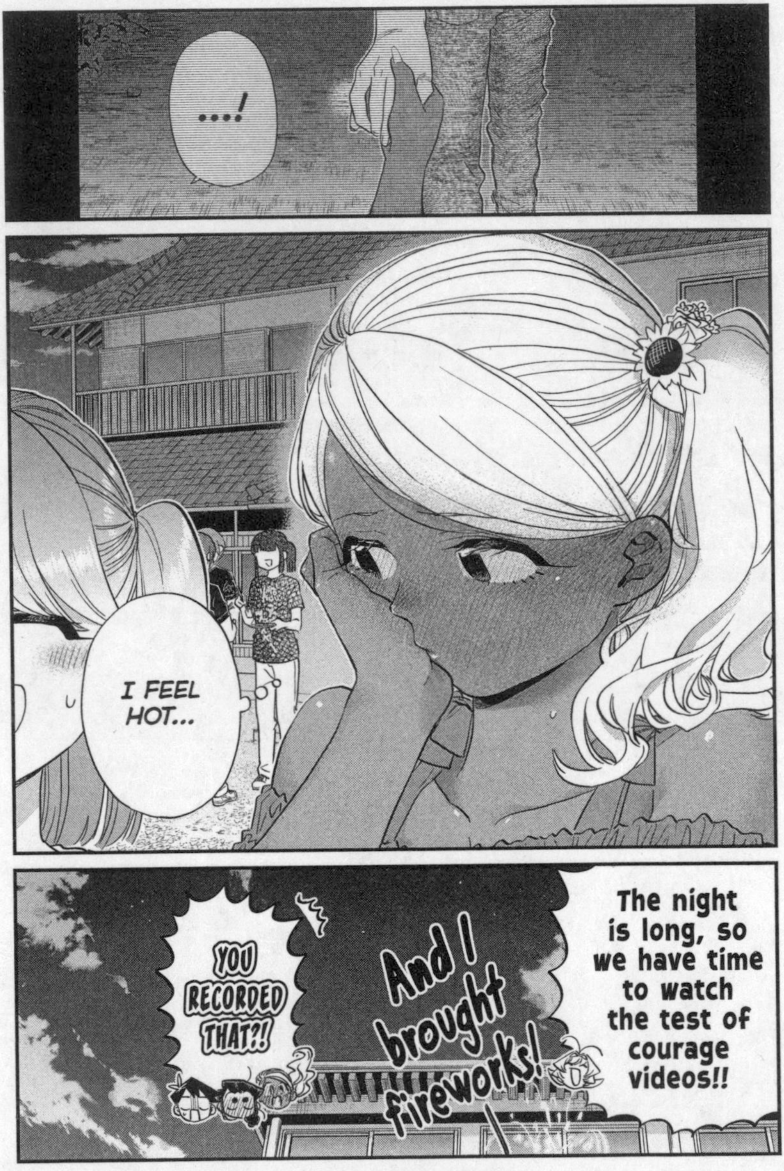
...!
I FEEL HOT...
The night is long, so we have time to watch the test of courage videos!!
And I brought fireworks!
YOU RECORDED THAT?!

Communication 181 — The End

Komi Can't
Communicate

Komi Can't Communicate Bonus

Can Rei Make a Hundred Friends? America, Land of the Free

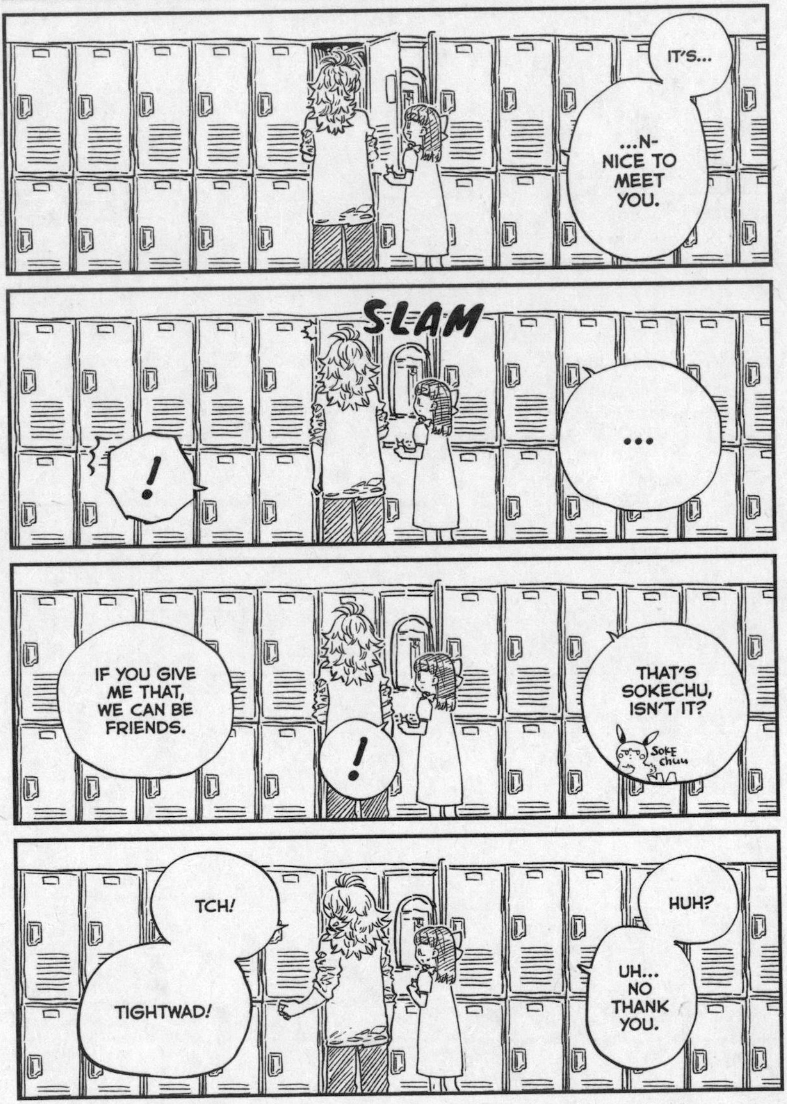
IT'S...
...N- NICE TO MEET YOU.
SLAM
...
!
THAT'S SOKECHU, ISN'T IT?
SOKE chuu
!
IF YOU GIVE ME THAT, WE CAN BE FRIENDS.
HUH?
UH... NO THANK YOU.
TCH!
TIGHTWAD!

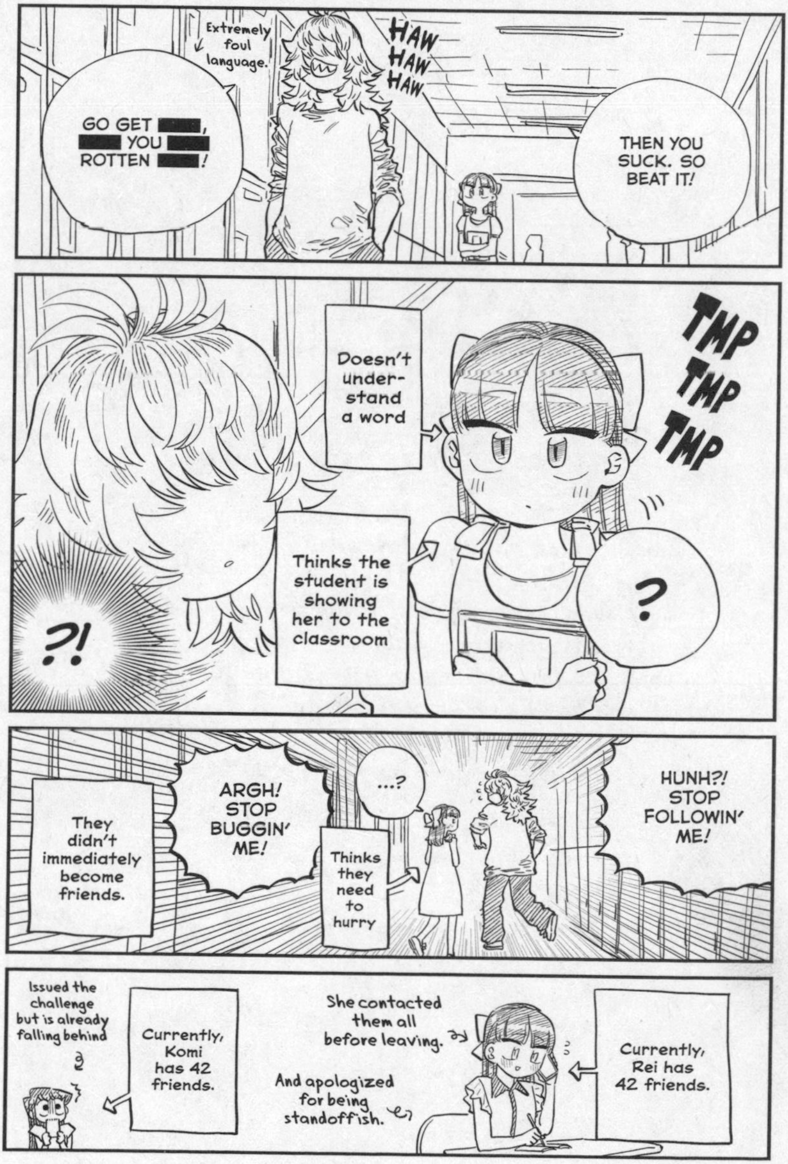
THEN YOU SUCK. SO BEAT IT!
HAW HAW HAW
Extremely foul language.
GO GET [redacted], [redacted] YOU [redacted] ROTTEN [redacted]!
TMP TMP TMP
?
Doesn't understand a word
Thinks the student is showing her to the classroom
?!
HUNH?! STOP FOLLOWIN' ME!
...?
Thinks they need to hurry
ARGH! STOP BUGGIN' ME!
They didn't immediately become friends.
Currently, Rei has 42 friends.
She contacted them all before leaving.
And apologized for being standoffish.
Currently, Komi has 42 friends.
Issued the challenge but is already falling behind

Tomohito Oda won the grand prize for *World Worst One* in the 70th Shogakukan New Comic Artist Awards in 2012. Oda's series *Digicon*, about a tough high school girl who finds herself in control of an alien with plans for world domination, ran from 2014 to 2015. In 2015, *Komi Can't Communicate* debuted as a one-shot in *Weekly Shonen Sunday* and was picked up as a full series by the same magazine in 2016.

Komi Can't Communicate

VOL. 13
Shonen Sunday Edition

Story and Art by Tomohito Oda

English Translation & Adaptation/John Werry
Touch-Up Art & Lettering/Eve Grandt
Design/Julian [JR] Robinson
Editor/Pancha Diaz

COMI-SAN WA, COMYUSHO DESU. Vol. 13
by Tomohito ODA
© 2016 Tomohito ODA
All rights reserved.
Original Japanese edition published by SHOGAKUKAN.
English translation rights in the United States of America, Canada, the United
Kingdom, Ireland, Australia and New Zealand arranged with SHOGAKUKAN.

Original Cover Design/Masato ISHIZAWA + Bay Bridge Studio

Published by VIZ Media, LLC
P.O. Box 77010
San Francisco, CA 94107

10 9 8 7 6 5 4 3 2
First printing, June 2021
Second printing, July 2021

viz.com

shonensunday.com

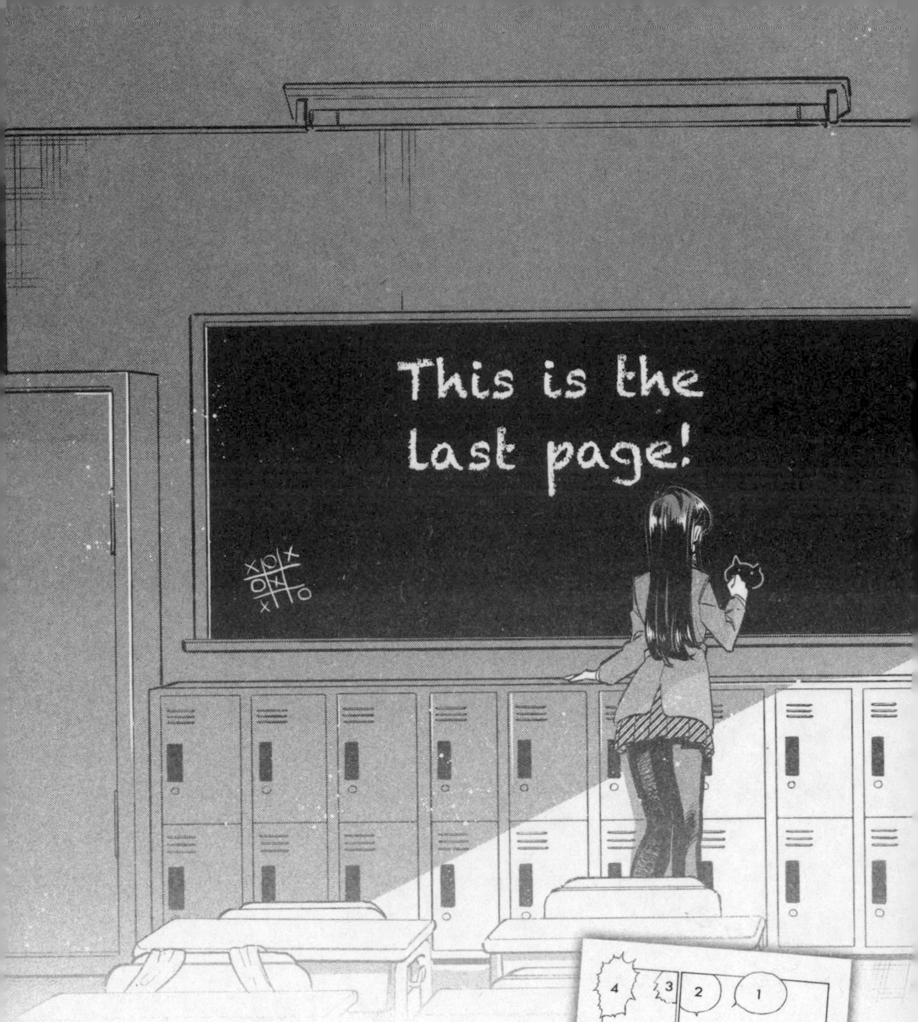
This is the last page!

Komi Can't Communicate has been printed in the original Japanese format to preserve the orientation of the artwork.

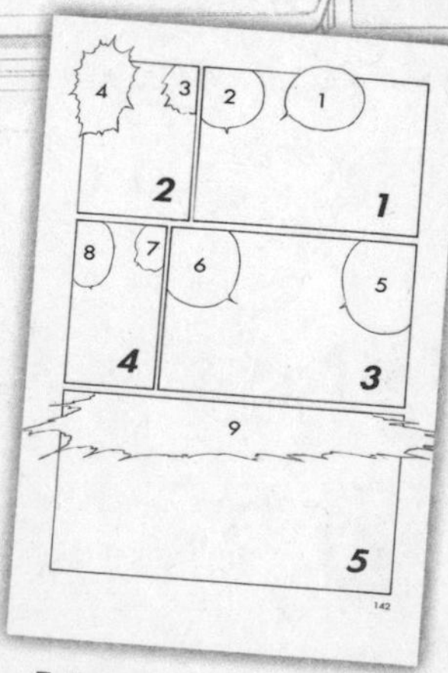

Follow the action this way.